Tinker, Tailor,
and Textile Worker

Tinker, Tailor, and Textile Worker

*Class and Politics in
Egypt, 1930–1952*

Ellis Goldberg

UNIVERSITY OF CALIFORNIA PRESS
Berkeley · Los Angeles · London

University of California Press
Berkeley and Los Angeles, California

University of California Press, Ltd.
London, England

Library of Congress Cataloging-in-Publication Data

Goldberg, Ellis.
  Tinker, tailor, and textile worker.

  Bibliography: p.
  Includes index.
    1. Labor and laboring classes—Egypt—Political
activity. 2. Textile workers—Egypt—Political
activity. 3. Communism—Egypt. I. Title.
HD8786.G65 1986   322.4'4'0962   85-16472
ISBN 0-520-05353-2 (alk. paper)

Printed in the United States of America

1 2 3 4 5 6 7 8 9

To my father and mother

Contents

Preface

This is a book about workers and politics. I first began to think about the questions discussed in this book not in an academic setting at all, but on a warm July evening over fifteen years ago when the shop steward in a factory where I then worked assembled the entire night shift for a dinner break discussion on the war in Vietnam. The talk went on for well over the half-hour allotted for a meal and provided the steward, an ex-Communist, with an ample opportunity to challenge the preconceptions of most of the younger men about war, American foreign policy, and the class nature of American society. Similar discussions occurred every night and made it clear to me that factories and the men who worked in them were not what they appeared to be from the outside, at least not if you were there for the long haul, as I then believed myself to be.

Two of the basic assumptions that inform this study became clear to me that night: first, that men in factories think and talk about major issues of the day as they impinge on their lives, and second, that alongside the formal hierarchical structure of authority in both the union and the factory there could exist a different and overtly egalitarian political authority that provided the basis for challenging things as they were.

The world of the factory, however, is not the only world of work. Six years later, while a secretary and typist in a small office of a large university I came to understand how different were the worlds of work and the degree to which the nature of the work process could condition the relations between workers and their reactions to those in authority and to work. In each case we wanted more pay, easier conditions, less-demeaning forms of authority; in each case we reacted either individually or collectively; in each case we confronted a gulf of incomprehension on the part of our employers about what we wanted when it came to specific trade-offs of hours, pay, pension rights, breaks, the timing of work, and the like. Yet I was most impressed by the differences in the two settings. Walking into an office was, even after a year, a far different experience from walking onto a shop floor, where there always seemed to be a certain sense of commonality (if not solidarity). The office, unlike the factory, was also made up almost entirely of women, and how we were assigned our jobs, how we did them, when we helped each other, as well as the friendships and social ties between us were all markedly different.

It was only later that I realized that what I had experienced others had already written about, analyzed, and dissected. When they have done so, however, it has usually been in terms that divorced the economics and sociology of work from its political importance. I set about to remedy this failing.

There are several people whose help I wish to acknowledge. I owe a real debt to Bob Bennett, the night foreman at Albers Milling Company, for showing me how effective and thoughtful a leader of men on the shop floor can be. He also made it clear to me how that effectiveness actually comes about. Gaile Wixson (my own costeward at the University of California) and Rachel Meserve were and are friends who showed me the different ways people deal with work in an office. They helped me to keep my job as well as to understand it.

Afaf Lutfi al-Sayyid Marsot, Kenneth Jowitt, and Bent Hansen all spent a good deal of time and energy with me on the doctoral dissertation that preceded this book. Their criticisms were intelligent and useful. I owe special thanks to Professor Hansen for sharing material from his own library and for attempting to save one political scientist from making outrageous errors in economic history. I owe him an immense debt. Karen Paige made many suggestions as a later reader and these have immensely strengthened this book.

This work could never have been attempted without the prior work of Egyptian scholars, not all of whom I have had the pleasure of meeting. Ra'uf ʿAbbas has not only written on the period but also generously shared documents in his possession with me. Rifʿat al-Saʿid spent hours in discussion and lent me documents as well. Jamal al-Banna shared his thoughts and a variety of original sources. So, too, did Fathi Kamil.

Taha Saʿd ʿUthman, Muhammad ʿAli ʿAmir, Muhammad Jad, and
Hasan ʿAbd al-Rahman were willing to speak for the record, and their
memories and analyses were useful and pertinent. ʿAtiya al-Sayrafi and
Muhammad Mitwalli al-Shaʿrawi were not only helpful intellectually
but also were especially gracious in their willingness to accept guests in
their households with all the generosity of Egyptian hospitality. I must
also thank Ahmad Sadiq Saʿd for several illuminating discussions.

I owe a special debt to many friends who contributed their time and
energy to make this book possible. Joel Beinin and Zachary Lockman,
who also study Egypt and have been engaged in similar research, have
been a source of support and knowledgeable dialogue. Barbara Geddes,
on the other hand, knew nothing about Egypt but was always willing to
take time from her own work on Brazil to give me stylistic criticism and
to point out the aspects of this work of value to someone outside the
field of Middle East studies. Joseph Zeidan not only taught me introductory Arabic many years ago but has remained a good friend and aided
me in checking the transcriptions. Carolyn Hughes is another old friend
without whose generous and expert help the maps of the Cairo area
would never have been done. Susan Oleksiw did a marvelous job editing
the copy, and although I have never met her, I think of her (and her
yellow slips) often.

I have been allowed to consult numerous official and semiofficial collections for this study. I owe a personal thanks to M. Raymond Didier,
who allowed me to see several collections of documents from the Suez
Canal Company. The staff at the Ministère des Affaires Etrangères and
the Ministère de l'Economie et Finances in Paris generously allowed me
to see the consular reports from Egypt. In Britain the Public Records
Office provided me with access to the British diplomatic files. I cannot
neglect the staff of the Egyptian national library, Dar al-Kutub, without whose willingness to cooperate this study could never have been
written.

Financial support for this book came from numerous sources: the
Fulbright program and the French Ministry of Higher Education, the
American Research Center in Egypt, the Regents of the University of
California, and the Center for Middle East Studies at Berkeley. The Po-
litical Science Department at Berkeley provided me with enough com-
puter time to allow this book to go through several revisions, for which
I am deeply grateful.

Aside from the experiential, intellectual, and financial resources ex-
pended by others for which I am indebted, there remain the emotional

debts. Maxime Rodinson provided me with an example of intellectual honesty, political commitment, and personal kindness that I shall never forget. Without my son, Louis, this book would have probably been finished sooner, but certainly far less well. Peg Benson appeared in my life as I was just beginning to revise my dissertation into a book. She turned a chore into a delight, something she also did for the rest of my life.

A Note on Transliterations

There is always a problem in deciding how to transliterate from Arabic. Because this book is aimed at the nonspecialist, I have reduced the transliterations, with one exception, to the barest essentials. The transliterations in the bulk of the book provide the correct vowels. No diacritical marks are used except for the ʿayn and medial or final hamza. The exception is the select Arabic bibliography at the conclusion, which does give a complete transliteration according to the Library of Congress system. Names that I believe are generally known are given under the generally known form and all transliterations from other sources are preserved when cited directly.

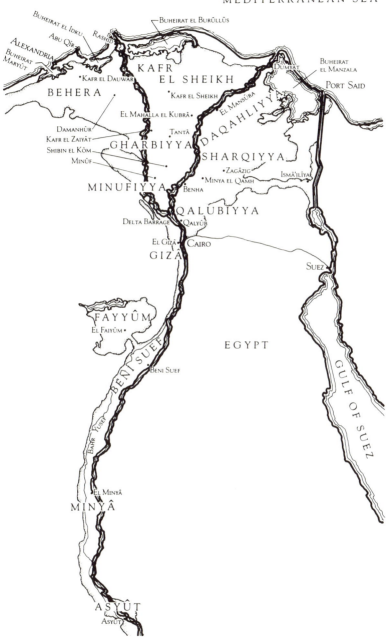

MEDITERRANEAN SEA

Buheirat el Idku
Buheirat el Burúllús
Rashíd
Abu Qîr
ALEXANDRIA
Buheirat Maryút
KAFR EL SHEIKH
DUMYAT
Buheirat el Manzala
PORT SAID
Kafr el Dauwar
BEHERA
Kafr el Sheikh
El Mansúra
El Mahalla el Kubrâ
DAQAHLIYYA
Damanhûr
Kafr el Zaiyât
Tantâ
Shibin el Kôm
GHARBIYYA
Minúf
SHARQIYYA
MINUFIYYA
Zagâzig
Ismâ'ilîya
Minya el Qamh
Benha
QALUBIYYA
Delta Barrage
Qalyûb
El Gizâ
CAIRO
GIZA
Suez
FAYYÛM
El Faiyúm
EGYPT
BENI SUEF
GULF OF SUEZ
Beni Suef
Bahr Yusef
El Minyâ
MINYÂ
ASYÛT
Asyút

Map 1. Egypt—The Nile Valley

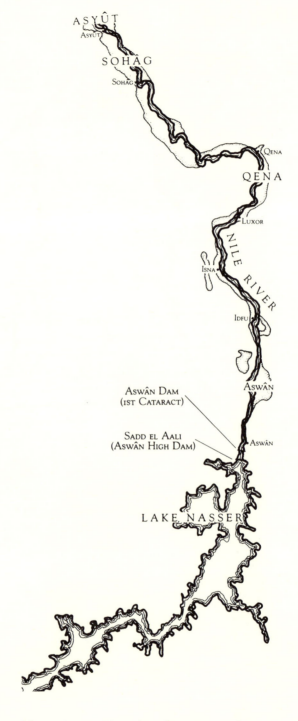

Map 1. Egypt—The Nile Valley (*continued*)

CHAPTER ONE

Introduction

THE ISSUE

Although the materials on which this book is based are drawn from recent Egyptian history, this is not really a book about Egypt at all. That it
sheds light on some important problems in recent Egyptian political history has less to do with the particular sources used than with the general nature of the question asked. I began this book in an attempt to
answer a question that seemed to me quite simple, but I rapidly came to
understand that it did not have an easy answer: What is the relation between work and politics and what in particular are the politics of an
emerging "working class" likely to be?

This is a question that has preoccupied political leaders as well as
academic researchers, and many of the suggested answers lead to more
questions. Are workers driven by economic necessity to adopt a particular global political vision? Is there an inexorable logic to the social reality of class that drives the politics of capitalist societies? Or is there
simply a continuum of minutely distinguished political positions that
workers might take, limited only by the historical setting of when and
how industrialization occurs, who gets to a particular group first, and
what ideas make sense in a particular culture?

None of the answers implicit in these kinds of questions satisfied me
although all had been suggested when I began this study by trying to
understand why a particular group of Egyptian workers—textile workers in the suburbs of Cairo and Alexandria—was so closely identified

with the Egyptian Communist movement throughout the 1940s and until the political landscape of Egypt was significantly changed by a military coup in 1952. What rapidly became apparent was that although my basic question was easy to ask, it was difficult to handle, especially at the level of analysis implicit in its formulation. Was I asking about Communism and the politics of revolution, or was I asking about the politics of workers? What I took to be the first question soon developed into the second.

In the case that initially drew my attention, it was not enough to formulate broad theories about "the workers," or "the masses," or the effect of the indeterminate social change that creates "unrest"; rather it was necessary to come to grips with a more pressing issue. Why did these workers come to accept Communist leadership when other Egyptians and other workers did not? Why did almost all contemporary observers identify textile workers with Communism on the basis of the behavior of this relatively well defined social group? Precisely this close identification seemed to suggest the need for a clear analysis rather than extensive description or documentation.

As I shall show, these workers chose Communist leaders and many of the leaders on the factory floors chose to become Communists, but despite the hopes of the Communists or the fears of the police, the Communist movement never assumed the leadership of the entire work force or even of the organized trade union movement. The textile workers were neither the vanguard of a revolution nor an anomaly meriting only description rather than analysis. They were part of the Egyptian work force and saw themselves as part of the Egyptian working class. How far did the two coincide?

In searching for a way to grasp the question that first drew my attention, I came to see how difficult it was even to frame the problem. In any discussion of work and politics we are talking about how groups of people make real but limited choices in situations that are largely not of their own making. Workers do not make the investment choices that create the factories in which they work; they do not create the plant administration or even choose the communities from which labor is drawn.

Workers nevertheless make individual and collective decisions that significantly shape subsequent decisions about investments, plant administration, and the sources of labor. In discussing any problem under the general rubric of work and politics, then, the range of possibilities for analysis becomes quite large.

The scope of inquiry is especially large when the writer is also concerned with the political choices of workers that might actually influence the nature of a polity or economy. Not only values but also the direction and scope of causation then become important factors. Marx, for example, believed that what men experienced at work would in many ways shape their understanding of the political universe in which they lived. So, too, did Lenin, who considered large-scale industry inseparable from the reservoir for Communist recruitment. Other writers have believed, on the other hand, that the factory is only a microcosm of the larger social world in which workers live and the factory thus reflects the conflicts of that world far more than it structures them.

In writing this book I have begun with a set of analytical tools that explain how factory employment molds the politics of workers, without assuming that the mere fact of wage employment itself is significant. We can easily describe factors of the work world such as market segmentation, authority structures in production processes, and industrial policies, but we have not thereby concluded a political analysis. Rather we have only begun a description, for we have only just uncovered the matrix within which different kinds of ideas make sense to different kinds of workers. Moreover, we do a disservice when we describe the appeals to which ordinary people respond as ideologies, reserving the term theory for ideas discussed in books such as this one.

How can we turn description into analysis? I begin by proposing that even the "world of the factory" must be seen in far sharper relief than students of the third-world working class have hitherto looked. It is no accident that in larger factories impersonal forms of authority are coupled with highly mechanized production and relatively unskilled workers, just as it is no accident that in very small workshops personal ties predominate over any other form of authority.

Organization theory suggests to us that different forms of production will employ different modes of authority; theories of labor market segmentation suggest that we shall find distinct kinds of people engaged in different processes of production. From this it follows logically that we shall tend to find some kinds of people (women, blacks, rural migrants) subordinated to different forms of authority. Authors who have studied the link between work and politics, however, have not gone further than this and often not quite this far, contenting themselves with the demonstration that the politics of the factory are indeed class politics, or that the politics of particular groups in the work place (unskilled, semiskilled, or highly skilled) reflect external political orientations (radicalism, conservatism, business unionism).

If, however, we are to go a step further, at least to suggest how the

experience of the work place influences the larger political arena, two more views must be considered. The first view, drawn from political science, holds that organizations mediate between the perceived needs of the members of an organization and the world within which authoritative decisions governing the fulfillment of those needs occur, that is, between voluntary mass organizations and the state. One immediate concern of the organizations of workers must be, then, the policies of the state, and (as the other side of the coin) trade unions, for example, must provide a resource for political entrepreneurs who wish to control the state administration.

The second view concerns the relation between the world of production and the world of politics outside the factory. We need to address a quite basic question, one that is at the core of this study: How do people understand their larger world given their experience in a particular part of it? This is not a demand for a psychology. Rather it is a first attempt at the subject of this book: It suggests that our view of the world of politics and the allegiances to which in general we subscribe is composed of a heightened picture of the authority relations we experience every day, our available collective resources to change it, and the success or failure of our past experiences.

A study like this one is by the nature of its material suggestive rather than exhaustive; nevertheless it seeks to incorporate several dimensions missing in other work, especially the suggestion that the evolution of the relations of authority at least in the sphere of capitalist mass production owes as much to the actions and desires of the workers as it does to those of the owners. Studies of labor in other areas make similar claims. Eugene Genovese asserts that the Old South was a world made at least in part by slaves, and E. P. Thompson tells us that the world of the English working class was one the workers made themselves. The contemporary world of Egyptian politics (and of other third-world countries) may also be one made in large part by the working class.

Although there is an underlying assumption in this study that the world of the factory that will unfold before us is one of "class conflict," it is far more important to underline that a simple phrase like that one is far too open to cast any light on the question to be answered. It is not important that we identify conflicts of interest between owners and workers, either in the factory or outside it. What is important is that we understand the specific, concrete, and regular forms such conflicts assume in terms of the political perspectives of different workers' organizations.

It is remarkable, after all, that even though the basic demands of workers in different industries—oil, sugar, textile—were quite similar, they were shaped by very different perceptions of the workers' social and political universe. Textile workers, oil workers, and sugar workers signed contracts governing hours, wages, and promotion opportunities that would have seemed mutually intelligible and yet each group of workers seems to have placed those contracts in a different context and voiced demands in significantly different vocabularies. Using different ways of understanding their situation, workers were led into different and on occasion momentous political engagements. To say that different groups of workers understood their situations in different ways might suggest what I call a vulgar pluralist approach as far off the mark as the vulgar Marxist framework. It might seem, and probably did to contemporary observers, that differences in status or occupation translated directly into the political allegiances of workers, just as "class" might for a simplistic Marxist approach. To so argue, however, again makes workers simply unconscious agents of a larger structure and limits our understanding of how they acted politically.

Rather than reproducing differences in where and how they worked, workers and especially local leaders actively sought ways to comprehend their situation and change it, often changing their ideas about their world in the process. Leaders arising from the shop floor and workers' organizations engaged in search behavior, which on occasion meant discarding theoretical premises, radically changing them, or simply refining an existing understanding to confront a new reality.

I do not believe that work translates directly into politics or that the political commitments of workers' organizations are completely fortuitous. Rather I believe that political commitments are contingent upon and consciously shaped by workers (and their leaders). In this way workers gain resources from the world of politics to change the reality of both economics and authority in the work place, even as their image of that larger world is derived from their experiences in the work place. Barrington Moore has suggested that workers understand injustice quite well. Here I would like to assert that workers have a sharper sense of equity as well, albeit a contingent one. Workers in different industries have fairly clear ideas about what would constitute justice or equity, how much justice or equity they are likely to get, and how much it will cost in any situation. The picture of the present and the picture of the future, I contend, are based on the existing opportunities in the worlds of work, worlds that vary greatly in the ease with which they allow men to unite, to communicate, or to struggle.

It makes sense to suggest that our vision of the world is related to the world within which most of our daily activity occurs. This is a position rarely considered within the Marxist tradition, for it is at variance with one strongly held belief of Marxist intellectuals, namely, that workers exhibit "false consciousness" when they do not become revolutionaries. Nevertheless, Marx and Lenin believed not only that classes structured the social world but also that people drew conclusions about the entire social order on the basis of experiences determined by the nature of classes in society. Consequently Marx and Lenin also believed that those who worked in different industries or even in different parts of a single industry could draw distinct conclusions from their experiences. Changing industrial settings could thus mean changing conclusions. Lenin, indeed, seems to have been almost obsessed with the idea that workers might, over time, reject the Bolsheviks if their promises were not confirmed in the workers' experience.

In my view workers do what everyone else does, including readers of this book. They take the ideas at hand and the available resources at their disposal—two things that vary widely depending on the social origins of the workers and where they are employed—and see what they can do with them; they search for allies and attempt to refine their understanding of the small world of work and the larger world that contains it. If they achieve an initial success, they hold to their initial analysis, but if they do not they look for new ways to comprehend, new ways to organize their own efforts, and new allies. Workers are thus interested both in the rules by which the conflicts in which they are engaged are played out and in the outcomes of those conflicts, although it cannot be said which takes precedence or whether individual or collective outcomes are more important. Concern with the rules is more interesting to us, however, for it is this concern that effectively links struggles around authority *in* the factory with struggles around authority *outside* it—that is, that links work and politics, which is the essence of this investigation.

Because this book represents a radical departure from the ways in which we have hitherto understood the relation of work and politics in the third world and because it attempts to draw on other studies in new ways, I shall briefly review other treatments of the relation of work to politics. In order to present a new and very different picture of the emergence of Communist and other worker-based organizations in the third world, I must first dispense with analyses based either on observations of peasant life or on positing a dramatic difference in the way elites and nonelites think about the world.

THE FRAMEWORKS OF ANALYSIS

THE POLITICS OF COMMUNISM

Most of the literature on Communists and Communism, including that on Communist parties in the Middle East, takes far too broad an approach to be useful here. Too often what is called Communist influence is linked to larger issues such as the collapse of the old order, its replacement by a revolutionary regime, or the search by such regimes for political support after coming to power. In this study, I am not concerned with how Communists or other groups of political leaders come to power or the aftermath. Since the trade union base of the Communists was both well defined and persistent, it makes little sense to explain their attractiveness at an inappropriately high level of analysis—for example, that those who support Communists are the disaffected, the extreme, or the deranged. Rather than focus on Communism, I shall focus on workers, which enables me to broaden the terrain even as the focus of the inquiry becomes narrower. After all, if all workers, or even all industrial workers, had been quickly won over by Communist leadership, then the answer to my question would be simple: Communism is the appropriate ideology for proletarians, just as it claims to be. It is possible that the workers might at first turn to non-Communist ideologies and, blinded by false consciousness, take longer to find the proper direction.[1] Then we might expect to see a "learning curve" as an ever-greater number of workers in the economy turned to appropriate leaders after older leaders consistently failed. If no workers had been led by Communists or if at least only some had been occasionally so led, then again the question would be easy for it would be apparent that another ideology was the appropriate one—nationalism or religion.[2] The problem as it presents itself from the sources simply does not allow for such simple answers. The Communists were entrenched in certain industrial and geographical settings, and other leaders with distinct orientations were entrenched elsewhere. Communists, nationalists, and Muslim Brothers competed for membership in many locales, but not everywhere did they find an ear.

Although we have many interpretations of Communist movements that explain why workers listened to them, none suggests the limits of Communist appeals. Communists might have seemed plausible leaders to those who were miserable and poor and hated the rich and the powerful. Those who had been alienated by the rapid progress of social change Egypt was experiencing might have been drawn to a radical ideology.[3] Communists might have attracted followers because they were able to make their own vision of revolution coincide with inchoate millenarian yearnings of precapitalist masses.[4] It might even be that if none of these explanations alone can account for the appeal of Communist leadership among textile workers, then perhaps all of them put together will provide an explanation. Sometimes, indeed, social scientists are like chefs. Textile workers might have simmered in a stew made up of a slice of envy, a cup of ignorance, a dollop of poverty, a pinch of charisma, all brought to a boil by the effects of colonial intervention on a previously stable and traditional society.[5]

THE POLITICS OF WORKERS

We need a more effective approach to the question of what makes sense to workers, especially to different kinds of workers—a social group that is well defined. How can we link specific groups of workers and their concerns with *patterns* of administration and authority, with particular ways of making a living wage, and with the politics of the state? Scholars have developed various theories in order to answer such questions in a Western setting.

The heart of the problem is discipline. Workers are subject to a dual discipline, that of the constituted authority in the plant and that of the labor market. To change the nature of the discipline to which they are subject, they must come to grips—individually or collectively—with the politics of the plant itself and the world that contains it. They must therefore conceptualize the nature of the internal discipline and that of the external discipline and then seek allies who will aid them in reconstituting that authority. We should not view discipline in this context as "legitimate authority" or overall administration; nor is it purely coercive. In the first type of discipline, jobs may seem secure but tenure is related to administrative politics; in the second type even highly capable workers may face unemployment or insufficient weekly incomes. In Egypt in the 1940s these distinctions in discipline existed in a single industry: textile workers in the gigantic state-owned combines at Mahallah faced the first type, whereas workers in Shubra faced the second type.

Three recent studies of labor and laborers, each from a slightly different perspective, attempt to explain the politics of workers in terms of relevant features of the work place. In no case are all the workers presumed to have similar politics now or expected to have them in the future. On the contrary, each study is designed to explain why workers, in the same industry as well as in different work settings, have different political visions. These three books, *Manufacturing Consent* by Michael Burawoy, *Contested Terrain* by Richard Edwards, and *Work and Politics* by Charles Sabel, represent a significant advance in our understanding of the politics of the shop floor, methods of work administration, and the choices of workers with respect to political philosophies.

All three are based on European or American empirical studies, something for which I do not intend to apologize or explain. If the level of analysis they posit is valid in those cases, then it should also be valid in other, "third-world" cases, for these authors make no assumptions about culture as explanatory factors. I shall consider "culture" an explanatory variable only when it meets two requirements. First, the term *culture* can be used to refer to a literary or artistic form that has a direct bearing on a worker's view or actions. Quranic philosophy, classical poetry, and historical philology are interesting subjects, but they are not relevant unless they are discussed by workers. If there is reason to believe that workers entertained particular ideas that are peculiar to their "culture," then it may be useful to discuss these ideas and their consequences. Second, the term *culture* may refer to the elements that define the working class as a group. This means that we must understand what Egyptians in the 1940s meant when they thought of workers. Who were workers? How were they recognized by other workers? To what could they aspire, and how could they (or should they) engage in collective action? Again these are questions that must be answered empirically from sources in working-class life.

Let us now look at the three studies mentioned above. Burawoy argues that the confines of the production process define the parameters within which we must understand the politics of the work place, especially the ways in which workers cooperate with owners and managers and the limits on that cooperation. For Burawoy, production is a game with many players; it coordinates disparate interests in a routine fashion. It is this sense of cooperation within the broad limits of production that makes work under the direction of someone else bearable.

The core of this process is what the workers and Burawoy call making out: "a series of games in which operators attempt to achieve levels of production that earn incentive pay, in other words, anything over 100 percent."[6] Making out not only makes work tolerable by giving it some of the qualities of play but also creates a culture that "provided the basis of status hierarchies on the shop floor, and it was reinforced by the fact that the more sophisticated machines requiring greater skill also had the easier rates."[7]

What enables a worker to rise in the status hierarchy? Innate skill, experience, the ability to get along with others who bring needed materials, the ability to work out compromises with others on the same job or the same machine, and the willingness to share secrets of making out or even the excess production itself on occasion. Ability and learned skills as well as leadership abilities, in short, seem to be the factors that help some men to rise, through perceived excellence in making out, to the top of the world of the shop culture. These are the shop elite, the natural leaders. Those who share knowledge of how to make out are especially respected by newcomers, who tend to fear they will never master the intricacies of the piece-rate system or of any system that requires workers to learn the secrets of a particular set of machines.[8]

If status is related to skill, the skills that provide high status do change over time. Once workers tried to stay with one job until they mastered it and resisted transfer; now, in the same shop they try to get better-paying, more skilled (and more difficult) jobs.[9] This shift benefits management by decreasing the cost of training for difficult jobs with high rates of turnover; yet it has occurred as the unintended consequence of the workers' own activity, their winning of a firm union contract.[10]

Making out and how workers successfully make out form the basis, for Burawoy, for understanding workers' politics. Certainly the experience of work acts powerfully on the consciousness of the worker, for Burawoy shows that how workers act in the plant, their "plant politics," is almost entirely explained by the labor process itself. Yet over time, even if the actions of the workers are molded by the desire to make out, things do change. Making out remains the goal, but the rules by which it is governed change. In Burawoy's view they change largely at the initiation of the company. New rules are made, imposed, and these lead to a new routine of making out. This brings us to the crucial question: How do workers in any environment make out?

Since making out partakes of the nature of a game, workers make out in some structured way. Thus what conflicts arise and how they are organized (between workers and owners or among workers) are important. Unfortunately, the rules that govern making out remain largely outside the scope of Burawoy's study. He focused on the shop, not on the firm or the union. Consequently Burawoy stops at the threshold of a critical question: How does life in the plant affect workers' view of the world outside it and where do they find the resources to change it?

To answer this question we need to learn how the rules that govern making out come into existence. Clearly such rules are a part of the structure of the firm. In *Contested Terrain* Richard Edwards raises this issue and discusses the rules required in various enterprises or activities.[11]

Edwards argues that there are three forms of control in shops: the personal authority of the owner; the flow of the work process; and the bureaucratic structure of the firm, especially the procedures for promotion, wage decisions, and work rules. Edwards links these forms of control to the size of the firm and suggests that increasingly larger capitalist firms need increasingly more institutionalized forms of control and these firms allow management of labor to "proceed without need of, and (except in exceptional circumstances) without benefit of, the conscious intervention of the personal power of foremen, supervisors, or capitalists." [12]

Edwards suggests how we may discover the life of workers in a plant. We must understand that they are engaged in a constant struggle over power in the factory. The struggle over power is a struggle over the rules by which the game of making out is played. It is clearly an unequal struggle, but it cannot be as one-sided as Edwards suggests. This becomes especially clear in Edwards's discussion of control. For Edwards different forms of control are introduced by management in response either to the need of the firm for cheaper methods of control or to the constant but almost mute "resistance" of the workers to earlier forms of control. [13] Nevertheless, workers have a clear idea of what they do not want and of what might be a better system of organizing work.

From the Pullman strike of 1894 through the U.S. Steel strike of 1919 through the Lordstown strike of 1972, the question of discipline is, in Edwards's analysis, far more important than the problem of wages, hours, or benefits. In fact, in the case of the 1919 steel strike, Edwards explicitly refers to relatively well paid workers whose major concern was abusive foremen, "autocratic" systems of control, and the arbitrary exercise of power. [14] While Edwards admits that unions welcomed bureaucratization of the work place, he considers the institution of new forms of control largely the result of company decisions rather than the result of the desires of unions and their members, the workers. [15] Contrary to Edwards's approach, I hold that only through empirical research can we discover whether workers or owners were more interested in the new method of administration. [16]

Edwards goes on to show that the three different forms of control affect different kinds of workers in systematic ways because the forms of control are related to firms' distinct processes of production or specific requirements of their markets. According to Edwards, the three forms of control can be correlated to certain work processes. Workers in the secondary sector of an economy will be subject to personal control; those in the subordinate primary sector will be subject to technical, pro-

cessual control; and those who work in the independent primary sector
will be subject to bureaucratic control. These sectors refer to ever-larger
firms, which also happen to have ever more stable sectors of the market
and consider a trained work force an increasingly important factor in
reducing costs.[17] This point is extremely important for its theoretical
and political ramifications.

There are several distinct approaches to the problem of labor market
segmentation and how to define it. It is not my intention to explore
whether labor markets are or were segmented structurally or limited by
design. Clearly at some points in recent Egyptian history, Egyptians
were denied jobs because they were Egyptians. At other times there
simply were not enough skilled Egyptians to fill certain positions. What
is clear is that in Egypt as elsewhere certain kinds of people routinely
worked in certain kinds of jobs, were more likely to get those jobs than
others, and had difficulty moving from one industry to another.

Even if, as I suggest, it is true that labor markets are segmented outside the United States in ways similar to those inside the United States—
among what are called secondary, subordinate primary, or independent
primary sectors (or whatever other labels are attached)—it would be a
mistake to assume that the mere fact of segmentation tells us very much.
Obviously, it would be wrong to suppose that the firms that occupy secondary, subordinate primary, or independent primary sectors in one
country (the United States) are the same as those elsewhere in the world
(Egypt). Nor would it be correct to assume that those who supply the
labor for firms in one sector in one locale (blacks, women, immigrants)
will be the same as those who supply labor for that sector in another
locale, where labor might be drawn from different social groups (peasants, artisans, children). What is important, however, is the understanding that just as the rules of how the game in the factory is played will be
the dominant concern of those working there, the rules of those games
will vary over time and place, and who plays the game and what assets
each worker brings to the play will also vary widely and systematically.
These understandings thus define the critical empirical questions for
any research on workers and politics: What are the rules, how can they
be changed, and who plays?

If workers enter different firms as part of well-defined groups, it is
clearly incorrect to assume that they are always willing to remain part of
the labor market from which they come. They may wish to play under
different rules, and this may be done in several ways. They may change
themselves or they may challenge the rules by which the old game is

played or they may try to adopt a different game entirely. All strategies will be tried. How can we learn how those who have entered under one set of rules try to change the rules? In *Work and Politics* Charles Sabel poses ideas that help us here.

Sabel is interested in how workers shape and reshape the work place, for he tells us "workers' ideas of self-interest, born of the principles of honor and dignity they bring to the factory, can be transformed by workplace struggles . . . [and these] struggles, colliding or combining with conflicts in the larger society and between nations, can reshape technologies, markets, and factory hierarchies." [18]

In attempting to explain why workers "put up with the possibilities for work, often appallingly limited from a middle-class point of view, that capital offers," Sabel offers an idea that may explain their attitudes not only to a job but also to an entire system of jobs. [19] Sabel elaborates the idea that workers have careers and consequently must make decisions according to a broader perspective than they have usually been credited with in academic literature. He suggests that there is a "mesh" between "job characteristics and attitudes toward work," and that workers make decisions based on their forecasts as well as their interest in acquiring skills, moving on to the next job, or even engaging in collective actions. [20] Sabel then deftly proceeds to describe the ways in which different kinds of workers, in different labor markets, attempt to improve their lot (or at least hold on to what they have) by learning new skills, leaving old jobs, or challenging the rules of the game.

If Sabel's idea of careers at work is useful for understanding struggles in and around the work place, then it should also be useful for explaining workers' struggles to reshape the work place itself. [21] Rather than assuming that workers have limited horizons and no information about the world that shapes the environment of their work place, let us treat these as empirical questions: Can we discern particular workers' perception of their horizons; can we discover how much they know about the markets that shape the environment for the factory in which they work; can we understand how they conceptualize authority in the plant and outside it? The answer is yes, although in a third-world country such as Egypt we must be satisfied with indications rather than the kind of research data that would result from studies of plants in Europe, the United States, or Japan. Questions about authority are what politics and political science seek to resolve.

To speak of careers implies that different workers could anticipate the challenge of shaping their skills to a market in a fairly homogeneous

fashion, or that skills, once learned, can be applied in a variety of settings. In the third world such an assumption may be unfounded. Hence,
in this study it is necessary to make a clear demarcation that Sabel
misses: between skilled workers and artisans. In chapter 5, I shall explore the artisan world in some detail and in chapters 6, 7, and especially 8, I shall explore that of skilled workers. Sabel tends to collapse
the artisans and skilled workers of contemporary Europe into a single
category. I have separated these categories in this study. The difference
has to do with the social framework within which the relevant skills are
learned, employed, and marketed.

The world of the artisan, the craftsman, and (as I shall explore it) the
servant is made up of dense social networks. Skills are transmitted directly from father to son or within a family in some way, or often not at
all. As I employ the term, the skills involved are those of the small-
commodity producer whose wares or services are sold directly to the
community in which they are made, rather than being marketed within
a larger or even national (or international) economy. As a result, the
bonds between artisan or servant and client are as dense as those among
artisans: these bonds are not only the bonds of interest but also of patronage and may even be quasi-familial. Even if contemporary craftsmen
in Europe and the United States seem similar in some regards to what
can only be called the traditional artisans, there is in reality little congruence between their worlds or their world views. Artisans live in a
world in which not only what they make but also the skills by which
they produce and the world for which they produce are constantly
under threat from machine production. Their skills—basket weaving,
pottery throwing, cooking, animal driving, ironing, and even cloth
weaving—may have only the most limited possibilities of adaptation to
industrial production. Unlike plumbers, electricians, mechanics, or even
carpenters, many artisans do not have skills that can be adapted to new
uses when the old markets die out. As such they face not only psycho-
logical and economic difficulty at times of rapid industrial and economic
change but also crisis.

Different sets of workers will then call on the state in different ways to
help them make their skills into a "career," and different kinds of skills
will be useful to state officials as they chart policy. It thus becomes imperative to look at the state and especially at state officials as active players in a game that involves workers. Rather than see politics at the level
of the state as either the outcome of initiatives by the owners or as a
balance between contending social groups, here workers and owners, it

makes more sense to see that workers as well as owners have resources with which to bargain with political leaders in the state bureaucracy, which has its own distinct preferences. Because workers not only vote but also may control physical access to a productive enterprise, they may be able to make demands on a firm that make the firm vulnerable to state officials. Thus workers and politicians need not necessarily be antagonists; sometimes they can be allies against the employer. Workers demanding justice from the government may not be as naive as they are sometimes made out to be. They may see state officials in an unwarrantedly good light; they may also be offering them a deal.

THE STRUCTURE OF THE STUDY

Around the themes developed above, I shall explore how workers view the political world they live in, both at their place of work and outside it. To learn how workers make out, I shall examine who gets to make out, where, under what rules and how malleable the rules are, and under what conditions. To understand what workers are willing to do to change themselves or the rules, I shall consider the kinds of careers they are pursuing. In order to fully appreciate what constitutes a career for blue-collar workers, I shall explore how they perceive the world that shapes the factory, both politically and economically.

How accurately workers understand these questions is less important here than determining what characteristics of their world they consider significant in pursuing their own careers. It would be easy to show that workers had little understanding of the local or international markets for their products or of the political intricacies of either Egypt or the international state system between 1930 and 1950. It is unclear to me that those in power understood these questions more correctly, for they disagreed often and profoundly about them; it is certain, however, that they knew more. But knowing more, as any introductory text on organization theory makes clear, is not necessarily helpful, for we must still determine the salient characteristics of the environment. In this regard workers and owners, trade union leaders and party officials, and peasants and landowners were often alike. What counted was what was salient, what stood out, and on every side there was a constant struggle to learn more about the world that was Egypt and the world that shaped Egypt from the outside. In the end, I was impressed by how much the workers often did know both about the world at large and about their own career choices.

To explore the questions and themes presented above, I have chosen four case studies that include significant differences in the production process. Given the nature of labor market segmentation, these studies allow me to focus on the mesh between who works in a place and the kind of discipline that exists there, as well as the degree to which the work process itself encourages making out in solidarity or as individuals. The studies also allow me to focus on the kinds of resources workers bring to their struggles in the factory, those from outside the firm as well as those from inside. By looking at workers' resources, by considering how they conceptualized the job as a resource (for themselves, their family, their village), and by determining opportunities for advancement or for changing jobs, I shall be able to relate the picture of the world expressed by their union leaders to their own lives.

It is gratifying to note that the use of an analytic framework grounded in Europe or the United States yields useful results and suggests ways in which Egypt (as well as presumably other third-world countries) differs from the capitalist core. This in turn clarifies an important part of what ought to be central to comparative politics: If an analytic mode is suitably abstract, then it should enable us to pierce the complexities of different societies. This frees us from the fashionable assertion that every society requires a different analytic framework. This is the norm in Middle East studies and it is useless, as useless as the position arising from the dependency school, which asserts that our results should be the same everywhere, for it is the same "world system."

Briefly, by looking at artisans, sugar workers, and tobacco, petroleum, and texile workers, we find a pattern. The elements are similar to those discussed above, but the arrangements are distinct. Workers, especially in larger factories, did try to make out. It was not always possible. Sometimes the machinery was too old and antiquated; sometimes it was too new and speedup was constant. In some places, moreover, jobs were insecure because of rapid technical change, in others because of extreme market fluctuations. Sometimes the state had an overriding interest in a firm for fiscal or strategic reasons; sometimes the state was the employer; and sometimes the state found private owners a convenient target for "purely" political reasons. In each case, influenced by these constraints, workers conceptualized the world of work and the nature of discipline at work differently.

Let me now return to an earlier question. Where were the Communists strong? They were strong where the world matched the description by Marx and Lenin, not in terms of the plant, but in terms of the lives of the workers: in the midsized, subordinate primary, market-sensitive area of textile production in and around Cairo, where portable skills and strong demand enabled workers to stand up to the boss and where workers had to rely on themselves because they could find few allies. Why were the Communists not strong in the large tobacco factory at Giza, the basic industrial plant of the oil refinery at Suez, or the giant sugar mill at Hawamdiyyah (or those of the south)? Because other strategies worked better, made more sense, or brought greater rewards for less risk (which is probably just another way of saying the same thing). In the course of the case studies and the conclusion I shall return to the differences between these work environments and the men who worked in them.

CHAPTER TWO

What Did It Mean to Be a Worker?

In perhaps every blue-collar setting there are certain commonly held ideas about who workers are, what they can expect, and how they can attain their expectations. In one sense, these ideas form a significant part of the working-class culture of any society. Yet it would be a mistake to believe that these ideas, because they are part of a larger cultural whole or are expressed in its language, can be deduced from the cultural and especially the literary or philosophical corpus of a society. In fact, members of a working-class culture may show greater similarity to the same group with a different language and religion than to members of other classes with the same linguistic, ethnic, or religious background. Considerably more research is needed on the definition of working-class cultures. Nevertheless, it would be a mistake to assume that similarity in outlook leads to common interests. Indeed, that was the historic error of European social democracy in the pre–World War I era.

In this study the focus is on how different groups of workers in trade unions and on occasion outside them evolved political strategies to understand their world and change it. All participants saw themselves as workers; all believed that workers had a political community to which they were bound; all believed that workers could aspire to decent treatment at work as well as higher earnings; all believed that only through some form of social organization and political association could workers achieve their aspirations.

Workers developed different strategies for achieving their goals, and this suggests not only different environments and hence possibly different interests but also competing ideas about organizations, their memberships, loyalties, and aspirations. Just as the "higher" cultural tradition has many, often contradictory, ideas about how to respond to the way of the world, so does blue-collar culture. In this chapter I shall explore two aspects of working-class culture. First, I shall examine what it meant to be a worker in Egypt in the 1930s and 1940s in terms of experiences, responsibilities, and orientations. Second, I shall investigate some of the dimensions of how workers understood themselves, their role in society, and the political options open to them in Egypt between the wars.

I undertake this discussion for two reasons. I wish first of all to clarify the degree to which there was a sense of community or common identity among members of the urban Egyptian work force and to show the degree to which that sense of community both coincides with and differs from a Marxist and essentially structural idea of class. Second, in light of the case studies that follow, I consider it necessary to show the existence of competing ideas, from which workers chose those that best explained their situation. Workers were not passive recipients of ideas, whether those of the dominant cultural tradition or those of revolution; rather they were active participants, even if often in a limited way, in a process of defining a political identity for themselves.

WHO WAS A WORKER?

Let us begin by answering the question, Who was a worker? More precisely, who did workers recognize as other workers? Four main characteristics defined a person as a "worker" socially and culturally, with a significant bifurcation *within* the category of "worker." Egyptians treated as compartments within a single category what we regard as two distinct groups. Workers were male, urban, spoke the Egyptian dialect of Arabic, and got their hands dirty.[1] Within this group a distinction existed between those who worked on or around machines and those who did not. In the United States a person who did not work on machines would cease to be a worker and become an "artisan" or craftsman, but this is definitely not the case in Egypt in the 1930s and 1940s.

Some of the people discussed here are not usually considered workers—
such as sugar workers or craftsmen—in the sense of the English word,
but these groups are accepted as workers in Egypt. The vocabulary of
the political leaderships including the left was not limited to class terms.

To say that the Egyptian worker was male, urban, spoke Arabic, and
got his hands dirty may seem obvious. But what it meant to have those
characteristics in interwar Egypt is not self-evident. What did it mean to
be a man in working-class society at the time? Certainly the peasants
had clear concepts of masculinity, strength, and the like. These were tied
to a desire to expand the amount of free time and to use it for private
recreation, often watching or participating in sports activities. On the
basis of the positions taken in the working-class press, I have inferred
that masculinity was associated with two main interests: sports and
family. A man was expected to maintain a family (a nuclear family was
preferred here, I suspect, though this one was larger than the nuclear
family currently popular in the West) and he was also probably an avid
follower or player of sports.

Those who believe nothing changes in "eternal Egypt" may be surprised to discover that only two generations ago the current mania for
soccer, and especially the Friday afternoon Ahli-Zamalik matches, did
not exist, and in many circles the growing interest in spectator sports
was considered dangerous, possibly un-Egyptian, and probably un-
Islamic.[2] For example, in the 1930s and 1940s weight lifting was extremely popular, and Damietta had three weight-lifting clubs.[3] The
Congress of Trade Unionists, in which Fathi Kamil played an important
role, was nominally led by ʿAbbas Halim, also a sportsman, and at least
one of its public gatherings was a banquet in honor of a star Egyptian
boxer.[4] Boxing and weight lifting seem to have garnered the particular
censure of the Muslim Brothers, which considered them an obstacle in
the way of the moral regeneration of Egypt. No doubt these two particular sports were already popular on Friday afternoons, for the Muslim
Brothers suggested that lessons in religion and Muslim culture be developed to replace the widespread popularity of boxing and weight lifting,
which contributed to the alienation of the people from their jobs.[5] The
factories and unions had their own sports teams, especially for soccer,
and the sporting life probably played a role in tying together workers in
different parts of the two major cities as well as in different industries.
We know that one of the highlights of the 1946 sports season was the
soccer match between the Cairo and Alexandria unions,[6] and we know
that the workers' sports federation was finally banned by the state.[7]

Masculinity as well as a love of sports contributed to the popularity of such games. Certainly ʿAbbas Halim owed part of his position in the trade union movement to his sports prowess as well as to his royal connections. Halim is alleged to have horsewhipped a small factory owner for firing a worker, and his willingness to resort to his own hands won him a certain prestige.[8] As I shall show further on, Halim owed the rest of his standing in the trade union movement to his ability to provide funds for union organizers and offices. No one ever seems to have taken him seriously as a figure interested in the well-being of the workers, and many who worked with him did so for avowedly ulterior reasons.

The role of the family in defining masculinity may be self-evident, but it is worth pointing out that the family at that time was already, in essence, the nuclear rather than the extended family. Peasants left the countryside to find jobs in urban areas and sent money home, and Upper Egyptians as well as Nubians kept links with kin in their villages of origin, but overall workers lived with their families. Moreover, in the press and in the demands of the workers, one finds direct and indirect reference to the nature of the worker's family: It was large, even very large, by our standards but relatively independent as a unit. As we shall see in chapter 7, the petroleum workers were able to win demands not just to increase the level of wages but also specifically to increase the income needed to support larger families. Supporting one's own family was an extremely important part of the self-definition of an Egyptian working-class man.

The characteristic of speaking the Egyptian dialect of Arabic may also seem self-evident for workers, but it is not. Just as peasants tend to be locally parochial, workers may tend to be national (not international) in their outlook. In the early part of this century many of the skilled workers were European, and Europeans were not only in positions of management and control but also in positions of blue-collar skill and authority through the 1940s. The political elite was by no means homogeneously Egyptian, if one takes language rather than birthplace as an indicator of nationality. Those of Turkish descent, for example, still spoke Turkish as their first language; others, even if Egyptian by origin, were more comfortable in French than in Arabic; still others were obviously Syrian or Lebanese even though they spoke Arabic. Speaking the Egyptian dialect of Arabic did not necessarily make someone a worker, but one who did not speak it was not at all likely to be a worker. Immigrants from further east were Arabs and even Muslims, but they were also usually professionals or capitalists like the Shurbagis, the

Shushas, or the Sibahis of the Shubra area. Eloquent speaking may have been a virtue and some, like Muhammad ʿAli ʿAmir, cultivated it, but eloquence was probably less important than content.[9] Good expression was admired but clarity was important. ʿAbbas Halim may have been admired for his strength and stamina, but he was also despised for his poor command of Arabic.[10]

In addition to the national language, the workers used forms of popular culture. The workers were thus as clearly Egyptian as the leading cultural figures were sophisticated Arabs or serious Muslims. Those to whom culture invariably means the most recondite art will perhaps be appalled or amused when I mention the flourishing in working-class life of what was essentially doggerel—*zajal* as poetry, rather than the classical Arabic *qasidah*.

Zajal has had its great practitioners such as Sayyid Darwish (around 1919) or Bayram al-Tunisi (in the period with which this book is concerned), but even the casual reader of the working-class press notices that this form was widespread, and used the common speech and common sentiments. Hardly a major union function or an issue of a union newspaper failed to include at least one poem from a worker in this form.[11] The textile workers' union had a poet laureate in Fathi al-Maghrabi, who published an entire volume of *zajal* under the title *I Am a Worker*, but he was not alone. A good example of the form, and far from uncommon in its sentiments or its rhyme, is found in the newspaper *Al-Damir*.

> I weave in silk but dress in cotton cheap;
> I grow fresh fruit, but porridge's all I eat;
> See something nice? The workers get no treat.[12]

This poem is typical of *zajal* concerned with workers. Bayram al-Tunisi wrote a similar poem that reached a much wider audience.[13]

The content of such poetry is important, for it reflects the political beliefs common to those who perceived themselves as workers; moreover, such poetry is based on a clear apprehension of the difference—not just in status but also in economic situation—between those who work with their hands and those who do not. The union and its leaders were fully aware of the value of such presentations and used either *zajal* or *qasidah* to capture the support of the local audience in political campaigns or union struggles.[14]

Egyptian workers were most conscious of class differences in the urban environment. Despite the line about growing fruit in the *zajal* quoted above, the working class had a decisively urban cast. Workers lived in a self-consciously urban environment rather than a self-consciously Muslim one. Jacques Berque may be right to consider the mosque as the symbol of the city (and especially the traditional city); it certainly is so architecturally and morally. It is the café, however, that distinguishes the city, for it is not only a place where the small luxuries of tea, coffee, and tobacco are consumed, but it is also the most available public space for free congregation in the city. One is tempted to suggest not only that the café was the locale for most of the socializing of workers but that cafés, far more than mosques, were the dominant social arena of proletarian districts.[15] For workers, who were for the most part men without offices, meeting halls, clubs, or other facilities, most public social life was lived in cafés. The workers did not meet in the mosques to plan strategy; they met in the cafés. Workers met in coffeehouses to plan street demonstrations;[16] successful demonstrations and strikes were celebrated in cafés;[17] and finally they were arrested in cafés en masse. One could even be hired in a café, for employment agents would frequent certain cafés in order to find prospective employees and far more workers were hired in this way than through the local offices of the labor department.[18]

In chapter 5 we shall see that even in provincial and outlying areas, such as Suhaj, the workers met in a café in town; they were townsmen who met where ordinary and secular town business was conducted: in a café. Meeting in cafés was not always highly thought of, for the café as a locale carried no prestige and did not enhance one's reputation. As we shall see in chapter 8, Taha Fauda voiced strenuous objections to the tendency of workers to spend their free time in cafés, and drunkenness and smoking, which are café-related activities, were forbidden in stricter Islamic circles.[19] From cafés workers often carried out peculiarly urban forms of social protest, namely, street demonstrations and hunger strikes. This was especially so in Cairo, the center of government, where it is apparent from written and oral sources that the workers and their leaders considered street assemblies to be an entirely normal and appropriate state of affairs.

It may seem surprising that I have not included being Muslim as a defining feature of being a worker. Many workers, like many Egyptians, were not: They were Coptic. To be Arabic speaking and Egyptian, however, often implied a cultural affinity to Islam and it is clear that for many workers Islamic holidays were accepted as Egyptian ones. There was nevertheless a confluence between speaking Arabic, being Egyptian,

and being Muslim, and religious and religion-oriented leaders attempted
to take advantage of this confluence to expand their following among
workers. All the workers wanted paid holidays, and where companies
recognized Christian holidays the workers wanted Muslim alternatives
(or, if the truth be told, probably Muslim additions).[20] The desire to
celebrate one's own holidays rather than someone else's is common in
disputes over holidays and wage advances, and one tram worker put the
matter clearly.

> The constitution of the Egyptian state specifies that the official religion of the
> state is Islam and that the Hijri [Islamic] New Year is an official holiday. All
> nationally owned enterprises respect this as do the state bureaus, but the
> Cairo tram company denies this and thus the Muslim workers who work at
> the Cairo tram repair depot demand to be permitted to leave work at 4:00
> P.M. to celebrate the Hijri New Year in equality with their foreign workmates
> who are allowed such a demand during their holidays.[21]

State-owned enterprises and government offices are presumed to set the
example for how employees should be treated, and the company is here
criticized for treating Muslims differently from non-Muslims and for
denying the integrity of their religious and cultural orientations. Although many of these demands were phrased in terms of Muslim holidays, it would be naive to think that most workers wanted the day off to
pray. Some did, but most wanted the day off for the same reasons other
workers anywhere want paid days off.

A worker also was one who worked with his hands, and as we shall
see in chapter 3, being a laborer defined not only workers but the continuity between handicraft and mechanized production. Generally speaking, those who did not get their hands dirty were not considered workers even if they called themselves workers. Taha Sa'd 'Uthman was a
worker because he was engaged in the hurly-burly of production, but
King Faruq, who was called the First Worker by his propagandists, was
obviously not really thought of as a worker. Between these two there is a
whole range of white-collar and professional figures, but it is clear from
the electioneering in working-class districts in the late 1920s that no
one seriously considered these people workers. On the contrary, the
workers were often admonished to choose parliamentary representatives from among their "own" rather than from the ranks of those who
had helped them.

Within the ranks of those who worked with their hands, there were
two groups: artisans and industrial workers. Further, the distinction between the loose associations of artisans and the tight organizations of

industrial workers in similar lines of production was reproduced in the terminology of the union movement. Textile workers were in different unions depending on whether they were manual or industrial workers; those who drove conveyances with engines were in different unions from those who drove animals; cobblers were in different unions from the employees of the BATA shoe combine. We find this distinction between unions reflected not only in the names of the unions but also in the description of the craft. Artisans often referred to themselves by fairly old Arabic names for craft workers: cobblers, weavers, tinsmiths, brass workers, barbers, cooks, and the like. Other workers referred to themselves as workers in an industry, such as textile, metal, or ship scaling, or in a particular company. Muhammad Jad, a carpenter in a fairly large shop, made it clear that in his mind there was a significant distinction between artisans (such as himself) and industrial workers, for he did not consider artisans to be "real" workers.[22] Artisans, in his mind, were not real workers because they did not have the potential to combine that characterized industrial workers. Jad is a Communist, but what is important is that the distinction he draws is a political one, not a social one: the nature of the organization and the stance of artisans.

The characteristics I have described above produce a composite portrait that corresponds to an archetype I refer to as the *gada*ᶜ.[23] The *gada*ᶜ was recognized by those who organized workers as the ideal type of worker, and was sharply differentiated from both the peasant and the intellectual (*fallah* or *muthaqqaf*) by urban workers. *Gada*ᶜ is an Egyptian colloquial term best rendered by the Russian *molodets*; there is no English equivalent, although the expression "good ol' boy" might once have been close. In effect, the *gada*ᶜ is someone whose life experience and courage lead him to take correct stands in the face of difficult choices. He is a man of inferior status, but his experience sets him apart from other people of low status. This experience enabled these men to overcome their political differences; their similar class background (not just social status) gave them a common language. These men respected others who were like them but had different organizational commitments. They could also do things that would be clearly labeled opportunistic if done by those of higher status or different experience.

I found a very clear conceptualization of the *gada*ᶜ when I spoke with "Shaykh" Hasan ᶜAbd al-Rahman, who had been president of the cab drivers' union in the late 1940s. He sharply differentiated leaders such as Fathi Kamil of the tobacco workers at the Matossian plant from leaders such as himself or other Communists and non-Communists who had worked with their hands. Kamil, essentially a white-collar employee, may have been a wage earner but he was not a proletarian because he lacked hands-on experience.[24] The word *gada* also occurred repeatedly when I was talking to Muhammad ʿAli ʿAmir, and it seems to characterize his life also.

One effect of this particular sense of the social status characterizing Egyptian workers led to what can only be described as an opportunistic shifting of political party membership from time to time. Almost all Egyptian working-class leaders joined political groups with which they professed not to agree because of concerns urged on them by fellow workers, other *gidʿan*. The number of Communists who joined the Muslim Brothers for brief periods between 1946 and 1948 seems to be quite large. Invariably this was partly because Muslim Brothers membership seemed to promise police protection; in addition, joining this group was not seen as a compromise of one's inner convictions, which is evidence of the relative (although real) leftism of many of these working-class leaders as well as of their heroic vision of themselves.

Heroism can be a complex subject. To say that the trade union activists had a heroic vision of themselves or to say they acted in a consciously heroic manner is to describe how they looked at themselves and to assert that they often took risks beyond those their work mates thought prudent or reasonable. It is not to assert that their vision of themselves was always correct, that anyone else in their society saw in them a heroic ideal, or that they acted with foolhardy disregard for the consequences. Clearly they were not always as courageous as they may have thought themselves to be; their low status made them unlikely objects for admiration by the larger society and they did not have the literary or propaganda apparatus to change that. Moreover, heroism is distinct from foolhardiness. The hero takes real and extraordinary risks, but a hero is successful by defying conventional wisdom; he is not the suicidal victim of overpowering forces. Just as the classical hero goes into battle with sword, shield, and horse, so these trade union activists sought out powerful allies or patrons as well as building organizations before engaging in a trade union struggle. Precisely by mobilizing hidden resources that only in hindsight appear to have been clearly available do heroes overcome their opponents. Clearly, heroic action is not the monopoly of any one political or social group, and different ideologies can motivate heroic behavior.

Different leaders utilized the heroic aspect of their own lives and their heroic moments in different ways. Some, especially the nationalists and Muslim Brothers, tended to see the heroic moment as a tool by which to pressure an incumbent elite to bargain with them, even if at the expense of those actually leading strikes and demonstrations. Others, more often Communists, attempted to fuse the heroic moment with sustained organization in the hope that heroism could be activated and extended as needed. This particular form of personal heroism has its underside. It made organizational commitments, even on the left, often weaker than personal commitments between leaders with similar backgrounds, and in a sense it was a mirror image of the personal relations among Egypt's political elite.[25]

The role of status in this self-perception is not something I wish to stress but it can hardly be denied. Echoes of it appear in complaints from the trained textile workers who had the equivalent of high-school degrees, fairly advanced education at the time. The word *class* implies a view of social stratification based on an objective reality—ownership— coupled with a sense of common experience. It is a view from the inside looking out. The word *status*, on the other hand, is a social designation—and implies a view from the outside looking in. Status has to do less with common experience than with commonly ascribed attributes. The clearest definers of status for our purposes are education and dirty hands, and the two markers were generally regarded as linked: Higher education meant cleaner hands. The left propagated a class vision; the Muslim Brothers, a status vision. Both were grounded in Egyptian reality of the period. The most poignant example of the deep gulf between status attributes and class experiences is in the newspaper published by the Muslim Brothers. "The worker is held to be a lesser thing than a clerk," technical school graduates were quoted as saying, even when the worker makes more money.[26] These technical school graduates, who would be considered workers after they entered the job market, wanted workers' wages but the status of officials because they were educated. This struggle for status and the affirmation of the values of culture and religion attracted such men to the Muslim Brothers.[27]

COMPETING WORLD VIEWS OF THE WORKERS

The characteristics that define the worker by extension define a large group of people and many subgroups. The most effective way to identify and describe these subgroups and their competing views of the world in which workers lived is perhaps by describing their positions on three

key issues for trade unions: first, the manner of organization (how workers should associate); second, the relation between workers and owners
(what workers ought to see as reasonable expectations); and third, the
nature of power in Egypt (who is the enemy and how should he be
confronted).

ORGANIZATION VERSUS MUTUAL AID

The oil workers, in creating their union, sharply differentiated it as a
niqabah from a *jam'iyyah*; they saw the two as quite distinct forms
of association. The textile workers were conscious of creating a union
organization (*niqabah*) similar to that which existed in Europe and different from some forms of association (*jam'iyyah*) prevalent in Egypt.
Moreover, this distinction had been propounded by elements among
the Egyptian Communist party as early as 1931.[28] Husni al-'Urabi published his short pamphlet *What Are Unions?* that year in an edition of
two thousand copies.[29] Although the impact of the pamphlet itself may
not have been very wide, 'Urabi was well known in Egypt and his ideas
were clearly current at the time. His pamphlet contains an extremely
cogent analysis of the situation confronting workers in the interwar period, with a fine delineation of who might help them and to what degree. 'Urabi, unlike his publisher, clearly considered workers to be those
involved in urban mechanized production.[30] 'Urabi viewed workers as a
distinct social group that had only a limited capacity to act on its own
behalf in Egyptian society. The workers' movement thus had to rely on
workers themselves, the educated elite (*al-mustanirun*), and the state,
which he called the servant of the people.[31] According to 'Urabi, one
particular problem in Egypt is creating a stable organization because
workers do not distinguish clearly between unions and mutual-aid associations, which are called *jam'iyyat*.[32] Thus, workers often give the
name *niqabah* "union" to something that is closer to a mutual-aid and
benefit group, or *jam'iyyah akhuwiyyah*. There is little doubt that such
informal groups existed in Egyptian factories and we even have documentary evidence of their existence. In 1942 *Al-Yara'* published what
purported to be an account of a printing worker's diary dating from
the previous decade. In 1934, according to the diary, this anonymous
worker had a sick daughter and created a *jam'iyyah* with his work mates
for ten piasters, which he promised to repay when he collected his weekly
pay envelope. He was unable to do so, much to his chagrin, because his
pay had already been reduced to repay an earlier debt.[33] It is apparent

from this story, first, that workers in the factories preserved a set of social relations to help them overcome the problems of illness, death, and
even lack of cash; second, the factories tended to cooperate with workers' creditors in ways that hampered the associations in their efforts to
deal with the problems of the workers. Mutual-aid associations were
culturally sanctioned and were more than the purely occasional and
spontaneous loans that work mates in a European or American factory
might give a fellow worker down on his or her luck. Nevertheless, company rules could play havoc with the associations, leaving workers either to complain in vain to the company or to create new organizations,
such as unions, that would take the place of the older associations and
societies. ʿUrabi was clearly arguing for the latter choice and he pointed
out that unions are distinguished from mutual-aid societies by three
features: unity, permanence, and a social basis in production.[34] Union
members are wage workers; and soldiers, the self-employed, and the
family of the owner cannot form unions in the sense in which ʿUrabi
uses the word.[35] On the basis of ʿUrabi's definition of a union, most of
those who participated in the "union movement" described in chapter 5
ought not in fact to be considered part of the larger movement for workers' rights.

ʿUrabi's perception of two distinctly different approaches to workers'
self-defense was not limited to Egypt, for the same perception appeared
in Lebanon. The Lebanese Communist and trade union organizer, Fuʾad
Shamali, published a similar analysis in Lebanon in 1929.[36] Lebanese
workers, who were more likely skilled workers or craftsmen rather than
industrial workers, evidently were torn between organizing mutual-aid
societies and trade unions, which were largely under the aegis of the left:
"Some workers," according to Shamali,

> believe that the trade union is a welfare society; actually it is the reverse: wel-
> fare societies distribute alms [sadaqat] to those in need, help poor families,
> teach poor youths in school, and undertake other benevolent activities. As to
> the trade union, while being an economic force, it is also a political force
> from which the working-class parties gain moral strength in their fight for
> the interest of the working class; it is, in the hands of the workers, a weapon
> that they brandish in the face of the despotic capitalist oppressors, who have
> no other purpose in life than to pile up money in their coffers in order to
> assuage their unhealthy appetites.[37]

It is striking that here again one finds a union activist pitting the concept of union organization against that of social solidarity and asserting
that organizations are to be preferred because one lives in a society torn

by class rather than in a society united by mutual obligation. Thus organization, social vision, and political stance are closely linked.

These views about the manner of organization were widely debated
within the Egyptian working class. Union publications often carried the
debates, for the textile workers' leadership actively urged the superiority of the union organization over the self-help or mutual-aid association. Generally speaking, mutual-aid associations were thought to be
the hallmark of craftsmen and artisans and were even considered appropriate for them. In an article entitled "Unions in Egypt and How They
Are" in *Al-Yara*, the author made precisely this claim.

> The success of this form of union requires a broad, cooperative program and
> significant benefits, which accrue to the member; it cannot basically be a
> popular [i.e., political] program, especially if you find that the preexisting
> customs of craftsmanship [*maqalid al-ta'ifah*] give the workers a tendency to
> associate in a *jam'iyyah* . . . this will be so especially in situations where
> members of the trade do not work for a wage but by the piece or on consign-
> ment or commission.[38]

Not all those concerned saw a difference; many tended to see all associations of workers as similar. Thus in the editorial "Legitimate Rights"
we find the more common nationalist approach that just as all those
who worked with their hands were workers, whether artisans or proletarians, so too all their associations involved *ta'awun* or mutual aid.
For the writer of this editorial the problem was to persuade workers to
accept any form of cooperation because their desire to support their
families from their own efforts made cooperation difficult.

> Mutual aid is generally perceived as being a reduction in the severity of fate
> because only the poor and weak assist each other and [thus] the pride of the
> worker misleads him to rely only on himself . . . [but] mutual aid is the most
> important element of success and prosperity and one of the necessities of life
> and thus one satisfies his pride and adopts better words for mutual aid such
> as *jam'iyyah*, *niqabah*, or *rabitah*.[39]

At bottom, the distinction is between charity and mutual aid, and
one can draw a clear demarcation between left and nationalist or even
religious views. Nationalists as well as leftists could see (but did not always) a distinction between the kind of organization typical of industrial
workers and artisans, but only the leftists made the imperative of creating trade unions a key part of their program. For the left, trade unions
existed to fight for the relatively unrestricted rights of the members and
as such were largely the representatives of the workers rather than the
means by which they dealt with sickness, injury, or old age. Unions, for

the left, were sharply differentiated from the social life of the workers. For the nationalists and even the Muslim activists, on the other hand, the union played an important role as the social matrix for the workers. The imperative to create an association separate from the social lives of the members was carried out fairly consistently, though not as completely as the left might have wished. This imperative was closely linked to the way in which the union leaders saw society. Organizations are fine for struggling for relatively unlimited rights in conflict, but are less appropriate in situations in which boundaries are less certain. This latter situation was characteristic of the artisans and also of seasonal workers. The uncertainty over boundaries was expressed in theoretical form by contending visions of the relation between worker and owner, to which we now turn.

WORKERS' RIGHTS VERSUS OWNERS' OBLIGATIONS

After the fight to replace fraternal associations with unions, the left waged a far more bitter struggle over how to characterize what the workers were fighting for. Were they fighting for their own relatively unrestricted rights, or were they fighting to get the boss to recognize his obligations to the workers? This was one of the major ideological disputes between the Leninists and the Muslim Brothers, and one of the thorniest issues for the nationalists. The idea of mutual obligation between worker and owner made sense in the restricted world of the craftsman's workshop, but made less sense in a world where bureaucratic authority broke through personal relations. Both parties in the dispute saw the issue clearly. Reporters of the leftist newspaper *Al-Bashir* focused on this issue in their report of an intraunion dispute in which both Muhammad ʿAli ʿAmir and Jamal al-Banna were ousted from the textile workers' union in 1950.

> The union executive board fired President Muhammad ʿAmir with the excuse that he is a troublemaker. . . . Then it fired one of the propagandists of ʿatf for the workers who is well known for his antagonism to them, namely, Jamal Afendi al-Banna, who assures the workers that he is neutral between the two contending currents.[40]

The link is clear: Jamal al-Banna is a propagandist for the idea of ʿatf, but such an idea is a disguise for antiworker sentiment.

Like the not-dissimilar concept of equity or *insaf*, ʿatf could be stretched to apply to a variety of situations. Wherever the employer could be presumed to have a duty to his employees or could be made to have such a duty, the idea of ʿatf was invoked. This was especially true in the state-owned sector, where the workers voted for the Wafd and were rewarded with relative economic security. A clear example of the concept occurred in 1935 when a group of workers at the Arsenal were rehired four years after their ouster by Prime Minister Ismaʿil Sidki. Sidki had fired them for political demonstrations against his constitution and they were rehired as the Wafd began to regain power. As late as 1935 when Nissim was prime minister and Nahas was waiting in the wings, the bulk of the workers had been rehired but without seniority for the time spent off work. The Wafd press admonished the government on behalf of the workers.

> Perhaps those in charge have already taken care of this matter with the due concern for fulfilling the equity due the workers in the Tursanah and outside it, for these latter are most in need of equity among government workers.[41]

In another instance the *Al-Ikhwan al-Muslimun* newspaper commented favorably on the sympathy the oil workers won from state officials in contrast to the lack of ʿatf from the oil company officials.

The ideas of *insaf* and ʿatf were common to the newspaper of the Muslim Brothers and almost completely absent from the Communist press. Thus Ahmad al-Sukkari of the Muslim Brothers visited the minister of social affairs to ask for succor [ʿatf] for workers during the late 1940s.[42] The workers at the Sibahi plant in the period during which the Muslim Brothers and the Communists were battling in Shubra al-Khaima are reported to have asked the local authorities for "their due."[43] Another demand for "due" or *insaf* is reported by Suez Canal workers and a special objection is raised by the Muslim Brothers against the ability of a government agency, the Irrigation Administration, to obtain a religious declaration against the workers.[44]

Two concepts were in opposition; both occasionally were tied to the same word, *haqq* "right," but they were in essence mutually antagonistic. One was a concept of relations between worker and owner rooted in the social world of the artisan; the other was a concept of relations rooted in the social world of large-scale private capitalist production. Supporters of the first concept rejected equal hourly pay in favor of piece rates, which allowed the stronger or faster or more skilled worker to get ahead. According to this view, equality was "anarchistic" or "communistic," and insensitive to substantive differences of individual need. Thus we find *insaf* differentiated from *musawah* in similar ways. *Insaf* was defined as "giving every one who has a due his due with just division and honorable proportion."[45] Equality here is thus an empty word, and the concept of right is clearly one of mutual obligations or due rather than unrestricted individual rights that conflict.[46]

This conception of rights and equity embraced by the Muslim Brothers, among others, was certainly the customary one in Islam. Thus the *Encyclopedia of Islam* defines the term *hukuk* as "legal rights or claims, and corresponding obligations, in the religious law of Islam."[47] The same source gives *insaf* as implying "the idea of 'to grant rights' . . . to 'assure others the same right that one claims for one's self.' The idea thus presented corresponds strictly to equity."[48] This was more or less the classic and, if one is willing to grant the word the stature it deserves, traditional view of rights and equity in Islamic jurisprudence. But it was not the only view of rights Egyptian Muslims held by the 1940s.

The clearest indication of a different and fundamentally civic conception of right is found in an article written by Taha Saᶜd ᶜUthman and published in *Al-Damir* under the title "Politics Is a Right of the People, Not of Specific Individuals."[49] Taha Saᶜd's argument is that the Egyptian people have begun to fight for their economic rights, and in the course of this struggle they have occasionally been on the point of abjuring their political rights and their commitment to the parliamentary regime.[50] This he says occurred because the political leadership of the country turned "freedom into slavery and equality into exploitation," thus turning *freedom, equality,* and *parliament* into unpopular terms. Egypt is in a difficult situation, he continues, because it has left politics to the politicians ("as if it were a trade or *hirfah*"); such a conception of politics can only lead to dictatorship. Although the law forbids unions as organizations to be politically active, it is incumbent on union members as individuals to utilize their political rights guaranteed by the constitution.

At the time of the article, the textile workers had recently attempted to elect Faddali ᶜAbd al-Jayyid to parliament. His campaign did not succeed, but it did indicate the strength and cohesion of the union at Shubra. Clearly Taha Saᶜd had a firm basis for his views. What is impressive about Taha Saᶜd's argument is his definition of the nature of rights: Rights are a potential to act that inheres in all individuals. Taha Saᶜd clearly evokes a sense of the antagonistic interests at play in the economic and political arena. He by no means holds out the idea that there are mutual obligations that might bind employer and employee; rather he holds that a common field of political action exists, a field that is

open to both sides where both will attempt to increase their opportunities. This is a radically different conception of how workers and owners
relate to one another and an extremely clear popular conception of the
nature of citizenship.[51]

To understand why such different views of the relations between
workers and owners and of the role of the popular masses in the political system arose, we must place these views within the larger context of
the competing analyses of Egyptian society and the relation of Egypt to
the world. We shall now turn briefly to the alternative analyses of colonialism and imperialism on the one hand and of classes and the nation
on the other.

COLONIALISM, CLASS, AND CLASS STRUGGLE

For the left the dominant factor in Egyptian life was colonialism, and
the left linked this problem to its perception of Egyptian political reality.
The views of the left appeared regularly in the journal *Al-Damir* in late
1945 and early 1946. At this time *Al-Damir* was being published by
the textile worker leaders from Shubra, who were in the final stages of
becoming full members of a Communist organization. The views expressed in this particular journal stand out because they are the views of
trade union leaders who were still in touch with workers and who considered themselves a genuine and Leninist-oriented left. It is not important that there may have been more cogent or even more correct (from
the point of view of a Leninist party) analyses. What is important is that
this group of trade union leaders had a particular view of the Egyptian
situation and attempted to convince other trade union activists and potential allies of that view. Two articles stand out: "Unemployment . . .
the Problem of the Hour and Economic Colonialism" and "The Nationalism of the Workers."[52]

In "Unemployment," the author offers a structural explanation for
Egypt's problems. Unemployment, certainly a pressing problem with the
post–World War II winding-down of production, was becoming acute.
Framed in Marxist terms, the argument is by no means out of touch
with what was happening. Greater demand for goods sparked the expansion of the capital plant and employment.

> It was impossible to deny factories the labor force they needed to fulfill the
> long-term demand created by the Allied armies, which thereby increased
> local demand and made production go up. These factories and workers es-
> sentially welcomed the wartime process because they benefited from it, espe-

cially in the increased imports of modern foreign machinery. In fact these capital inputs took up all the available work force and even caused a net inflow from the countryside because of the demand for labor.[53]

This whole process is deemed "quite natural" and what is problematic is its cessation because of the decline of demand after the withdrawal of the armed forces and the political decisions of the colonial power, Britain, to forbid Egypt (and Egyptian capitalists) to continue production at the old rate and to sell to local markets in nearby countries and continue the progressive transformation of Egyptian capital stock. There is, therefore, no internal crisis in the Egyptian economy but rather a critical situation imposed by outside forces. Rich Egyptians are laying off workers, as directed, in order to spread fear and enable English or American colonialism to trample Egypt. The author of the article then suggests that if progressive capitalists are willing to "deepen their analysis" of the situation, the workers are willing to go along with a campaign to buy Egyptian and thereby save the home market, wages, and employment.

Two important themes emerge in this article: first, the interest of the Egyptian workers is clearly separate from but may nevertheless be linked with the interests of the Egyptian capitalists. Second, colonialism represents a set of political decisions with structural rather than personal origins and consequences. It is clear that there is danger from foreign dominance, but that dominance is manifest, not in the personal decisions of foreigners who work in Egypt or in their relatively privileged position, but in a system and structure that prevents Egypt from carrying out a "natural" sequence of capital expansion and development. In 1950, the left and many of the workers would look back on the war years as a kind of golden era when demands were won easily and strikes were neither as difficult nor as dangerous as they became during the period of rampant unemployment of the postwar era.[54]

In "The Nationalism of the Workers" Mahmud al-ʿAskari makes a similar argument in an attempt to redefine the nature of national unity against colonialism, which he calls "our number one enemy." According to al-ʿAskari, the workers are "nationalists before anything else because they understand the real meaning of nationalism." Praising the workers for their consistent struggle against colonialism "in any form," al-ʿAskari calls them the vanguard as early as 1919 and goes on to say that they remain the vanguard "because on them alone falls the burden of freeing the national soil." Al-ʿAskari suggests that the blazon of the workers is "unity" in the struggle against colonial domination. Unlike unity of the ranks as preached by the Wafd, which suggested the workers wait for the ouster of colonialism before they make social demands, al-ʿAskari suggests that anticolonial unity is the desideratum of the workers and is damaged by the failure of the bourgeoisie to strengthen the workers. This would best be done, al-ʿAskari suggests, by "total, complete unity in the struggle" and safeguarding existing wage levels, employment levels, and production levels. If this is done, workers in turn may support not only students, peasants, and small traders but also the national bourgeoisie. The workers will support the "nationalist capitalists but not aid those who are unjust or help those who are inimical." Here the Wafd vision of unity against colonialism is reversed, and clearly different interests appear to be at play: the capitalists may or may not support social reform. If they do not, then there can be no antiimperialist unity, and yet the workers' leaders are willing to support the capitalists in the interests of "freeing Egyptian industry from the danger of foreign capital."

The importance of this assessment of the Egyptian situation is not its degree of accuracy but rather how much it differed from the stand of the Wafd or the Muslim Brothers.[55] Where the left saw a "natural" and systemic-structural set of problems rooted in the nature of a developing capitalist economy, the Muslim Brothers argued that the origins of the workers' ills were cultural and largely personal. Where the left perceived the possibility of a political alliance between workers and owners, the Muslim Brothers suggested an inherent corporate identity of interests between workers and managers in the same economic sector. Where the left suggested that expansion of the Egyptian market regionally and internally might be the basis for avoiding bitter conflict within the Egyptian political community, the Muslim Brothers argued for a commitment by the state and the firm to increase benefits in order to avoid pushing workers to join independent and possibly antagonistic interests.

The Muslim Brothers identified colonialism as the core of Egypt's problems and then defined as the relevant aspect of colonialism for the workers the lack of interest evinced by foreign supervisors in the welfare of their subordinates. For the Muslim Brothers, as for the Wafdist officials, the workers were themselves too simple to know their own interests and were prone to "outbursts." For the Muslim Brothers, society was essentially in equilibrium and its main problem was that of replacing an ineffective elite, the British, with a new and effective one: Muslim Egyptians. It is for this reason that the concepts of ʿatf and insaf figure so clearly in their analyses and that they describe strikes and demonstrations as "outbursts." The words *sympathy*, *equity*, *understanding*, and *concern* describe human characteristics rather than structural relationships. Thus Muslim-oriented literature tends to describe the workers as "oppressed" rather than "exploited," a preferred Communist adjective. These words point to two different ways of looking at the same situation: the word *oppressed* suggests a failure of human interaction and may be solved by changing the personnel of the system, whereas the word *exploited* refers to an inherent structural relation.

STRATEGIES AND ENVIRONMENTS

The different world views sketched out above were found to be appropriate to distinct settings, so that even men who shared the four characteristics that define the Egyptian worker might follow different courses of political thought and action. In an ideal-typical exposition, we find three strategies for dealing with the demands of workers as a group. The first is a heroic reliance on the workers' own resources to create their own organizations dedicated to fighting the owners. To do so also means opposing any tendencies within the organization toward long-term accommodations with the owners based on short-term and partial agreement that would limit the ability of the workers to expand the definition of their own interests. The second strategy is to rely exclusively on the good will of the employer as a partner in a larger community and to vigorously oppose any tendencies to create separate and exclusive ways of expressing any interests of workers themselves in an antagonistic framework. The third strategy is to recognize that workers and owners are opposed and unequal. It is then possible to advance the interests of workers by relying on the extraeconomic actions of political patrons, which would, of necessity, be controlled from the top of an organization relatively resistant to the day-to-day concerns of workers.

In reality, these three strategies represent three important dimensions of union existence, and all schools of ideological thought may employ aspects of these strategies at different times. Each leadership chooses aspects of the strategies that are reasonably consistent among themselves and appeal in systematic ways to the membership. At least in the early industrialization of colonial countries like Egypt, aspects of the strategies seem to cluster in particular groups. One cluster, linked to a Leninist model, suggests an underlying belief in the creation of coherent and formally structured organizations to fight for relatively unlimited rights of workers in conflict with owners in a system of structured economic relations. Another cluster suggests a belief in the reliance of the workers on social association coupled with occasional acts of spontaneous mass movement in which the workers attempt to replace one elite with another so as to redefine a set of existing personal relations. This particular cluster presumes a culturally specific orientation with religious-ethical overtones. A third cluster is similar to the second but is essentially secular and suggests a belief in the creation of a ramified social association in which political patrons (rather than a universalist religion) help to redefine the personal relations that cause social antagonism. These three clusters also seem to be related to a perception of the workers' organization as a union or mutual-aid society or a combination of the two.

Let us consider the problem from the point of view of union militants or leaders (the union elite, if I may so use the term). The existence of social conflict in the factory is clear enough: owners and workers are competing for the income produced at the factory and it appears that one can benefit only at the expense of the other. In order to protect an existing situation or to improve it, it is necessary to determine its cause. This means determining the critical features of the conflict. Thus, as a first step, it seems plausible to suggest that the source of capital in interwar Egypt is the cause of the conflict between labor and capital: namely, foreign colonialism. Having defined the nature of conflict and suggested its dominant features, the union elite must choose a way to confront it. If the source of the conflict is foreign, then the mode of confrontation must be national. This is especially so when conflict is not seen as inherent in the patterns of work, but is sited in the personal relations between members of different occupations, such as workers and foremen. Existing social bonds between those who share a culture and merely happen to be in different occupations must be strengthened because these bonds provide cohesion in the face of conflict over norms. In such cases, the hypothetical analysis could run, conflict is best concluded either by adopting new norms of personal behavior or by the substitution of those with proper norms for those without them.[56] Thus conflict should be resolved, not through the structure of the plant, but by appealing to outside forces to remove the conflict itself: that means, specifically, intervention against the expression of conflict. Parenthetically, it should be noted that the foreign owners see things in the same light from the other side: they wish the workers to adopt new norms and wish to intervene against the expression of conflict until they do so.

The Muslim Brothers held that conflict in the factory, an undeniable fact, was rooted in the personal outlook of the managers, and social association of the workers provides the basis for their cohesion in the struggle over norms. They thus contended that the dominant members of the community (the *shaykhs* and those who had taken the *hajj*) would also be the dominant leaders. The mode of struggle therefore was a demand for justice, with a tendency on the part of the leadership to use blackmail (the threat of violence) to mediate between workers and managers.

On the other hand, the Leninists believed that conflict was rooted in the structural conditions of the factory, and that formal organization was the appropriate mode of creating cohesion among the workers. Organizational specificity took precedence over multiply stranded social association. The mode of struggle related to this position was the relatively unlimited struggle to expand the rights of workers, with a recognition that alliance with those of opposing interests might be possible if areas of mutual interest could be found, such as expanding the market for Egyptian production.

In some situations, however, conflict appeared to result from immediate policy orientations of a management that was liable to change under pressure from the state. Here, unlike our first case, conflict did not seem to arise from the innate dispositions of the managers but rather from policy decisions within a given context. In such contexts one finds a tendency either to make political deals with political patrons to put pressure on policy makers through the state or to deal directly with the managers to trade streamlined control of the work place for benefits. The former stance accords most closely with that of the nationalist Wafd and ʿAbbas Halim and the latter with the social democracy of Fathi Kamil. These two strategies may be understood as collapsed versions of the cultural (and here Muslim) strategy on the one hand and the structural (and here Leninist) strategy on the other. The difference appears to be that the actual recourse to the test of strength in the more extreme cases generally does not occur. The first stance does indicate, however, a set of preferences on the part of policy makers, whereas the second stance assumes a structured trade-off of costs and benefits between opposing interests. The Wafd-Halim strategy has echoes of the cultural critique of the Muslim Brothers and other nationalist figures but uses a more clearly defined network of patronage to reach its ends, whereas the social-democratic strategy presumes that labor peace is worth the price of higher wages and better benefits.

If we assume that these opposing strategies—especially culturalist versus structuralist—have a quality akin to ideal-typical variations, then we cannot avoid seeing more or fewer aspects of any or all of them in real cases. More importantly, this ideal-typical analysis can help us understand why men formally committed to a particular organization, such as Salamah in the Muslim Brothers, were able to move rapidly away from such a commitment when the situation changed. As an example, let us briefly consider the contrasting cases of Salamah and Kamil. Salamah was a member of the Muslim Brothers and Kamil was a social democrat. Salamah's arguments regarding the oil companies, it may be recalled, were not entirely cultural; indeed they seem in some ways to have been less cultural than those of the nominally non–Muslim Brothers at Hawamdiyyah. Rather, they leaned on the cultural as a determinant of policy decisions. When a new set of policy makers came to the fore—as occurred in foreign-owned industry increasingly after the Free Officers' coup in 1952—Salamah's own position gradually came to be that of the state. In a situation in which a regime was willing to share what had been foreign profits with the workers in the form of increased benefits, someone like Salamah could easily see the triumph of his particular analysis. Hence it was fairly easy to move into a position of leading the state-dominated trade union federation even as the organization of the Muslim Brothers was being smashed by the regime. For Fathi Kamil, on the other hand, the determinants of policy decisions were rooted in contradictory (but not necessarily totally antagonistic) interests of workers and owners. Workers thus had interests that required an independent and autonomous organization if they were to bargain with a particular set of policy makers. According to Kamil, workers are the same everywhere and share more with other workers even across national boundaries than with other members of their own national community. Within the corporate framework of national unity held by the Free Officers, Kamil's social-democratic position was a problem. The Free Officers were willing to increase the share of labor in income and benefits, but were not willing to share political power. Fathi Kamil was committed to a particular view of how to win increased benefits, but how much the workers got remained paramount. In this he was unlike the Leninists, whose total opposition to an identity of interests made them a danger. Fathi Kamil, only a problem, was therefore kicked upstairs.

The three groups we have examined underscore our basic point: we are not looking only at different settings, or different vocabularies, or different idiosyncratic approaches to problems of organization. Rather we are looking at the different strategies that are appropriate in different settings and have different consequences in moments of political crisis. Some of these consequences are intended; others are not.

CHAPTER THREE

Economy and Society: Conflict and Change

In order to understand workers' politics we need to understand as much as possible the different ways workers in Egypt made out. This means we must also understand the various sets of rules governing discipline in different kinds of enterprises; in addition we must determine what kinds of workers were likely to be employed under those rules. We must investigate this last question first, that is, we must investigate the growth of the demand for industrial labor in Egypt (especially in the context of the demand for other kinds of labor) and the sources from which labor was drawn, especially the communities in which workers lived and the skills they brought to their jobs.

The theory of labor market segmentation predicts in a general way what kinds of labor and hence what kinds of workers will be needed in particular industrial settings, but the level at which the theory operates is far too general to be more than a starting point. It is all very well to say that the mass production industries for a large, stable market may well require the least-skilled workers of a society. The actual levels of skill considered "least skilled," the actual sources from which such "unskilled" workers are drawn, and the political and social resources of such workers will vary widely, as will the importance of mass production in the overall economy of any particular country.

As the idea of "careers at work" in different labor markets suggests, workers may participate in different labor markets, but they do not make any of the fundamental decisions that govern the creation of the labor markets themselves. They do not make decisions about capital allocations, which create the demand for industrial labor, and they do not form *de novo* the communities from which labor is supplied. The prior existence of a community or social group, on the one hand, and decisions about where and how to employ capital on the other hand sharply limit the framework within which workers or would-be workers can exercise choice.

What we see at a glance in Egypt is what we see elsewhere in the third world: peasant communities in the agricultural sector often producing for export and a long-established artisan sector along with a growing industrial sector that uses equipment and labor in ways similar to those of the developed capitalist world. Even if we also examine tables of quantitative data, any picture drawn along these lines is unhelpful.

We cannot assume who is an "industrial" worker or what is the experience of "industry," nor can we even assume that the experience of being a worker is most intense in the most mechanized industries. We must begin instead with several empirical questions. What were the major industrial establishments in Egypt? How did they differ in terms of stability of employment? What kinds of discipline did they employ? Whom did they employ? Did labor markets link up individuals with employment opportunities, or did an entire family undertake to provide labor for one position? How much mobility from market to market or even within markets was there? I do not wish to answer these questions as might an economist; instead, I intend to use them to explore how workers, confronted with a world they did not make, understood the world and sought to change it. Because the orientation of this study is toward industrial workers and because industrial investment was largely linked with foreign capital, we need to examine the patterns of investment in Egypt in the pre–World War II period; we shall then be in a position to suggest where the demand for unskilled, semiskilled, and skilled labor was likely to develop. Finally, we shall consider how this demand was satisfied and the relevance of the particular sources of supply.

CAPITAL INVESTMENTS: WHERE MEN WORKED

Despite a widespread misconception that Egypt has "always" been a hydraulic society, the creation of a centralized irrigation system around which state power could be exercised is fairly recent. In large measure investment in agriculture in the nineteenth century created an irrigation system that was amenable to central control and a corps of officials to undertake the task. This investment originated almost entirely outside Egypt, but shaped the growth of industrial production in that country. Further, this investment led to the demand for new kinds of labor and thus created new labor markets in Egypt as well as the opportunity for more extensive movement between or within such markets. Most of this investment was directed either into agriculture itself or into marketing, processing, or transporting agricultural products.

Before the nineteenth century, decisions about investments in the countryside and in the cities were largely if not entirely local matters. According to one scholar, from Pharaonic to Mamluk times "at the social and administrative level, flood control and irrigation were and continued to be managed locally, by the mass input of the total, able-bodied rural population of a basin unit."[1]

In the period after the Occupation of Egypt by Britain in 1882, however, money as well as expertise flowed into Egypt, to fund agricultural development as well as industrial production. After 1900

> there was a vast flow of foreign currency into the country, no less than 160 new companies with an authorized capital of LE 43.5 million being founded between 1900 and 1907, as compared with a total paid-up capital of LE 13,885,000 for all companies (save the Suez Canal) in 1899. . . . This money was almost entirely invested in land banks, mortgage companies, and the like and scarcely at all in manufacturing.[2]

More precisely it can be said that this money went to support an infrastructure that secured Egyptian agriculture a place in the world market.

> A study of the distribution of foreign investment at the beginning of the 20th century shows that the bulk of imported funds found employment in banking, land and urban development, transport and public utilities and other amenities necessary for the commercialization and urbanization of the country.[3]

Yet few of the improvements in techniques seem to have benefited the bulk of the rural laboring population for

> despite increased drainage, more farm animals, improved water supply, and large-scale imports of chemical fertilizers, crop yields did not grow rapidly enough to compensate for the fall in land per person . . . by 1940 output per worker in agriculture was still below the 1914 level.[4]

Throughout the early twentieth century there was an increase not only in investment in agriculture but also in population—both on the land and in the rural towns. In addition the fragmentation of landholdings and the loss of smaller holdings because of arrears in taxes and debts increased the number of peasants who entered the labor market throughout this period.[5]

Although there was industrial investment in Egypt before the turn of the century, observers in the 1920s recognized that it was not of the type to turn Egypt into an advanced capitalist country and the investment of that earlier time was largely the result of foreign funds flowing to the country.

> Industry as understood in England is unimportant in Egypt. There are neither huge industries nor trades such as coal, steel, engineering, cotton, wool, building, etc. as is the case in this country. The sugar industry is probably the most important, yet it is wholly undertaken by foreign corporations.[6]

Modern writers generally agree with this characterization of the Egyptian economy, at least through World War I, although the more recent writers give the word *industry* a broader scope.

> Industry in Egypt during this period [1882–1914] consisted essentially of three elements: namely the remnants of the traditional craft industries, the two main industries based on agricultural raw materials—cotton ginning and sugar crushing and refining—and those industrial undertakings evoked by the development of Cairo and Alexandria as modern commercial cities.[7]

The cotton and sugar industries and oil production had employed mass production techniques and thus needed large amounts of unskilled labor. Cotton gins typically required less investment than did the sugar refineries, which generally led to the gins being owned by Egyptians and the refineries by foreigners. Gins and mills apparently required the same kind of unskilled labor and found it by introducing machinery directly into the countryside. In so doing these industries generated a seasonal demand for labor that enabled most of the work force to remain in village society; they do not seem to have encouraged workers to learn new skills.

There is little doubt that employment in the gins and mills was widely regarded as an option for a peasant family rather than for an individual. The cotton gins, for example, are reported to have employed significant numbers of women (for fourteen to eighteen hours a day), but the women represented a family labor commitment, for they were "replaced from time to time by another member of their family but the employer takes no steps to insure that individuals are relieved at intervals."[8] It is less clear if the sugar mills employed women or whole families on a rotating basis, but it is nevertheless true that even in the year-round labor force of the large sugar refinery at Hawamdiyyah any position belonged to a family, whose members successively filled it. The freedom for such substitution points to the extremely low level of skills involved and thus to the exceedingly poor bargaining position of the workers. Such workers were, however, the majority of the unskilled work force in Egypt at the time.

The industries of agricultural transformation employed approximately 120,000 workers, primarily poor peasants or landless laborers, for the duration of a harvesting season. These were the people who were Egypt's "industrial" workers for a long time and they brought with them their ties to their own specific villages and their personal sense of what was right and wrong. The cotton ginning and pressing factories employed 40,000 men and women from October to April; the cottonseed oil presses and the grain mills (both industrial and nonindustrial) employed 50,000; and the sugar industry employed almost 30,000 workers between December and May. Many of these firms were owned by foreign-based firms, by Europeans who immigrated to Egypt, or by Egyptians with close ties to foreign markets, and were all part of the process by which Egypt was linked to the world market.

Although foreign ownership or entanglement was a salient feature of such firms, by itself this does not distinguish this sector of activity. What is important is that these investments were in areas well suited to industrial production. These firms were engaged in providing standard products for a large and relatively stable market; they therefore required large numbers of unskilled hands. Other unskilled labor was required in the infrastructural sectors. The investments in the public utilities also date from this period, although the transit, transport, and energy systems tended to grow while the ginning and milling industries did not.

It was not until the 1930s, however, that large-scale light industrial production came into being. When it did it grew rapidly. This development was related to the shift to import substitution, which itself was tied to the formation of a nationalist-capitalist group centered around Bank Misr. This group

> succeeded in breaking the monopoly of foreigners on business . . . established the long-delayed cotton textile industry [and] laid the foundations for a more diversified economy, [although] it certainly failed to alter in any fundamental way the colonial character of the economy.[9]

Not all these firms with machinery were necessarily what we might call independent primary producers. In the 1930s large-scale machine production was introduced to substitute for handicraft production locally as well as to develop completely new products. Often such machine production was intended for a large, stable market for standard goods, but it was also used occasionally simply to expand the output for small or unstable markets or markets for nonstandard goods. Thus the effect of machine production on workers' wages, conditions, and chances to learn new skills and follow new careers differed widely from industry to industry or even from firm to firm. Sometimes the introduction of machines led to a rapid loss of jobs, whereas at other times it led to a rapid expansion of investments, which also generated increased demand for labor. In the case of the cigarette industry, employment dropped dramatically between 1910 and 1930 while production increased. In the case of textiles, industrial employment and production increased rapidly from the 1930s onward, although not always smoothly. It is by no means clear that we can really lump all the mechanized textile workers together, for some produced coarse cloth to meet the demand for cheap goods while others produced finer cloth for smaller, less stable markets.

COMMUNITIES AND CRAFTS: WHERE DID WORKERS COME FROM?

Who made up the population of Egypt, and especially the laboring population? In the cities there were merchants, artisans, religious scholars, domestics, slaves, and servants. In the countryside there were landowners, peasants, and the landless. Let me now turn to these two broad groups of communities.

ARTISANS AND CRAFTSMEN IN URBAN AND RURAL BUSINESS

In the popular view competition from foreign imports had completely displaced "traditional" craft production in Cairo and other urban centers at the turn of the century. Certainly particular branches of handicraft production had suffered from foreign competition in the period after the Occupation in 1882, but that does not mean that craft production as a way of life had ended. That U.S. production of automobiles has been challenged does not, by any means, imply that industrial production itself is no longer dominant in the United States; rather, other branches of industry have been developed as old ones decline. So it was in Egypt. Artisan production, which had been dominant in Egypt's urban life in the past, remained dominant well into the twentieth century, especially in terms of the numbers of people employed in artisan, handicraft, or merchant shops.

The world of the small craftsman, like the world of the peasant, is a traditional one in the sense in which the term is used by American sociologists, political scientists, and anthropologists. In this world we find a clearly defined career and perception of the craft labor market. Artisans, craftsmen, and merchants live in a world in which the ceaseless exploration of practical knowledge is necessary but is undertaken in essence by collective trial and error. Artisans learn and the "art" progresses: without the sharing of the myriad specificities, there is no progress. The price for such progress, however, is dedication to the craft itself and the ability as well as the willingness to limit entry into the craft.[10] Once he has entered the craft, the apprentice is assured that his progress will be sure and steady even if not quick. Where any of these features is absent, the craft itself often quickly degenerates, although artisans may well try to enforce the rules of the craft long after the productive structure of society makes it uneconomical to do so.

Cairo was and remains full of such people, and their world is by no means a halfway house between rural "tradition" and urban "modernity." It is the world of urban "tradition," and it remains vital, not because it is held over from the past, but because the structure of craft life itself is a world of tradition. Perhaps no one has expressed this better in regard to Cairo than Janet Abu-Lughod:

> Type 3 [the Traditional Urbanite], however, constitutes the missing link in Cairo's puzzling ecology. Even today it accounts for more than half of the city's population. Failure to conceptualize adequately this third type—not as some intermediate point along an urban-rural continuum but as a separate dimension—accounts for the frequency with which irrelevant questions and meaningless hypotheses are framed about the Middle Eastern city.[11]

We should expect to see quite different orientations not only toward time and discipline but also toward association between workers in the craft and other groups because the conceptual orientations and resources at hand are clearly different. We must therefore differentiate the elements of the urban work force.

Without suggesting that life in Cairo was immemorially the same, I shall consider a few descriptions of artisan and mercantile life before 1882 as a way of discovering the world of the small craftsman. If Jacques Berque was correct that it was urban life itself taken as a whole that was most distinct from rural life, then the distinctions between urban dwellers were initially less important than their differences from those in the countryside. At one point "a journeyman would be designated with the general term sani^c which means both laborer and craftsman." [12] The word was used for a person working in a glass factory or a silk-weaving shop, but also for one in service of a "bride-comber," a woman who dressed brides and took care of other arrangements for weddings. [13]

The capital reserves and capital employed were relatively low, especially by our standards, and shops were small. This may be a general feature of artisan production, but it has certainly been the case in Cairo for a long time. Before 1800 there was already a great division of labor and the average workshop employed two or three workers besides the owner. [14] Artisans were differentiated from merchants, shopkeepers, and those who possessed book learning. Socially they were known as men who made things and were paid wages. [15]

The urban craftsmen associated through a series of guilds, which helped preserve the situation of the artisans from decay and gave the state easy access to them. These guilds took the typical form for craftsmen, artisans, and merchants, and were not dissimilar from any other forms by which men monopolized their crafts.

> The guilds existed in the second half of the nineteenth century . . . [and] performed important public functions. Thus throughout the century the shaykhs of the guilds controlled and supervised the guilds' members' activities and ensured that the instructions of the government were carried out; they were made responsible for misdemeanor of their guilds' members; they supplied labour and service to the government and private employers; and they arbitrated disputes among the members of the guilds. . . . It was the function of the guilds to restrict the number of persons exercising a certain trade, and in many occupations the guilds kept a monopoly of their trades until the last decades of the nineteenth century. [16]

The guilds, it is apparent, had a dual role: they were a link to the state and they served their members by limiting employment, for which they had state sanction for coercion. [17] The individual price for the service rendered the members was too high to ensure that individuals would pay. Thus, the state was as necessary for the maintenance of the guild—the protective form of association for craftsmen—as the guild was for the state. Craft production remained the norm for urban production for a long time, and the very notion of labor or workers remained for a long time imbued with the notion of small urban producers in handicraft or artisan production rather than large-scale industrial capital production. In many locales craftsmen were the initial nucleus of an urban industrial work force.

Most urban production and service continued to be carried on in small shops by men who had few or no employees. Even by 1907, when productive inputs in the agricultural sector had already had a major impact on prices, population, and work, urban production was still little affected by machines. By 1907 there were four hundred thousand "industrial" workers in Egypt, but they were overwhelmingly in "small-scale" industry and were still referred to by the same word, *sani^c*, used hundreds of years earlier. Work was

> carried on in workshops, or in booths, by handicraftsmen working on their own, with the help of a few apprentices. In fact, and in spite of its name, it [small-scale industry] is the most important category, for it employs the greatest number of workers and spreads its network over all the towns and large villages of Egypt.[18]

It is important to keep in mind that the particular products of craftsmen and artisans differed from those that had been so produced in the past, but such producers still dominated the work force and sometimes output itself. The key areas of such production were

> building, weaving, and its derivatives, dyeing, metallurgy and ironworks, wood and its derivatives, tanning, shoemaking, milling, chemical industries (soap, oil, candle-making), and artistic crafts (jewelry, fine carpentry, embossing, etc.).[19]

In general these were goods for immediate and local use, but not always. Some artisan goods were sold throughout Egypt. The same man who made these goods or provided the service had to market it.

> In most cases the Egyptian industrialist is also a trader. He manufactures his goods and markets them himself, either wholesale or retail. And it is a constant fact that, since he keeps no books or has only the most rudimentary accounts, he is unaware of the cost of production of the goods. . . . As his main concern is to ensure his livelihood and that of his family, he limits his horizon to satisfying that need and neglects all that could promote the progress and vitality of his business.[20]

Those interested in large industrial undertakings denigrated such a world view. Artisan and craft production was nevertheless seen as the repository of important social values centered on the family. Owning a small workshop and supporting a circle of dependents either by birth or by apprenticeship, artisans were presented by some authors as the ideal and idealized core of Egyptian urban civility. The very title of one of

Yusuf al-Siba'i's stories, "A Contented Fellow," suggests that its central characters live a life to be cherished and emulated. These three residents of the Mediterranean town of Damietta are two carpenters, "Osta" Ibrahim Zeinhom and "Muallim" Ali, and Zeinhom's wife, Zakiya.[21]

Even as late as 1937, 52 percent of all "industrial" establishments employed no one other than the proprietor, and another 40 percent employed fewer than five people.[22] To the degree that politics became urban mass politics, these were the men who would at first be available for mass protest, and for these men to protect their situation they needed a tie to the state. Conversely, for a party like the Wafd, which was largely unable to rely on its opponents to play the political game by the routine parliamentary or constitutional rules, access to such a group was necessary.

PEASANTS ON THE LAND AND IN THE FACTORY

Besides artisans, who made up a significant portion of the "working class" on their own and were available for recruitment into large-scale industrial production, there was also a large reserve of peasant labor. As we consider accounts of peasant life at the time of the Occupation and thereafter, we should remember that in Egypt as elsewhere accounts of peasant life tend to follow one of two Western literary traditions: all pastoral or all brutish.[23] Berque is lyrical in his description of village collectivity.

> The harvest takes place in an atmosphere of collective emulation, with practically no individual initiative. The peasants move in groups from one plot, *qibala*, to another. The whole of the land is dotted with plots, each with its proper name, connected with those of the village. . . . Cheerful bands harvest from dawn to dusk.[24]

Recent research has begun to undermine this rosy picture.

Berque's overall point about a collective identity, however, is valid. Clearly, villages had some sort of collective identity, even if that identity was primarily manifested in opposition to the exactions of the state. Peasants identified themselves with a particular region or even a particular village, and mutual aid within the horizon of that village and its social world was a fact of life. Perennial irrigation, cotton production, and more money did not immediately change this picture, according to Berque, of "the village's collective personality," which was "primarily a refuge from legality."[25] Most of these villagers lived in far from rosy conditions, and although anthropologists may celebrate the villager's

unity with nature in picturesque terms, poverty and uncertainty determined many of his responses to events. Collectivity coexisted with the
uneasy personal hatreds that were, along with envy and avarice, the
closest expressions of class war in the peasant universe.[26]

The peasants may have produced for a capitalist market, but they did
not entirely live in one, for although "they produced for the market . . .
that market did not include their own labor force."[27] As late as 1939,
only 17 percent of the land was under money rent.[28] The peasants were
typically "avaricious," according to one anthropological account of
the time.[29]

In Upper Egypt at least, harvesters were all paid in kind through this
period (the 1920s), as were many craftsmen and tradesmen in the village. Cash was used for transactions between but not within villages.

> The custom of paying in kind is a very ancient one, and is not confined to
> harvesters only. The village barber is also paid by his fellow-villagers in this
> way, with beans and corn, and those who thus remunerate him can demand
> his services for shaving and haircutting for a year. . . . This rule applies also
> to the ferryman, who, when the fields belonging to a village lie on the op-
> posite bank of a canal, conveys over the cattle and laborers every morning,
> and brings them back just before sunset.[30]

The water carrier in the market was also paid in kind.[31] Moreover, these
habits were not limited to Upper Egypt, for barber-surgeons in the Delta
were also paid in kind.[32] Markets in the Delta were evidently also places
of barter as well as cash sales.[33]

The life of peasants was marked by more than the absence of a full
range of market incentives. Peasants were also subject to direct coercion
on occasion. Despite the formal end of corvée labor, peasants still had to
perform unpaid labor for officials, often for the private benefit of the
officials.

> It is usual, if not obligatory, for a fellah who wishes to stay in the good graces
> of his ʿumda to work for him several days without pay.[34]

Village solidarity still existed, and the sense of norms of justice rooted in
the village remained, even if the countryside itself could no longer support a society in which those norms were realized. These norms often
concerned land or other communal issues, but in general were framed in
terms of the existence of customary rights.[35]

Clearly these peasants provided the least-skilled labor in Egypt. They
had the skills of the hoe and pick ax, skills that entail a certain learned
rhythm of work, even if not of production as a process. There was a

large reservoir of such men in Egypt and the possibility of making ready money must have been attractive to them. Yet for most, their skills were not transferable to the new industrial enterprises, where work might be as repetitive as in the fields but demand a familiarity with different and far more dangerous implements. The peasants' chances for advancement in the new industries, given their almost total lack of education and their easy replacement, was limited. Though not all unskilled or semiskilled work was extremely low paying, most of it was, and all of it lacked opportunities for peasants to climb the skill ladder.

It is difficult for us to appreciate fully the skills of such workers not only in a transitional social setting (between farm and city) but also in a transitional age from the world of animal power to that of mechanical power. Lack of knowledge, of skill, of familiarity with the industrial setting, was more than a barrier to a rising income; it was often a source of real danger. The unskilled of this time and place did not have even the abilities we assume among the "unskilled" today, who are expected to read, write, and be familiar with the operation of machinery. The absence of these skills often had tragic consequences. *La Bourse Egyptienne* carried, almost daily, reports of workers who burned themselves to death, mutilated themselves, or electrocuted themselves (or their co-workers) because of their unfamiliarity with even the simplest precautions for working around machinery, electricity, or both. One report will illustrate the real level of knowledge many unskilled workers had. Mustafa al-Ghitawi was ordered to clean up an electric transformer and proceeded to do so with a broom and a can of gasoline; he was killed when a static discharge ignited the gas. What appears to have happened is that a European chief engineer gave an order, which was transmitted through a subordinate to a worker who had no idea of the dangers of electricity.[36]

In 1931, Harold Butler in his report on labor conditions noted that although most factories had placards and notices regarding unsafe conditions, most workers were unable to read them. He suggested using pictorial posters, which were then evidently not in use.[37] The world of the factory was a desirable one from the point of view of income, but it remained dangerous and unpredictable in other ways.

TYPES OF DISCIPLINE: HOW ARE MEN DIRECTED TO TASKS?

There are clearly a variety of ways by which work is coordinated and men are persuaded to perform the tasks that are presented to them. I shall briefly present two approaches, one characterizing the artisan world of work and the other the industrial world of work in Egypt.

The world of the artisan was a world of dense social interaction. The shop of the craftsman was his own world, often coextensive with the master's authority in a family. Craftsmen's relations were complex and based on face-to-face contacts with customers (or clients) and other artisans and merchants. The single person, master in his shop as in his family, set the tone for the urban economy as he did for urban society.

Not all observers considered this to be a good arrangement, but its prevalence clearly determined what the work place would be like: family discipline expanded into it and defined activity there. The artisan's business was distinct from other businesses, just as his family was distinct from other families. Precisely because it was *his* it was different, rather than because it ran in a different way or produced something distinctive.

> Each individual from among the masters of these crafts is individuated by the establishment of his own workshop and keeping its administration independent, and by working in it (in general) on his own or with the aid of a single helper.[38]

These craftsmen were found not only in the large cities such as Cairo or Alexandria. They were even more typical of the smaller towns and cities in the countryside, whether in Upper or Lower Egypt. In some places they existed with no direct foreign competition and probably little indirect competition from imports.

> The small factories that I saw dealt with rice, silk, furniture, and shoes. My guide told me they are almost entirely in the hands of natives and that there are very few foreigners in the city. . . . [In one silk mill] all the looms were worked by hand by patient slit-eyed Egyptians and many small boys were employed.[39]

The nature of industrial production—the division of jobs into a large number of relatively small operations—was the same in Egypt as in the countries from which the industrial mechanisms were imported: this form of bureaucracy was built into the production structure. But the role of the foreman in Egypt did not follow entirely the pattern established in Europe, for in Egypt the foreman's role was largely unchecked by any concern for the maintenance of the bureaucratic integrity of the structure as a whole.[40]

The role of the foreman in Egypt was endowed with considerably greater power than would have been the case in many factories in the United States that needed to maintain a stable work force. This seems to

have resulted in part from a perception that the sociological origins of
the work force required it.

> The present disciplinary system at Mahallah which was conceived to deal
> with fellaheen fresh from an agricultural environment is now being applied
> to vastly different individuals. . . . As time has passed the system produces
> less and less results and more and more friction. . . . Full production cannot
> be realized under the present conditions because of the chaotic system of su-
> pervisory discipline. . . . The present labor control system in the mill con-
> spires to maintain a constant state of tension among the workers and an ever
> present danger of strikes. The supervisor is expected to maintain production
> through the agency of a rigid disciplinary system which is the consequence
> of the opinion held by management that the workers are "too ignorant to
> understand" and therefore must be ruled by fear.[41]

Management's goal of maintaining discipline in the work force also led
it to take other positions that opposed the interests of both workers and
owners. Workers were more willing to stay in factories and learn new
skills, for example, than were owners to have them do so. Again, Mahallah is an example. Further, all the textile factories established after
the 1930s were located in outlying rural or urban areas in order to maintain access to cheap labor in an environment that would inhibit labor
organization that would ultimately cause the price of labor to rise.

> The last point referred to earlier in the text is the large wage differential be-
> tween town and country, the average level of wages in Mahallah being ap-
> proximately 70% of that ruling in Cairo and 60% of that ruling in Alex-
> andria, and the fact that labour in rural areas is not highly organized.[42]

One can argue that there were other reasons such as humidity for choosing a remote locale like Mahallah, but these reasons do not apply to
other outlying areas such as those near Cairo, nor do they address the
possibility that employers were unwilling in many cases to pay wages
high enough to keep a stable work force. In fact, Egyptian managers do
not seem to have wanted to attract relatively well-trained workers to
provide a stable work force if that meant weakening management. Well-
trained workers were confident, independent, and often demanding
about both wages and the way in which control was wielded in the
factory.

Who was the worker preferred by management? We have a good picture, drawn in the 1950s, that holds true for an entire earlier generation.

> The most critical criterion is obedience and docility which Egyptians seem to
> equate with efficiency. A good worker is one who accepts authority, carries
> out orders, refrains from talking back to his superiors, and does not start

arguments with fellow workers. In short, employers want workers who are committed to accepting the unilateral authority of management. If they do not question the discipline of factory employment, do not break machinery or damage equipment, and are punctual, they will probably become permanent workers.[43]

This perception of the ideal worker, according to Harbison and Ibrahim, was especially common in the set of industries "Egyptianized" (foreign-owned companies that were bought out by Egyptians) in the mid-1940s, including the sugar industry. These new owners were characterized by Ahmad ʿAbbud. Presumably Abbud did not change the entire structure of control, although Harbison and Ibrahim indicate that he may have made them more personalized and less formal. According to these authors, wholly foreign-owned companies had more highly bureaucratized internal structures.

> The foreign companies usually had a formal plan of organization, a detailed set of rules and operating procedures, position descriptions and classifications, and fairly clear lines of demarcation between line and staff operations. The lines of communication were more formal, the regulations more rigorous, and the functional organization more impersonal than in their Egyptian counterparts.[44]

These firms were the Egyptian affiliates of what we would today call multinational corporations: Shell Oil, Socony-Mobil Oil, Heineken's Brewers, and Players Tobacco.

Although Harbison and Ibrahim give relatively high marks to the textile industries in Mahallah and Kafr al-Dawwar owned by the Bank Misr group, it seems that they were not significantly different from the Abbud-owned industries, and that in fact the national bourgeoisie in general placed considerable power in the hands of the foreman. I shall return to this point more fully in chapter 8.

The rigidity of the disciplinary system was in many ways a strength of the factory system as it attempted to make peasants act like industrial workers. If one believes that a man's character is shaped early in life, rigid discipline is appropriate in order to keep in a factory men whose idea of a "career at work" is to hold their own land. This form of discipline may also reflect a traditional belief on the part of the owner that the factory is "his," in the same way that an artisan views his workshop. Again, the choice of a rigid discipline may simply reflect an unwillingness to pay a sufficient wage to induce workers to remain in the factory, acquire new skills, and develop a new career, one that is different from the one in which they began.

If we place the "multinationals," which employed a relatively stable year-round work force (thereby leaving the sugar industry out), at one end of the scale and the small shop owner at the other, we would find that the smaller, Egyptian-owned mechanized firms embody some of the worst features of both worlds: a management jealous of its prerogatives, facing an unstable market, and anxious to use any extraeconomic appeals to keep wages low, along with the need for a skilled work force unwilling to put up with such a situation.

CHAPTER FOUR

To Build the State;
To Use It

It is impossible to discuss politics without discussing the state. Discussions of the state in the abstract or of political activity and its relation to economic activity are more properly the concern of theoreticians and I shall not enter into them here. For the purpose of this analysis, it is important to recognize only that the state is a large organization that has powerful means to act, some of which are peculiar to it; that it is staffed by personnel, some of whom are chosen in ways peculiar to it; and that it carries out policies, some of which are necessarily contradictory. Certain features of the Egyptian system, as it was formed in the early twentieth century, had specific effects on the various sectors of the industrial work force.

How did the Egyptian state work? What were its means? The means were the corps of professionals in the bureaucracy who carried out state policies in the "field," the army, and the legal system.

Who were the leaders and would-be leaders of the state? They were certainly politicians, but the areas in which they operated varied widely. Egypt had a parliamentary system, but none of the state's leaders was able to win power by skilled manipulation of parliamentary rules or parliamentary coalitions. Egypt had elections, but only rarely were they the deciding factor in which party held power; further, they were not entirely free or honest. The competence of the politicians came more in their varying abilities to work within the two great givens of the Egyp-

tian political system: the control Great Britain exercised and the resentment to that control and to the entire system that grew up during the
First World War and persisted until 1952.

What were the policies of the state? In particular, what were the policies of different political leaders in the state toward different sectors of
the economy? This last concern often led to contradictory outcomes.
The interest of the state in higher tax revenues, for example, sometimes
conflicts with the political alliances of those in its higher echelons. The
interest of the state in asserting its control over parts of the national
patrimony sometimes conflicts with the economic explcitation of that
patrimony. For these reasons a state may favor one part of the national
work force over another, just as it often favors one section of capital over
another. The state and politicians appear, therefore, as independent
actors to be won over by workers (or owners), and how this is done may
have a great impact on how workers (or owners) see themselves.

In the last chapter I indicated that Egypt did not have a centralized
and powerful state based on control of an irrigation system reaching
back to the Pharaonic era. It was the British who perfected and centralized the irrigation system so that it could become the basis for
greater state control in the countryside. That, in essence, is the problem
of the Egyptian state in the period between 1882 and 1952. The British
created instruments that the Egyptian political elite sought to use, and
the Egyptian political elite was willing to struggle fiercely over who controlled the state administration but not so fiercely that it might damage
those instruments. British officials did not always agree among themselves over what policies were best suited to their interests in Egypt, and
Egyptians did not always agree over what policies best suited their own
interests. Consequently one might find British and Egyptian officials in
odd alliances either over particular policies or over the creation of particular kinds of administrative tools.

THE STATE AS MEANS TO AN END

Max Weber gave considerable thought to the problem of defining the
state. In defining the state and especially what he called the modern
state, Weber was concerned primarily to explicate those features of this
large organization that distinguished it from other large organizations.
He considered the existence of large bureaucratic organizations in general to be the hallmark of modern civilization. Modern states thus share

many features with other organizations even as they are distinguished from them in other respects. What is distinctive to such organizations as states is not that they use force, argued Weber, but that they use force at the same time they attempt to prevent any other institution from using it.

> Ultimately one can define the modern state sociologically only in terms of the specific *means* peculiar to it, as to every political association, namely, the use of physical force. 'Every state is founded on force,' said Trotsky at Brest-Litovsk. That is indeed right. . . . Of course, force is not the normal or the only means of the state—nobody says that—but force is a means specific to the state. Today the relation between the state and violence is an especially intimate one. In the past, the most varied institutions—beginning with the sib—have known the use of physical force as quite normal. Today, however, we have to say that a state is a human community that (successfully) claims the *monopoly of the legitimate use of physical force* within a given territory. Specifically, at the present time, the right to use physical force is ascribed to other institutions or to individuals only to the extent which the state permits it.[1]

Weber's arguments about force and the modern state are nothing more than extensions of his theses about the uses of bureaucracy and rationalization. Katharine Chorley's analysis remains the most succinct.

> It is the application of science to warfare that has weighted the scale so heavily in favour of the political side which controls a professional army as against the party which controls only volunteers, however brave and even fanatical. The technical resources and skills of modern troops make it impossible for amateur soldiers, untrained and necessarily unequipped with instruments of modern war, to stand up against them if they are exploiting these resources to the full.[2]

When all is said and done, no matter how cleverly we discuss ideology, hegemony, education, reification, and the like, preponderant (if not monopolistic) control over the means of coercion *distinguishes* the state from other institutions in society.

States come to be and to possess the attributes mentioned by Weber, but just as society is not an undifferentiated mass of people or the economy an undifferentiated mass of laborers, so too the polity is not an undifferentiated mass of citizens. Any state must monopolize the means of coercion; win legitimacy (and this from different sectors of the population); and set both social and geographical bounds for the exercise of its monopoly of coercion.

What does this analysis tell us about Egypt? The power of the khedive—the title of the ruler of Egypt in the nineteenth century—was sharply reduced in two important areas. He was nominally the agent of an Ottoman sovereign and thus was in some regards limited in the decisions he could make independently. More important, given the increasing formal independence of the khedive, which ultimately led to the independence of the monarchy after World War I, was the question of the means at hand to put his decisions into effect. Although Muhammad ʿAli tried to build an army and a police force powerful enough to extend Egyptian power far beyond the Nile Valley as well as within it,[3] by the middle of the nineteenth century, the Egyptian state hardly seemed to have a real existence.

If we take the khedive as the dynastic representative of central power, then central power was in a precarious state in Egypt by the second third of the nineteenth century. It hardly seems likely that any Egyptian regime in the fifteen hundred or so years before the Occupation could actually make its writ run uniformly throughout the land. Certainly by the nineteenth century even the older prerogatives of the state were falling into desuetude before the growing economic power of local magnates and wealthier peasants as well as before the difficulty of creating a state apparatus that could supersede not only peasant norms but also peasant procedures.

If the village "headman" in Egypt, as elsewhere in the Middle East, is supposed to represent the state to the village rather than the village to the state, then state power was woefully inadequate by the time the Suez Canal was built. True, it was still possible to force thousands of peasants to dig the thing, but it was no longer possible for the state to appoint its own headmen, or *shaykhs*,[4] to ensure that decisions of the central government would be carried out with any uniformity in the countryside. On the contrary, by 1882, according to Baer, state control had largely broken down and there was a general rebellion in Upper Egypt.[5] Thus the urban state existed largely through accommodation with the countryside, and especially with the rural notables in the countryside, who possessed not inconsiderable economic power in their locales and began to find in urban power an attractive way to reinforce their local position.

By introducing a bureaucratic administration the British were able to restore a balance between the periphery and the central administration that favored the latter. Not only did the British send five thousand troops to Egypt to support the financial reforms that would allow the state to pay off debts contracted during the 1860s, but British officers commanded the Egyptian army itself.

The military was far more under the control of the British and its development much more carefully regulated. . . . The top positions within the army
were held by the British, and every effort was made to ferret out discontent
and deal with it firmly. The military crisis of 1894 only intensified these tendencies with the British administration. Egyptian officers could hardly expect
promotions unless they had demonstrated loyalty to British rule. The military, then, did not develop in as autonomous a fashion as the bureaucracy.[6]

The British introduced into Egypt an army that could project a powerful military presence and, to an important degree, deny its opponents
the ability to project their own military power. But this was not all that
the British did. As I suggested above, the state monopoly on violence is
only the hallmark of the state; it is far from the sum total of its means.
The colonial period introduced into the Egyptian state two other important means of rule: a corps of technical advisers and a new legal system.

As Tignor suggests, control over the new bureaucracy was more tenu-
ous than control over the army, but this new institution was no less important for projecting the state into society.

British irrigation inspectors were to become the arbiters of Egypt's agricultural life . . . [their jobs] brought them into contact with local Egyptian
officials—the mudir, the mamur, and the village shaykh. The inspectors
settled disputes over the division of water, determined with the aid of the
central office how often the land was to be watered and how frequently.
They arbitrated disputes over where private canals could be constructed and
whether pumping apparatus could be installed. When it is kept in mind that
irrigation water was the lifeblood of Egypt and that those unable to procure
water could not raise their crops, it is possible to understand the vast powers
exercised by these officials.[7]

If the state could interfere in such an important area of national life by
creating an inspectorate and laws, could it not interfere in other areas of
the economic life of the country? British irrigation engineers were able
to insert themselves at a key point in the economy, one that they had
created. Their technical expertise then became the basis for domination
over Egyptian society. This particular form of domination was what
Weber called modern domination, for it was governed by rules.

What were the rules? What was their origin? The rules came from a
new legal system that was national in scope even if not so in composi-
tion. This third institution was the Mixed Court system, perhaps the
most peculiar feature of Egyptian colonial life. The Mixed Courts were
essentially a way of ensuring that European interests would dominate at

the local level in Egypt and that those interests would be recognized within the framework of European rules of law, that is, by the terms of modern and European legitimation, regardless of the substantive impact of this formal mechanism on Egyptian society. Under the pretext that what was called Islamic law was not suitable to modern capitalist society, an effort was made to introduce Western law (either French or British) as the basis of the Egyptian legal system.[8] Briefly,

> by the turn of the century it was a commonly established practice for the Mixed Tribunals to assert the right to try every important case. The rationale behind the demand was that the courts had the right to try not only cases involving any foreign subject, but also cases involving any foreign "interest." As the Egyptian judicial adviser indicated in 1899, "the Mixed Tribunals have gradually established a principle (which is nowhere to be found in the law itself) under which they affirm their jurisdiction in all suits where a 'mixed interest' is discoverable although the actual parties to the suit may be natives. It is easy to understand with so vague and arbitrary a criterion of jurisprudence that the powers of these tribunals have been extended in an ever widening circle."[9]

The Mixed Courts and their law were strongest in the fields of capitalist economics. These courts saw themselves as the protectors not only of natural individuals but also of foreign companies (imbued with legal personality after all) even if only partly owned by foreigners.[10] For peasants and workers (many of whom came from peasant families), this foreign law meant they had to accept hunger, humiliation, and expropriation. Berque, as always, is eloquent.

> The legalism of the Mixed Courts excluded even the opportunities which the irregular economic activities of former days (humane, on the whole) had allowed the debtor. In five years, 50,000 feddans of a single province had passed, by distraint, for a wretched price into the hands of the creditors.[11]

A careful accounting may well show Berque's figures to be wrong, but that hardly matters, for it is likely that many Egyptians believed as he does.

In large companies, Egyptian law was finally declared—in line with the Capitulations—to be inapplicable. In a decision rendered by the appellate branch of the Mixed Courts in Alexandria in 1924, the largest industrial company in Egypt was specifically declared to be not subject to Egyptian law because it was not an Egyptian company at all but a French company on Egyptian soil.[12] An entire sector of the economy was thus not only staffed by Europeans but also dominated by Europe in the simplest sense: the Egyptian state apparatus existed only to enforce foreign law. Clearly the question of who could make rules was critical and this in turn would determine if the state would serve any national purpose at all. The question of rules thus came to link two critical concerns: those of the workers and those of the politicians. If the state can determine under what rules a firm may exist, it can also at the same moment determine what rules a firm may apply internally.

THE LEADERS CONTEND FOR CONTROL

The world market of which Egypt was a part was centered in Europe. It clearly served some Egyptian interests but could be made to serve others.[13] Marius Deeb makes a good case for the manner in which Egyptian control of the Egyptian state (and especially its apparatus for marketing cotton and for providing agricultural credit) was in the interests not only of most of the large landowners but also of the midsized landowners (who seem to have been what we might call the rich peasantry) and the educated intelligentsia.[14] These interests initially coalesced into the nationalist movement called the Wafd. Later they were to separate.

The dynamite to dislodge the British from the commanding heights, however, could only come from a more popular source. It came from the peasants and urban working class, and represented a response both to nationalist agitation preceding World War I and to the specific grievances regarding the state and the economy rooted in the conduct of the war.[15] Seizure of peasant livestock and draft into the Labor Corps led to significant discontent with British policy in the countryside.[16] The wartime experience, some observers felt, had itself contributed to the peasantry's combativeness and also to their sense of just where foreign power was most vulnerable: in its transport system. Its transport system was thus subjected to repeated strikes and to sabotage through the March-April uprising.

> The thousands of natives who have been drafted by the Labor Corps have learned discipline. They know how to dig trenches and drive trucks. This peasant, for so long singular, seems to have picked up a national consciousness.[17]

The authorities chose to interpret the 1919 revolution as xenophobic, despite conflicting evidence. Certainly the French accepted this as the official British view.

> It is my belief that the English wish that we consider the open opposition to their policy which currently is manifest in Egypt as a xenophobic movement.[18]

This uprising included, however, a massive outburst of peasant resentment at Egyptian landowners.[19]

In urban areas, discontent was focused on foreign rule at least in part by prewar activity by nationalists such as Muhammad Farid who had seen workers in the factories turned into a distinct class by foreign capital for its own use; nationalists had sought to rescue these workers from their "ignorance" so they could assume their rightful place in Egyptian society.[20] But even though the 1919 revolt signaled mass disaffection with and a sense of oppression by foreign domination, its repudiation of English policy did not, in fact, correspond to a revolutionary ideology; and certainly urban Egypt was in large measure responsible for this.

Muhammad Anis suggests that there were two distinct stages to the 1919 revolt. He differentiates the rural impulse from its urban counterpart. The former amounts to a radical rupture with the old regime, and is eventually replaced after a brief period by a more moderate urban-based and middle-class movement.

> The 1919 revolution is really divided into two stages: first, is a violent revolution that occurred in March after Sa'd Zaghlul and his three comrades were banished to Malta. This was a relatively short period of time but it was the revolution that the British military forces opposed with full vigor as it was the stage in which the peasants actively took part. . . . A second stage followed that began in April and it was, in terms of time, a relatively long stage, during which the peasants withdrew from revolutionary action, and the revolution became limited to Cairo and the urban centers and in which the urban elements such as the students, employees, attorneys, and workers played the critical role.[21]

It was during this second phase, in the early 1920s, that the trade union movement made its greatest advances and that Wafdist officials became prominent in its ranks.

The revolution of 1919 thus brought to the fore the three main actors in Egyptian politics between 1919 and 1952, namely, the king, the British, and the nationalist party, the Wafd. In the order listed, it is immediately apparent that the progression from king to Wafd implies an ever-greater diffusion of interests and strategies along with an ever-greater universe of personnel to tap for government positions. Egyptian parliamentary politics were no less diverse than those of any other country, and they were structured by features not dissimilar from those in many other countries: complicated as the maneuvering of the parties might be, the executive and the army could easily short-circuit the electoral process. Consequently even nationalist politicians initially committed to electoral politics could decide to support the interests of the throne or the army to get to power. In a simple view, the throne stood for the interests of the largest landowners and pashas, while the army stood for the interests of the British.

The tableau of Egyptian parliamentary politics thus appears to oscillate between periods in which for a variety of reasons the Wafd came to power through relatively free elections to periods in which it was summarily ousted from power, whether by royal fiat or by British demand. Early in this period, the Wafd generally came to power when popular discontent was at its peak, for example, after the 1919 revolt; later, during World War II, the Wafd came to power because it was the only political force in Egypt willing to cooperate with the Allies in any way whatsoever.

Almost all prime ministers, whether Wafdists or not when they assumed the position, had been in the Wafd at some point in their career and all considered themselves nationalists. In general, the Wafd spoke in the voice of a secular populist movement and was in power in the early 1920s and later 1920s. From before the end of the 1920s into the early years of the Depression, the premiership was held by one or another man who was more interested in promoting foreign investment than domestic consumption. This was an unpopular economic policy and was usually accompanied by authoritarian measures, including suspension of the constitution, fraudulent or limited elections, mass jailing of opponents, and limitations on trade union activity. Beginning in the early 1930s there was a continual alternation of Wafd and non-Wafd politicians in power, with the latter generally associated with authoritarian government.[22]

This brief survey of Egyptian parliamentary history should indicate how various groups of politicians viewed the workers. Some clearly saw the workers as potential supporters; others saw them as enemies; still others saw them as neither clearly one nor the other. Let us now examine in detail the Wafdist and non-Wafdist views of workers, including how nonconstitutional politicians and the British looked at this unruly social group and what kinds of benefits they were willing to give its members.

THE POPULIST VIEW

Despite the British view about the xenophobic nature of the Wafd party or its "revolutionary" character, the Wafd had what were fairly limited goals. A secular nationalist movement, the Wafd was by no means interested in changing the market system: its leadership was far too closely tied to the market—whether as large landowners or rich peasants—to do so. What it did seek was a state strong enough to make decisions based on Egyptian interests. The tie between the nationalist movement and the masses of Egyptians was based less on "primordial sentiment" than on a cultural unity and pragmatism: the Wafd, in office, would make decisions beneficial to Egyptians that the colonialists would not or could not make.

This is certainly the bond with the labor movement, both in the countryside (as in Upper Egyptian sugar mills) and in the cities. As long as the Wafd needed mass support to threaten British dominance, and as long as foreign capital rather than Egyptian paid the price, the nationalist movement under the Wafd was able to give the workers significant benefits. In return, the Wafd attempted to ensure that no independent working-class organization was formed. The Wafd was relatively successful in its approach, particularly to the urban work force, and there is reason to believe the party was stronger in the cities than in the countryside.[23] Unfortunately, the problem with pragmatic appeals is that when promises are not redeemed, the supporters become disillusioned and this seems to have occurred in the urban areas.

The majority of the activists in the nationalist movement—Wafdist and non-Wafdist—courted the labor movement. In so doing, however, they expressed a specific vision of its role in Egyptian society as well as a vision of Egyptian society itself. Generally, labor was seen as a social and economic stratum whose interests would be advanced by the general advance of society. Only in a few instances do we find nationalists who believed that the interests of labor were significantly different from those of other groups in society, and never do we find nationalists who believed labor's interests were *antagonistic* to those of other parts of the Egyptian society or economy.

Probably the best enunciation of the general Wafdist view of the workers is to be found in Sa'd Zaghlul's address to the Wafdist trade union federation meeting in 1924. Zaghlul was not only the leader of the Wafd but also Egyptian prime minister at the time. He lauded the workers and claimed affinity with them, for they, like him, were of low status; they were the "rabble" (*tabaqat al-ra'a'*) who were especially pure and revolutionary because they did not seek official positions. They were not a competitor, in short, for the rabble is the most numerous class of the nation, which has no special interest and whose principles are everlastingly firm [*thabit ʿala al-dawam*], these principles being independence for Egypt and the Sudan. This class does not run after office or seek a place to fill nor have an interest to be gratified, but wishes only to live and keep the country honorable.[24]

Such an atomized view of the working class was convenient but it did not correspond to reality. Urban workers were already differentiated by occupation and use of machines. They were in the process of becoming organizationally differentiated as well. What was essentially an archaic vision remained a political desideratum for a long time, and was echoed in contemporary government literature: that the workers' movement had no interests apart from those of the nationalist movement, which included major property owners.[25]

The Wafd party organized one of the earliest labor federations in Egypt and was anxious to create trade unions in the urban work force almost as soon as the nationalist movement developed. In so doing the Wafd was more interested in preempting any other political forces from reaching a social group that spontaneously supported the Wafd. In 1924 the Wafd specifically faced competition from the Communists, but they were only one among several antagonists during the next several decades and did not really count until World War II. This Wafd federation was the General Federation of Workers Unions in the Nile Valley, and it promptly collapsed when the Wafd was forced out of power in 1924.

It is instructive, nevertheless, to consider several aspects of the federation for the light it throws on how the Wafd expected to organize the workers. Abd al-Rahman Fahmi, the president of the federation, is often called a terrorist, and there is no doubt he undertook to organize a secret quasi-terrorist apparatus for the Wafd. What is usually overlooked, however, is that he was in essence a military officer who had entered the service of a nationalist movement in search of a state. It was this former policeman who recognized the potential of the labor movement for the Wafd as early as 1919 and wrote to Zaghlul in October 1919, telling him that he had been involved in spreading unions across the land, and that every "trade" or *hirfah* (in Arabic) now had a presumably pro-Wafd union.

The Wafd would continue its ties with unions based on craftsmen and tradesmen throughout the pre-1952 period. These ties were based on the view of the nationalist movement as an all-encompassing political framework and on the view of urban workers as small producers, views that dominated nationalist Egyptian thinking for a long time, even as such production dominated the Egyptian economy. Saᶜd Zaghlul was not the only politician to court such workers.

Thus, at the Wafd national conference held in January 1935 to prepare the nationalist forces for the party's accession to power, labor figured prominently. ᶜAbbas Halim and a group of Wafd party activists including ᶜAziz Mirhum, Hasan Nafiᶜ, and Zuhayr Sabri filed a report on workers. The report had four parts: the relation of workers to the national movement, the activity of workers in the national movement, the rights already won, and a program for further goals of the labor movement. First and foremost the conference rejected the idea of an independent political role for the labor movement; rather, the labor movement was to be subordinated to the leadership of the national movement. Within the nationalist movement leaders outlined three main efforts against the Sidki regime, from which the nation was just gaining its freedom. All had to do with support of the labor movement for the Wafd and opposition to Sidki's repression: circulation of a petition to the king, sending delegates to the 1931 Madrid meeting of the Socialist International unions to publicize Egyptian repression, and election protests such as the ones at the Arsenal and railway workshops. The protests had led to the dismissal of hundreds of workers.

The report described the labor federation led by Fahmi as the golden age of labor and, of course, omitted any mention of the Communist-led federation it was created to supplant. The trade union movement itself was considered still wholly a part of craft production and the age of craft production was eulogized as a time when

> the crafts were not open to any and all, but the manual professions [al-sinaᶜat] were most often bequeathed from father and grandfather and people spent a long time becoming skilled in a craft so that they might become masters [muᶜallimun].²⁶

The dominant mode of struggle endorsed in the report is legal-political action: either legislation of wages and conditions or their administrative regulation, or state support for unions themselves. Only briefly does Mirhum mention "the gains of workers won without government interference" and those are characterized as unstable. Indeed they were, but hardly less so than administrative decrees, which admittedly depended on having a friendly regime in office. Of goals for the future, the report ranked high guaranteed work for workers, so that they might not be "hired and fired as the master wishes."

For those who doubted the importance of having friends in high places, and they were few, the Wafd showed it could keep its promises during its first week in power. The responsible authorities ordered the return to work of those fired from state workshops for anti-Sidki activity as well as amnesty from criminal judgments.[27]

Firings and reinstatements were not an uncommon element in the lives of workers who wished to support political causes. It is in this context that we must understand the appeals of Wafd politicians to the urban workers: the promise to protect those who supported the party and the likelihood at least of retribution for those who were harmed by its enemies.

The appeal of the Wafd as a nationalist party was inherently the promise to use the power of the state to defend the workers and to serve their interests. Although this was never stated in such bald terms, everyone understood what the promises of the Wafd were. Let us look at just one example of this. In 1937, ʿAbd al-Hamid Sanussi issued an appeal specifically "to Tram Worker Voters in the Ramlah District" (of Alexandria), urging them to vote for the Wafd. Sanussi's argument was fourfold: (1) it was technically illegal to fire workers for voting; (2) not all workers had to vote orally—only the illiterate need do so (he urged them not to be afraid); (3) he had served the workers since 1925; and (4) he had been reelected against tram company wishes since 1933, and his present opponent, supported by ex-Wafdist Mahmud Nuqrashi, had also opposed the popular doctor, Mahjub Thabit.[28] The Wafd could deliver, although it never delivered quite as much as its supporters hoped for. Thus the Wafd retained significant allegiance among the urban work force, but it was never interested in creating an independent union organization, for it feared the effect of competition.

The workers often expected considerably more than the Wafd political leadership either wanted to promise or found it prudent or possible to give. Workers, especially those in government industries, had high expectations for the Wafd in power, and considered the Wafd rise to office equivalent to a major political upheaval. In the words of one worker at the state-owned printing factory, the year 1935 was widely viewed as revolutionary.[29]

Another populist of some importance in the trade union movement at this time was ʿAbbas Halim. He is of special note because what separated him from the Wafd was primarily his personal ambitions as well as his familial relation to the king. In the interwar period he represented to trade unionists the possibility of following the general political orientation of the Wafd without being organizationally subservient to it. This option was favorably received by many trade union leaders.

According to his own account, ʿAbbas Halim began his career with the workers with his role as a mediator between two groups of butchers. How could such modest beginnings be parlayed into greater influence? With his personal power, ties to the royal family, and wealth, Halim was able to act for the workers—in certain limited ways—as could the state. In situations like that of Egypt in the 1930s, outlaws and strong-arm men are the alternatives to the state, and it is clear that Halim was able to call upon and direct this kind of force. Halim asserted he was able to end a "bloody struggle of thirty years duration" when a small group of Cairene butchers arrived in his office as part of his federation. Even the police had been unable to accomplish what he did, leading me to suspect he threatened to use force to resolve a dispute in the common interest; no single party had been able to bring this about.[30]

Moreover, Halim could (like the state) provide funds and officials. To provide even such limited mediation implied the existence of significant resources—resources that Halim could use to reward workers who acted in ways that helped his own plans. Halim in fact had a large personal fortune that enabled him to pay the expenses of union organizations.[31] This gave Halim considerable leverage, especially given the legal disadvantages under which unions worked as well as the difficulties members had in paying dues, not to mention attending meetings or providing organizational services themselves.

If the Wafd and ʿAbbas Halim had been acting more or less in concert until 1935, their alliance was shortly to wear thin, much to the dismay of many workers. Halim had always been interested in advancing his own interests and the Wafd was unwilling to brook competition. Opinions vary on which side should bear the major responsibility, but it seems apparent that neither Halim nor the Wafd wanted to risk a labor movement led by the other.

In 1935 a major battle for control of the labor federation, nominally under Halim's leadership as a member of the Wafd, broke out and almost every union in Egypt either took sides or split down the middle. What had been a wobbly but unified movement was rapidly converted into two organizational centers, one the Higher Council for Trade Unions headed by Wafd politicians, and the other the General Federation led by

Halim. Neither was able to maintain a continuous organizational existence after the Wafd left office in 1937, although both continued in some form. The struggle for preeminence between the two centers was bitter and long lasting, and the unwillingness of either side to compromise wrecked the union movement.[32]

It is easy to blame Halim's "phony revolutionism" for the problems in the trade union movement, but the Higher Council of the Wafd was itself unable to do more than raise workers' hopes briefly and then dash them.[33] The revolution that workers expected from the Wafd in 1936 was as phony as anything Halim had promised, and made that year a watershed for the unions. After 1936 there is not only a generational renewal in the trade union leadership but also a political transformation, especially outside the state-owned industries. The strength of the Wafd among industrial workers at this point was largely in state-owned industry such as the Arsenal or rail workshops or in foreign-owned industry. The appeal of the Wafd as a guarantor of populist politics began to decline in at least some sections of the industrial work force. In part this was because of the nature of the relations between the state and industry. There is a certain ambiguity about the politics of state-owned businesses during this period, compared to those owned privately by Egyptians. As long as the British were dominant, there was a tendency to see state enterprises as subordinate to the British, but there was also a genuine tendency on the part of Wafdists such as Makram ʿUbayd to use state-owned industries to set wage and benefit levels, perhaps because as tax-supported industries they were thought to be free of the tyranny of the bottom line. According to the Wafd, the state was a reliable ally because both the state and the nationalists, unlike either the British or non-Wafd politicians, could set aside the concern with profitability. Instead, "the first duty of the state [was] its fatherly authority over all persons . . . and the duty of equity, which urges a return to the status quo and that all [fired] workers return to their jobs."[34] Ironically it was not until the British brought the Wafd to power in 1942 for reasons of international politics that the populist promises of the earlier period were kept. During the 1940s a law recognizing trade unions in the private sector was finally passed as well as several decrees regarding cost-of-living adjustments.

These reforms were associated with one particular Wafd minister, ʿAbd al-Hamid ʿAbd al-Haqq. His 1942 tenure as minister of social affairs was brief, and with the end of it, the gap between the actual policies of the Wafd and the wishes of its electoral urban base became

clearer. So popular was ʿAbd al-Haqq that union leaders actually attempted to take up a subscription to erect a statue of him.[35] After a year
in office he was replaced by Fuʾad Siraj al-Din, who was widely considered to be the leading representative of the landed elite and allied
"pashas" in the cities.[36]

NONPOPULIST AND ANTIPOPULIST VIEWS

Not all politicians were as anxious to wrest immediate independence
from the British as was the Wafd. Many politicians acknowledged that
the bulk of investment in Egyptian industry was foreign, and they therefore sought to enhance the position of the Egyptian middle class within
the framework of European preeminence. They believed that the best
means for strengthening the Egyptian economy and ensuring the growth
of the Egyptian capitalist class within that economy lay in working
closely with foreign capital. Those who took this view remained largely
anti–trade union in approach, although they also supported measures
to Egyptianize the economy, thereby benefiting some sections of the
working class by opening up more positions for skilled workers and for
white-collar employees.

The British, the palace, and many of the Egyptian large landowners
and factory owners came to share two interests that are related to the
views opposed to trade unions: the desire to maintain public order and
British supremacy, on the one hand, and "private" order or the internal
regime of the factory along with Egyptian profits, on the other. When
the Wafd recognized the political potential among the urban work force,
the British and nonnationalist Egyptians realized the dangers inherent
in an organized work force, organized and controlled by the Wafd or
independent but still allied to it.

One of the main opponents of the labor movement was Ismaʿil Sidki.
Sidki was not only a prime minister but also a founder of the Egyptian
Federation of Industry, and was interested in the "progress of industry."
He was a forerunner of what today is called the triple alliance between
national capitalists, foreign capital, and state officials. His political
methods were certainly dictatorial, but they were consistent with developing Egyptian industrial capacity by creating a favorable climate for
investment, which often included repressing demands for higher wages
or for interfering with the authority of factory owners.

Although Sidki changed the Egyptian tariff structure to favor Egyptian industry in some spheres, he also believed that cooperation with

foreign investors would benefit the Egyptian national bourgeoisie. An outstanding example of this position was Sidki's role in the agreement reached by the state and the Egyptian Sugar Company in 1931 when the home market for sugar was saved by raising the tariff on imports and setting a domestic wholesale price. In exchange, the state shared in the profits of the company. Since the sales price included the costs of cultivation as well as an excise tax, the state was heavily involved in the interests of estate owners as well as those of industrialists.[37]

Sidki had long favored policies tying together Egyptian and foreign interests. In 1922, after leaving the Wafd, he tried, while serving as minister of finance, to increase the level of Egyptian participation in foreign exploitation of mineral deposits. He insisted that any phosphate mining concessions be given to mixed companies rather than foreign ones and that one-half of the administration and one-quarter of the capital be Egyptian.[38] The French, to whom the scheme was proposed, found it impractical at the time, but by 1950 there were similar deals in the petroleum industry. Then the bulk of employees were required by law to be Egyptian and (to ensure that not all employees were laborers) they had to take home the majority of wages paid. Foreigners certainly did not believe that Egyptians were per se unwelcome partners. One industrialist, Talᶜat Harb, planned a trip to Paris in 1925 and French officials in Cairo attempted to get the help of their superiors at home in lining up meetings for him with French financiers.[39]

Those who opposed the populist Wafd during this period assumed that workers were likely to form unions. Further, these politicians assumed that unions would pose problems for national industrial development and they sought various ways to cope with the emerging organizations. As early as 1931, while Sidki was premier, a Labour Bureau was set up as part of the Ministry of the Interior (i.e., the police) under the direction of Richard Graves.[40] The office was responsible for enforcing existing child labor and safety laws as well as gathering statistics, preparing legislation, and learning "the causes of conflicts between labor and management."[41]

Harold Butler, an official of the International Labor Organization, visited Egypt in 1931 and suggested that the government resolve labor's ambiguous political situation. Butler noted in a report the anomalous legal situation of unions: they were "neither forbidden nor recognized." He suggested that unions be officially recognized, if only to provide the state and companies with a valid interlocutor.[42] Butler considered this an especially important reason. The state and companies both needed an interlocutor because most contracts until that time had been signed with the workers either individually or, on occasion, collectively, but never organizationally. Thus, there was no one to guarantee performance of a contract by the workers.

The difficulty in resolving the ambiguity lay in the confusion over what trade unions actually were. On the one hand, police officials feared that labor organizations could lead to nationalist support and even political unrest. On the other hand, those who worked with union leaders and had ties to the Labour party at home believed that unions could, at some expense to particular European interests, help safeguard the overall structure of those interests in Egypt.

The first view is reflected in a report filed in 1934 by the British ambassador, Miles Lampson. Lampson told the Foreign Office that the activities of Halim

> have for some time past irritated and preoccupied the authorities responsible for public security, who are of the opinion that his organization of labor syndicates and contacts with working-class elements, reflected in a recent minor epidemic of strikes, are subversively intended.[43]

The British were especially concerned that a wave of strikes might spread and the events of 1919 might recur with the added problem that the railway workers would deny British troops access to trains. Several letters deal specifically with the railway workers, among whom unrest was said to be "really serious, and [the] public safety is affected, apart from the fact that the men are being thrown in Abbas Halim's arms."[44]

An ongoing debate between Graves and Alexander Keown-Boyd, who headed the Office of Public Security, which was also in the Ministry of the Interior, sharpened after 1935 when it became clear that the Wafd would return to power. Keown-Boyd was a well-known proponent of the use of police power to curb the trade unions. He was widely disliked in Egyptian nationalist circles, where he was regarded as one of the English officials most responsible for political repression in Egypt. He appears, for example, in one of Bayram al-Tunisi's poems as an ominous figure in Egyptian political life at the time of the signing of the 1936 Anglo-Egyptian treaty.[45] By contrast, Graves believed that unions existed on a wide scale, but were organizationally "defective," thereby rendering little service to the members or to the employers, for whom they could have been a "convenient medium" for negotiations. From Graves's point of view, giving clear legal status to the unions would end the "dangerous anomaly" represented by 'Abbas Halim.[46]

Under pressure from London to accept a political solution to the problem of labor unrest, Keown-Boyd insisted that he did not "believe only in police repression" and argued for the creation of guildlike associations subsidized by the state. He considered existing unions "hotbeds of industrial unrest." Nevertheless, he did seem to favor repression for he proposed that all industrial disputes be settled by local police authorities, although this idea had already been rejected by London.[47] In a meeting arranged to reconcile Keown-Boyd and Graves, Keown-Boyd argued for a "modified form . . . [of] the old system of guilds and corporations" that had died out in the 1890s after the introduction of European labor codes, and, failing that, suggested the "Fascist cooperative system." Graves renewed his plea for a system to regulate the unions, "one which would offer protection against exploitation and lightning strikes." The only point on which the two men could agree was that Egypt should join the International Labor Organization if a "safe representative could be sent."

The personal differences of these two men represented policy differences rooted in differing political and organizational perspectives; at issue was how much independence unions could have and remain effective agencies of social control. The debate soon took on a note of urgency: only two years after this debate with Graves, Keown-Boyd became head of Egyptian operations for the Bradford Dyers Company, which led to the establishment of the plant at Kafr al-Dawwar. How labor was to be managed was of great practical importance to him in this new venture, which combined British and Egyptian capital in a new and unparalleled industrial complex.[48]

The dispute over how to deal with unions remained unsettled. Nothing was done. Doing nothing, however, was tantamount to leaving unions in the legal limbo that Butler had found so threatening. Despite the efforts of various officials and others, this dispute would continue, with new faces in the old roles, through the 1940s when fear of Communism replaced fear of nationalism.

CONTROLLING THE ECONOMY

If the attitude of those in the state administration—whether European or Egyptian—toward unions was ambivalent, the attitude of the state after 1919 toward capitalist enterprise was never so. The official policy was that the state was to aid in the development of an Egyptian-run industry even if the capital came from outside Egypt. Successive Egyptian governments—whether Wafdist or non-Wafdist—were concerned that Egyptians sit on the governing boards of all companies and that as much of the staff as possible be Egyptian. For the entire period, in fact, government policy was to encourage local capitalists on the premise that Egyptian capitalist industry would benefit the country as a whole. The state, as in the case of Bank Misr, was the guarantor of large local enterprise, and even if it did not invest directly, the state could create the conditions for the Egyptianization of foreign capital. Indeed, by the turn of the twentieth century the state was using its customs power in at least a limited way to influence the direction, growth, and ownership of the textile, sugar, tobacco, and transport industries, often by setting duties high enough to force enterprises to use local products (in the textile industry) or not to (tobacco). The state also ran one of the largest industrial enterprises in Egypt—the Egyptian State Railway—which provided 10 percent of the state budget.[49]

The concept of Egyptianizing foreign-owned industry became popular at this time. This was the practice of allowing Egyptian capitalists to buy out foreign properties on relatively favorable terms for the Egyptians, rather than nationalizing the companies without compensation. This strategy satisfied a wide variety of needs—local control, increased employment, enhanced production—and was therefore pursued by several successive governments beginning in the early 1940s, although the policy was probably more closely identifed with Wafd nationalism than with any other party.

Egyptianizing industry had its roots in the formation of the Bank Misr project, whose founders certainly saw themselves as part of a larger Egyptian nationalist movement. In 1940 the state had rescued the firm when it appeared to founder and so began the greater role of the state in the industrial economy. This policy complemented the state's already heavy involvement in the agricultural economy through dam and canal building as well as rail service.

CHAPTER FIVE

In Name Only: Artisans and Tradesmen

In the world of industrial production, the rules governing making out are effectively written down or at least increasingly written down as the outcome of formal processes of negotiation. In many third-world economies, however, such as Egypt in the interwar period and even down to the present, the rules that govern making out are neither written down nor the result of formal processes; the rules do not even exist apart from the direct efforts of the producers to market their output. Where artisan production or service employment is in competition with industrial production (either local or domestic), artisans and servants must often confront a crisis not only in their particular workshop but also in an entire industry.[1] In meeting such challenges, artisans and servants often must appeal directly to the state to set limits on the kind of competition they must meet.

These workers are often tied to their work and their market by an extremely dense social network and by the nature of their skill. As a consequence, they usually cannot move from one line of production into another. Unlike the skilled workers (whom Charles Sabel calls craftsmen), artisans and servants often do not have skills that would enable them to move from one line of endeavor to another as a response to competition from a new form of production. These two factors—the nature of their skills and the social network—differentiate the world of the artisan from that of the industrial worker in Egypt.

The basic idea of a trade union appears to flow naturally and historically from that of a guild. In fact, this is not so and the creation of modern industrial unions requires, as many Egyptian workers themselves
believed, a wholesale struggle against earlier conceptions of solidarity.
Indeed, the idea of solidarity between craftsmen and tradesmen is based
on ideas of labor, society, and political influence that differ from those
that form the basis for solidarity among industrial workers. The so-
called unions of craftsmen and tradesmen preserved older, more defer-
ential patterns of integrating into society those who worked with their
hands but lived in urban environments. These groups typically looked
to patrons in the state to act as mediators in their conflicts, which were
by no means invariably between owners and workers. Some conflicts
were between owners and owners; others between journeymen and apprentices; still others between all those engaged in a craft or a trade
and those who provided the means to carry out their business. In sum,
under the name of trade unions we have what might best be designated
by the archaic sense of the word *corporation*. These groups were concerned with problems of mutual aid and mutual accommodation rather
than with struggles for unrestricted rights. Theirs was a world of adjustment and compromise, and even in bitter conflicts this remained essentially a world of master and man rather than of elementally antagonistic
social forces. These associations used an older vocabulary to describe
themselves and their goals. Because they formed a numerically important part of a movement of those who worked with their hands, the artisans and tradesmen influenced the entire self-conception of that movement and its organizational forms, shaping the goals, vocabulary, modes
of struggle, and orientations of other workers, including industrial
workers.

Some scholars insist that the guilds and the guild system had completely disappeared from Egypt by the first years of the twentieth century and therefore cannot have played a role in the development of
industrial unions. Yet according to newspaper reports, guildlike associations continued to exist until a later time, although these associations
should perhaps not be considered true guilds. It is clear from mass circulation newspapers, as well as trade union newspapers and memoirs of
trade unionists, that the struggle to create trade unions in Egypt during
the 1930s and 1940s was a struggle against older ways of organizing
those who worked with their hands. Let us now consider more closely
the survival of the craft association, the features of that association in

this century, and the role of the association and federations of these associations.

THE SURVIVAL OF THE CRAFT
ASSOCIATION IN EGYPT

Much of what we know about guilds in the nineteenth century is summed up in Gabriel Baer's *Egyptian Guilds in Modern Times*.[2] Baer defines a guild as "a group of town people engaged in the same occupation and headed by a *shaykh*"; he suggests the phrase "head of a craft" (*ra'is hirfa*) as a functional alternative to *shaykh*.[3] The *shaykh*'s prominence was based on his mediating role between town workers and the state as well as among the town workers themselves; according to Baer, the *shaykh* was responsible for tax collections and the regulation of production. The role of the *shaykh* was clearly an important one; he guided the guilds for the economic benefit of the state and in turn ensured the guilds of state protection.[4]

Guilds may have been threatened by economic competition from modern forms of production, but they were not destroyed economically. The change in the character of the state and its economy after the Occupation in 1882 undoubtedly had an impact on the guilds, but the assertion that the guilds died out because they could not compete with imports from Europe no longer seems valid. Lord Cromer's famous statement that handicraft production had ceased to flourish by the 1890s or had disappeared seems to miss the mark.[5] Without presenting an exhaustive list, I suggest that many of the professions or trades that had guilds in the nineteenth century continued to exist through the 1940s in large numbers.

It was during this period, for example, that the Manual Laborers Union, allied to the nationalist Watani party, was formed at the direction of Muhammad Farid, the leader of that party. The Manual Laborers Union had 979 members when it was founded in 1909, the bulk of whom were craftsmen (47 percent were blacksmiths, carpenters, or saddlers). Even at its high point in 1912, when membership reached 3,139, about 18 percent of its members were cigarette rollers, still a manual craft, and the rest were primarily craftsmen. Only 6 percent were railway employees and approximately 9 percent were "mechanics." The largest single category of membership remained blacksmiths.[6]

In the 1930s two newspapers provided strong evidence of the large number of surviving craft associations. Both *Al-Jihad* and *Al-Yara^c* were, at different times, favored media for announcing union news, proposed meetings, elections, and so on. Many of the crafts organized in guilds according to Baer are listed in these newspapers. For example, in March-April 1935 almost all of the regular trade union news concerned reports on craftsmen or tradesmen.[7] There were construction workers such as carpenters, painters, and "ornamenters," often organized by town in the provinces or by quarter within the cities of Cairo and Alexandria.[8] We also find unions of barbers and hairdressers, tailors, vendors, cooks, musicians, saddlers, and cobblers. These were almost invariably organized by geographical area, especially by quarter in Cairo or Alexandria. Thus there appear to have been cooks' committees in such Cairene locales as ^cAbdin, Bab al-Sha^criyyah, or the Muski.

In early 1943 in *Al-Yara^c*, we read about barbers, cooks, store employees in provincial towns (such as Benha), café employees, and even gardeners. We also find mention of industrial workers such as printers, textile workers, cotton ginners, and the like. In addition to general mention, we also find substantive news stories about vendors, launderers and ironers (the ubiquitous *makwagis*, who seem still to be legion in present-day Cairo), upholsterers, bakers, hand-loom weavers, hairdressers, construction workers, and the like.

The existence of certain occupational groups is only one form of evidence for the survival of guildlike associations. The terminology and mode of organization adopted by union members are also revealing. In a meeting of the Gharbiyyah federation of unions in 1937, the trades mentioned are traditional services or crafts, and they are referred to in Arabic by older participial forms rather than by a complex genitive phrase. Thus we find coppersmiths (*nahhasun*) but not workers in copper; and masons (*banna^un*) but not construction workers; even older collective plurals such as *tuha* "cooks" are common. These older forms, drawn from classical Arabic, seem to refer to a corporate conception of an occupational group rather than a mere plural.[9]

Honorifics given to association leaders also indicate a traditional form of organization. For example, a union organization in Gharbiyyah province planned to unite with the car workers, led by "Comrade Muhammad Effendi al-Nimr, Shaykh of the Drivers of the Tanta." The title *shaykh* seems to indicate, not that a full-fledged guild of drivers existed in Tanta, but that honorifics, still popular in Egypt, were widespread in the trade union movement, drawn from a popular culture that was not far removed from that of nineteenth-century society. Thus al-

Nimr was not only an *effendi*, that is, one who wore Western clothing, but also a *shaykh*, as was a Communist trade union leader of taxicab drivers in Cairo a decade later.[10]

The brass smiths also used traditional terms: they called their group a *ta'ifah* (the classic Egyptian word for a guild), which by the late 1930s seems to have been used also as a general word for craft. Further, each member of the brass smiths' executive committee was explicitly designated *mu'allim* "master."[11] In Shubra Khit in the province of Giza, the heads of the unions in the local federation also used these forms. Mu-'allim Muhammad Sulfan and Mu'allim Muhammad 'Amir were president of the café workers and carpenters, respectively; the butchers and trappers were headed by Shaykh Qutb al-Ta'an and Shaykh Muhammad Musa. The president of the barbers was, surprisingly enough, known as an *usta*, a title one might have expected with a carpenter.[12] These groups have clearly preserved or recovered older forms of expression because they reflect the workers' view of themselves.

Finally, the mode of organization may also indicate the continuing influence of an older form of worker organization. An especially clear example comes from Gharbiyyah. In Gharbiyyah, the motor transport workers were organized by point of departure rather than by company or locale. Thus the Gharbiyyah chauffeurs' union meeting in July 1937 was attended by representatives from departure points in Tanta for Al-Sa'ah, Kafr al-Zayyat, Al-Suntah, Shibin, and the train station.[13]

The existence of these various groups as well as their titles and manner of organization point clearly to the survival of groups of workers organized according to traditional forms if not strictly in guilds. Furthermore, the evidence suggests that they existed in large numbers. Nevertheless, it is difficult to determine the percentage of such groups in the trade union movement over time or at any given moment, although much of Egypt's production was always handicraft. In the provincial areas, handicrafts were an important means of production and craft "guilds" were often the largest single sector of the trade union movement. In May 1935, the trade union federation in Mahallah, where large-scale industrial production had only recently begun, consisted of unions of workers in shoemaking, tailoring, motorized transport, nursing, hand weaving, ironing, baking, cooking, barbering, *tarbush* making, café waiters, and, of course, workers in the cotton factories.[14] Many of the unions in Port Said—a town that had had a union federation since 1920—were unions for craft and service workers as late as 1935 and were certainly craft associations rather than industrial locals.[15]

The "banding" workers and the Union of Canal Company Workers of Madame Graham were clearly older trades or simply mutual solidarity groups of workers in a particular office.[16]

Clearly the artisans and tradesmen continued to unite in organizational forms that suited their tradition and perception of their work. Even though we cannot calculate their precise numbers, we can estimate that they were large enough in number to have a major influence on those around them.

THE FEATURES OF CRAFT ASSOCIATION IN EGYPT

It might be objected that although all of the groups mentioned above are indeed craft unions, nothing makes them significantly different from craft unions in the United States or Western Europe, where craft unions still play a significant role in trade union organization. A look at the basic features of the business of handicraft production or of supplying services in Egypt may clarify the difference between European and Egyptian craft "unions."

First, most of the workshops or businesses on which these craft unions were based employed fewer than two workers besides the owner, if indeed they employed any staff at all. Second, in many cases, their capital was less than fifty Egyptian pounds, although a capitalization of less than one pound was by no means rare. According to the industrial census of 1937, for example, 48 percent of those establishments involved in cleaning and ironing clothes employed no staff, and an additional 41 percent hired one or two workers. None hired more than nine. The capital requirements for washing and ironing clothes were also quite low: 7.6 percent of establishments were capitalized at under one pound, and 91 percent at under fifty. These washers and ironers were represented by a plethora of "unions," usually at least one in every city, the *ʿummal kayy al-mulabis*. Again, 72 percent of the hairdressers employed no workers and 23 percent fewer than three. Their capital requirements were also typically low, probably being limited to sufficient funds to buy razors and scissors. Thirteen percent had no capital at all; 13.7 percent had capital valued at less than one pound; 82.9 percent had capital amounting to less than fifty pounds. Even in woodworking (which included working in cane) 84 percent of establishments employed only two workers at most; almost a quarter had little or no capital, and nearly 70 percent had capital worth less than fifty pounds.

Despite their modest size, each of these crafts was represented throughout the 1930s and 1940s by unions. Outside Cairo and Alexandria such unions could be simply associations of small producers and providers of services. The conclusion that the small workshop reigned supreme seems inescapable when we consider that although hundreds of thousands of Egyptians worked "in industry," fewer than 140,000 worked in establishments employing more than 10 workers.[17]

Certain other features undoubtedly played a role in shaping the craft unions. Practitioners of a craft were men who entered as apprentices and expected to remain for the rest of their lives.[18] Such men had an intense loyalty to their profession. Muhammad ʿAli Husayn, president of the cooks' union in Cairo in 1943, for example, had been a cook for twenty years before he became head of his union.[19] He had a high opinion of the role of cooks, for he asserted that cooks "perform important and honorable work for the household." From this it seems apparent that many cooks then were private servants as well as being employed by restaurants. His brother had been a successful cook and had enabled him to attend a primary school in Heliopolis for three years. Husayn had been a "member" of the cooks' union at least since 1928, when he was second secretary. The president at that time was ʿAziz ʿAbd al-ʿAziz, and it is indicative of the close personal bonds that characterized craft organization that fifteen years later Husayn still referred to ʿAziz as the union's leader and his own (raʾis al-niqabah wa raʾisi). It is hard to gauge the importance of loyalty to a profession or group, but the commitment of workers like Husayn to older ways cannot be easily dismissed.

Craft unions as well as their federations also had the characteristic of uniting groups that we in the West expect to remain separate. Craft unions in Egypt typically united owner and worker in one group. Thus, when Wafdist-oriented political activists formed a Committee for the Defense of Car Owners and Workers, they brought together owners, drivers, and workers in Gharbiyyah, Daqaliyyah, Sharqiyyah, Buhayrah, Qaliyubiyyah, and other provinces; together these workers demanded changes in the laws governing the use of agricultural roads.[20] As late as 1942, owners of and workers in barbershops were meeting to form "their own" joint union.[21]

Finally, craft unions were sometimes formed at the initiation of outsiders who carried the major burden of helping the union become established. The role of Mahjub Thabit in the founding of the Manual Laborers Union is an example of this. Thabit began his career as a physician in the popular Cairo quarter of Sayyida Zaynab where he gave free medical treatment. He later became an honorary adviser to the Manual Laborers Union, and after World War I he moved to Alexandria, where he again worked closely with the labor movement and especially with tram workers in the popular neighborhoods of Ramlah and Minaʾ al-Basal. He sat out the Wafd-Communist struggle of 1924, which he viewed as a government attack on the unions. He was, at various times, a counselor for unions of gas and electrical workers in Alexandria as well as for printing workers and train workers,[22] and for various trade union federations. He seems to have been a professional who sincerely believed in a life dedicated not only to nationalist organization but also to the idea of responsible behavior by those who have advantages. This belief was a powerful force for nationalist agitation in the 1920s and 1930s and seems to have been the role that most nationalist, including Wafdist, politicians adopted. Thabit was finally elected to parliament from the working-class area of Minaʾ al-Basal in 1927; as the French consul at the time indicated, Thabit's free medical aid to the poor was a major reason for his popularity.

Thabit's deep involvement with these groups of workers typified the conduct of many socially prominent men who either led or discreetly guided local unions. In the case of the upholsterers' union, nationalist leaders actually kept the union alive during much of its existence. The union was originally formed in 1919 and existed until 1923.[23] The official leadership in that period seems to have been a notable and politician who, from courtesy or rank, was addressed as his excellency. The union collapsed in 1923 because of a "misunderstanding." Sometime in 1924–1925, thanks to the activity of another leader, also called his excellency, the union was reformed. This leader was Muhammad Effendi ʿAbbas, and the union grew so large that it held election meetings in a movie house. It chose as its counselor the Wafd politician Hasan Nafiʿ, who was associated with the labor movement for most of the 1920s and 1930s. ʿAbbas seems to have been concerned with creating a viable and ongoing union organization. To do this ʿAbbas suggested issuing membership books to be carried by all members as personal records. This was routine in industrial unions such as Shubra. But this suggestion provoked violent opposition from the membership, which "misunderstood" the proposal and forced ʿAbbas and then the president to resign. By 1926 the union had disappeared again.

In 1930 the union was resurrected when it was reorganized by yet another Wafd politician, Husni Shintnawi. It was suggested then that the union support a small workshop and showroom, and even though three hundred pounds was offered by a leading upholsterer, the idea of the workshop seems to have caused dissension. This is surprising, for unemployment was clearly a major problem for upholsterers and furniture makers throughout the 1930s.[24] In 1938 the president, Husayn Effendi Yunis, announced that unemployment was the union's main problem, and he once again suggested creating a union workshop, this time using union funds. The resistance was intense, and the idea vanished.[25]

As this brief narration makes clear, Wafd counselors kept the union alive, and as soon as the union was formed it found Wafd politicians to act as its formal leadership. At the same time the members seem to have had a deep distrust of transforming their group into a self-sufficient union that would be able to check up on dues payments and to demand contributions. Rather it seems the Wafd politicians provided money out of their own pockets to keep the meetings going, provide amenities, and tie members to the nationalist movement.

The craft union in Egypt as it survived into the twentieth century thus had a membership of certain characteristics that distinguished the craft union or tradesman's group from other unions. Members were intensely loyal craftsmen or service workers, often of many years' standing in the trade or craft, who worked in very small shops or independently, requiring little capital to maintain a business. These workers were often the object of the efforts of professional men to improve the workers' position either in work or in other areas of their lives. The leadership of unions thus could just as easily come from professionals outside the craft or service as from the craft workers themselves.

THE PURPOSE OF THE CRAFT ASSOCIATION IN EGYPT

The craft union is clearly distinguished by its membership, but these unions are also distinguished by their avowed purposes. Rather than a group of workers of comparable skills fighting an economic battle, craft unions drew members from vastly different social, economic, and career levels. This diversity of membership combined with the nature of work for artisans and tradesmen led to certain aims for unions. These goals or purposes are evident in part during regular meetings. A union federation meeting in the provincial Upper Egyptian town of Suhaj in 1936 was attended by members of the union of cooks, barbers, car drivers, transport coachmen (*hudhiyyat al-naql*, which refers literally to coachmen or teamsters), the mechanical section (presumably motor vehicle drivers), electrical workers, janitors and messengers, café employees, and construction workers. The meeting was called by their president, Riyad Makawi, an attorney and president of the local Wafd organization. The first item on the agenda concerned renting out the buffet of the workers' club to the president of the local cooks' union for four pounds a month plus costs. This was agreed to; the union books were then balanced and a secretary chosen. Next, the construction workers' union, which had apparently fallen into disarray, was reformed and the new president thanked Makawi for his "beneficial services to the classes of the workers." Finally, Shaykh Amin Ahmad ʿAli, the local deputy for those of high religious status in the area, the descendants of Muhammad, urged the workers to perform good deeds and to obey God, the Prophet, and their deputies. The evening ended with Makawi accepting the applause and cheers of the assembly.[26]

In this meeting the members are subjected to moral lectures and other efforts to improve their character, and this is a typical part of the program of a union meeting. In every federation, union members had to listen to informative or moral lectures by their leaders. The Wafdist attorney Hilmi al-Jazar, for example, ran the Gharbiyyah federation for several years, sponsoring lectures on Western philosophy and medicine, among other topics.[27] Federation members once sat through a speech on self-reliance as a principle for human activity, with the lives of Garibaldi, Washington, Hitler, Mussolini, Duvalier, and Egypt's own Zaghlul cited as examples.[28] The union leadership assumed that members would benefit from these lectures and therefore union meetings were used as a platform for local intellectuals or political or social propaganda rather than as a forum for workers' economic or political concerns.

Related to this purpose of "moral uplift" was a concern with workers' and owners' rights and obligations. This should not be unexpected because these unions involved both owners and workers. The difficulties that union leaders could encounter in this area, however, are aptly illustrated by the comments of Muhammad ʿAli Husayn, president of the cooks' union in Cairo in 1943.[29] Husayn mentioned that he had had problems in explaining to his members their obligations to their employers.

> [I tried] to teach the worker in my union his duties toward the owner and what were the duties of the owner toward him, for many craftsmen [abnaʾ al-mihnah] believed that the law recognizing unions was only a weapon against the employer.

Husayn's ideas were already in conflict with those of industrial workers, which had probably begun to spread among some craftsmen. Moreover, the existence of a law gave employees rights that enabled them to look after their own interests without regard to those of their employers. Such a concern for one's own affairs is not necessarily the beginning of a larger consciousness of class.

Husayn's union, like many others, was still largely a mutual-aid society. During the month-long fast of Ramadan, for example, Husayn and other leaders of the cooks' union visited the local units and collected alms for the sick.[30] This type of union activity was considered basic to the unions for craftsmen and service workers.

Closely related to a concern with mutual aid and self-help was a concern for self-policing. It was only possible for craftsmen to help each other if there continued to be a craft; indeed the best way to help each other was to ensure that no single craftsman unfairly expanded into a given market at the expense of the others: work had to be shared equitably and that meant enforcing union discipline on those who might be tempted to become "free riders," benefiting unequally at the expense of those who kept the accustomed hours, services, or fees. In 1934 one newspaper reported that the barbers and coiffeurs of Shibin al-Kum in the Delta

> have been unionized for quite a while. Their union functions regularly and all the hairdressers show an extraordinary discipline in obeying the union regulations.[31]

The internal rules so scrupulously obeyed were simply rules to limit competition among shop owners. The unions sought to enforce the collective regulation of the trade in order to strengthen the position of all the members, but this often meant singling out and punishing a particular member for violating the rules. When need be, the courts, as in the case of Shibin al-Kum, were used to back up the unions' authority.

The effort to police its own members reveals the craft association's weak spots. Individual members were politically and economically weak and gained little or no strength in numbers. The collection of dues from many small shops and businesses was difficult, and members who were lower-level workers had a difficult time enforcing regulations against owners who were also union members. Since the unions were founded in part to overcome economic disadvantages, union leaders in the twentieth century sought a way to gain the necessary strength to enforce decisions of union leaders and members. Their solution was to appeal to the state to intervene and settle disputes or enforce decisions. A state court or agency could settle a wage dispute, enforce a regulation, or require a benefit for all workers. Thus the union sought to use the state as a substitute for collective organization. To aid this union effort, members had only to appeal to their leaders, who were often nationalist political figures or professionals with close contacts in government. A few examples will clarify the role of the state in aiding the unions.

The vendors of fuel oil and the large petroleum companies, which provided the fuel oil, carried on a dispute for fifteen years, during which time vendors went from being wage earners to piece-rate salesmen.[32] The most complete records cover the vendors for the Socony Vacuum Oil Company. Before 1935 the vendors sold kerosene from carts provided, as were all their implements, by the company and were paid three hundred piasters (three Egyptian pounds) per month. Vendors signed renewable contracts for three-month terms; there was no security of tenure. Kerosene was sold by a standard measure, the bucket.[33] In 1935 vendors were hired on a commission basis (8 millièmes per bucket) and in 1936 the duties of vendors were contractually changed to include maintenance of the carts, and the base price of kerosene was set.

In 1938 workers' complaints about reduced incomes were already reaching the state, and by 1944 the Labour Bureau under the Wafd government increased the commission to ten millièmes or one piaster per bucket. In 1948 a ministerial decree was issued, raising the commission another four millièmes and declaring the conflict ended. Nevertheless, the companies refused to allow vendors the cost-of-living adjustments that several pieces of legislation had guaranteed workers because, they claimed, the vendors were not workers.

Not until 1953, after the overthrow of the royal regime, was the issue finally decided. At that time the court established that vendors were workers and not merchants because vendors were not free to seek kerosene from other suppliers and because the company paid some of the costs of distribution. Thus the vendors were employees. The vendors, however, seem to have considered themselves employees but not workers. This is clear from the vendors' argument about the wage structure of the petroleum distribution process. The union argued that after wages and commissions are taken into account, income and status do not coincide, and they should.

> The union in its memorandum says, for example, that we sometimes find an
> assistant warehouseman earns a salary that amounts to more than the salary

of the vendor, although the latter is the superior of the former and that the salary of the vendor is sometimes greater than that of the warehouse official although the former is subordinate to the latter.[34]

The conciliation commission refused to accept the argument that salaries must always be strictly in accord with theoretical lines of hierarchy.

The itinerant vendors of Cairo in the 1930s sought help from the state for a different problem. These vendors proposed that the state license them in exchange for their controlling the traffic of vendors. Citing a system supposedly used "in Europe," vendors (of other than kerosene) proposed to police themselves in exchange for legitimacy. Specifically they proposed to refuse union membership to those found guilty of crimes, to license members, and to require special uniforms (similar to the uniforms worn by newspaper vendors); in exchange vendors would be allowed access to all streets and squares while carrying a maximum of two kilograms of miscellaneous goods.[35]

A surprising number of the records of the Labour Bureau deal precisely with what we would have to call internal union problems. The bureau intervened to regularize a work situation, penalize an employer, or legitimate the role of a union for craft and service workers, including those in traditional crafts. Thus it is not uncommon to find handwritten agreements such as the one between the makers of palm-fiber cartons and their workers, which describes piece rates for seventeen different kinds of cartons and includes a provision for a 12 percent raise. Wages, figured on the basis of one hundred baskets, went from a low of 81 piasters per hundred to a high of 450 piasters per hundred. The workers and masters, both groups illiterate, signed with their seals, not their signatures.[36]

Although unions were large and had a diverse membership with socially prominent leaders, they could not enforce regulations or policies against the members' wishes. Further, because the craft unions included both owners and workers in their membership, it was often difficult to establish a uniform policy even when that policy was clearly beneficial. To overcome its inherent weaknesses, the craft union came to rely on the state to confirm or enforce its decisions or to serve as a distant employer to whom demands were submitted. The need to win the state as an ally thus became one of the more important purposes of the union and one of the main reasons behind the choice of leaders not drawn from the ordinary membership.

THE RESPONSE TO THE CRAFT ASSOCIATION

Egyptian trade unionists and others were aware of the practices of craft associations and attempted to challenge them, but they failed to overcome these practices and often ended up employing them. The life of Muhammad Hasan ʿImara is a case in point. ʿImara had been apprenticed to the *shaykh* of a group of barbers as a youth. He later worked in a Cairo salon that employed both Egyptians and Europeans and had a union led by an Italian barber. Such an establishment was a rarity among Egyptian barbers. The union executive council as well as the membership was also mixed, that is, included both Egyptians and Europeans. This union

> fought to resist the guild [*taʾifi*] structure and began to fight in any manner destined to end the power of the heads of the guild [*shuyukh al-taʾifah*] even as it was concerned to better wages and honest intervention between workers and owners of salons.[37]

This union seems to have had no connection to any larger group, and was probably the legacy of a still relatively large Italian community in Egypt. The union collapsed, and ʿImara was not to hear of unions again for several years. When he did it was by the most improbable accident. ʿImara heard about a new barbers' union being formed from a friend who had bought a piece of cheese wrapped in the leaflet announcing the first meeting. ʿImara attended the initial meeting and was elected secretary, but the union federation of which it was a part was disappointing. The federation seemed like nothing more than the old guild structure, for it was composed of "brokers" who bought and sold workers. This federation was the Egyptian Workers Federation headed by Daʾud Ratib.

Early in 1930, ʿImara and a group of his associates expelled Ratib and elected ʿAbbas Halim president. To accomplish the task they took the membership rolls and official seals to Halim's house at night, evidently one step ahead of the police. Although Halim was on bad terms with the king, he was still a member of the royal family and a rich man; he could deal with the police relatively easily. The union then sent out handbills calling for a broader federation; Halim's prestige as an ally of the Wafd, a prince, and a sportsman helped greatly. Besides a small number of industrial unions, the federation seems to have attracted mainly crafts. ʿImara seems to have formed at this time the personal and political attachment to Halim that would remain throughout his life.

Halim was allied to the Wafd but not under its control, which favorably impressed many trade union leaders; he bankrolled the union federal bureaucracy. Dues, which were in any event not always collected, were set at only two piasters a month and only 10 percent went to the center. Halim made up the difference between the federation's income and its expenses. The federation had at least ten full-time positions and published its own newspaper (*Al-Safaʾ*). Halim's financial contribution, then, was not slight.[38]

Throughout the 1930s, when union activities often became a dangerous proposition, ʿImara continued to receive the benefits of having a patron and supporter like Halim. Although ʿImara formally rejected the practices of the craft associations, he and other unionists found it difficult if not impossible to carry on without some of the practices of craft unions. In fact the trade unions, largely craft in orientation, could not yet provide the basis for stable, self-sustaining, organized activity. The collection of dues was irregular, and union members rejected even such basic tools of administration as dues cards or books. Thus, the formal response of men like ʿImara might be to reject craft unions in principle, but these men used any of those practices that would help them achieve their goal of building trade unions to aid workers.

The craft associations of the twentieth century are perhaps best understood as a transitional stage. In the traditional form, the *shaykh* mediated between workers and government, but once the government changed, with the arrival of the British in 1882, the role of the *shaykh* also had to change. This left craftsmen and others without a mediator and forced them to draw on the group of comparable government influence: professional men such as attorneys and physicians and politicians in the nationalist movement. These individuals gained access to the government for the unions and carried on in a new form the role held by the *shaykh*. But whereas the *shaykh* had imposed the order of a more remote government, now union leaders dealt directly with the government and its agencies. Political parties recognized the advantages to be gained by assisting these unions, and the nationalist movement became a strong supporter of the associations for craftsmen and service workers.

Despite the criticisms of the supporters for a less traditional union, the craft associations met the needs of large numbers of workers and left a clear imprint on the labor union movement in Egypt. The unions of craftsmen and service workers brought to the trade union movement a strong sense of attachment to the nationalist movement, a pattern of personal attachment to leaders, and an understanding of the need for a politically independent trade union organization.

Although these workers seem to have had an excessive reliance on their "betters," perhaps it was only by relying on the personal good will and generosity of influential men that any association of those who worked with their hands could come into being. Reliance on the mutual obligations of social superiors and inferiors made more sense than taking on the entire structure of rural or even semirural society and the state. Isolated, impoverished, and dependent, craftsmen had little to work with. Even men like ʿImara who hoped to break down the older system of *shaykh* and laborer found themselves unable to break away from the practice of allying themselves with prominent and influential men. To speak then of guilds or guildlike structures persisting into the twentieth century is not to claim continuity with the remote past. Rather these structures point to the changes that the old guilds underwent and affirm that the significant break with the past for those who worked with their hands came, not at the turn of the century, but later, and this break was based on the creation of new forms of industry and new concepts of political organization and orientation.

CHAPTER SIX

Peasants in Workers' Clothes: Politics in the Sugar Mills

The formal organization of the process of industrial production does not by itself explain the politics of industrial workers. The industrial process may indeed substitute formal controls for the more personalized controls of the artisan world, but this more formal world of the industrial establishment also requires particular kinds of workers, and, ironically, the most highly mechanized sectors of the economy may well use vast amounts of unskilled labor. The relatively high degree of mechanization in the Egyptian sugar industry, for example, did not attract workers who were "proletarian," but rather drew in large numbers of workers who did not expect to be employed full time in factories. These workers, moreover, did not have the opportunity to acquire new skills for higher-paying jobs in the factory. Most of the workers in the sugar industry were peasants for whom the opportunity to regularly earn cash money constituted a significant resource, one they sought to pass on within the family. The politics of any union movement had to be intelligible within this framework, the world of the peasant.

Consequently, even though unions in the sugar industry engaged in the activities generally associated with industrial unions, such as strikes, signing contracts, and even negotiation between workers and management, these unions had a distinct character. Workers in these unions did not seek the new identity that others have assumed they would.[1] Rather, these unions were associated either with a nationalist party, usually the Wafd, or in one significant case with the Muslim Brothers. In both instances, however, the union preached a conservative doctrine of *insaf*, or giving each one his due.

The traditional nature of this work force and its isolation from the major urban centers of Cairo and Alexandria probably made it inevitable that the workers would rely on traditional figures to provide leadership and would define their struggle with the factory administration in terms of communal solidarity. In Upper Egypt those figures were primarily the local social elite and nationalists, and in Hawamdiyyah they were Muslim activists. The Muslim activists succeeded in Hawamdiyyah by identifying a potentially critical group in the factory—the foremen—the same group that was critical for textile workers. The Muslim activists saw the foremen as the key to implementing their vision of a unified Islamic community in the factory and to building an association of factory workers.

A traditionalist ideology, exemplified by close ties to the Muslim Brothers, made the union leadership militant and yet acceptable antagonists to the plant administration and the central government officials, especially in the period before the end of World War II. Thereafter, the leaders faced a crisis of redefining the nature of the union and its relation to the plant. The union leadership overcame this crisis by seeking new political allies to play the old game. The workers continued to make out, but in part they did so by state fiat, financed by government decisions.

NEW WORK IN A NEW INDUSTRY

Sugar mills were spread throughout Egypt, and I shall concentrate primarily on one, the plant at Hawamdiyyah in Giza near Cairo, although there were significant differences between the leadership at the Hawamdiyyah plant and the other plants in Upper Egypt. The failure of the nationalists to fulfill the workers' expectations in 1936 may have led Hawamdiyyah to become significantly different from the other plants. For this reason I shall present the case study in chronological order up to 1936, treating Hawamdiyyah as a separate instance by the beginning of World War II, when the Islamic-oriented union was formed.

The work force in the sugar mills numbered in the tens of thousands spread along Upper and Middle (southern) Egypt. Dispersion is one of the most striking characteristics of any industry based on transforming food crops, but it is especially common in the sugar industry because of the need to perform steps in the industrial process close together. The closer the steps between cutting and milling, the less sugar lost by fermentation in the cane. When the sugar industry was begun by Khedive Ismaᶜil about 1850, mills were generally small. In the ensuing forty years, however, the tendency in the industry worldwide was to larger and larger plants with larger amounts of machinery. By the time of the French-owned monopoly of the *Société Générale des Sucreries et de la Raffinerie de l'Egypte* in 1893, Egypt boasted several large establishments. Five mills and one refinery operated throughout the period from 1919 to 1950. From north to south, they were located at Hawamdiyyah (beyond Giza), Mattai, Abu Kurgas, Shaykh Fadl, Nagᶜ Hammadi, and Armant.

The cane mills were still enough of an oddity at the turn of the century to merit a description in an early Baedeker's guidebook.

> The sugar factories, which are a monopoly of the Khedive, follow each other in rapid succession. They are connected by the railway and short branch-lines, used in harvest times only, run from the plantation lying farther to the W. Their lofty brick and iron chimneys impart a very modern industrial air to the ancient land of the Pharoahs. Large barges with sugar-canes or with fellahin 'factory hands' are met on the river. The juice is expressed from the cane and then refined by being boiled twice in closed vessels.[2]

If towns such as Armant, Mattai, or Nagᶜ Hammadi stood out at all, they did so because of their mills, railway bridges, or railway stations. Baedeker's description of the source of the work force seems exact, for it is amplified in a contemporary discussion of the Egyptian economy.

> As long as they have existed the sugar companies have recruited from among the peasants living near the factories. Thus they are either small owners or agricultural laborers who work at an industrial job. The sugar company has an inexhaustible reserve among them because the fathers of the families request, without stint, places for their sons. The "sugar tradition" is established then, in one way or another, in peasant families whose villages or estates lie alongside the factories of the Company.[3]

Peasants working in factories, then, made up the 90 percent of the unskilled work force in the sugar industry.

These unskilled workers were influenced by the ecological and seasonal constraints of a growing cycle far more than workers in other food-based industries or even than workers in sugar production in other countries because the cane harvest in Egypt overlapped the period of planting. The harvest season ran from December to April, overlapping the planting season, which ran from mid-February to mid-March. The work of preparing the fields was no less arduous than cutting the cane or milling it: workers were required to till the soil twice and then plant sixty-seven hundred pounds of seed per acre.[4] The cane was grown by landless agricultural laborers on the large estates as well as by small landholders. So acute was the labor shortage that cane was sometimes not planted until May, and owners tried various schemes to shift the planting dates in order to avoid a labor shortage.[5]

The mass of unskilled workers were hired only during the harvest season, a time of peak demands on the strength not only of individuals but also of families. This was also a time of relatively great bargaining power for the peasants working in the sugar factories, for they could afford to strike. The peasants did not need to be sophisticated economists to understand that they could afford to disrupt the factory at least briefly, for they had alternatives while the factory managers had none. The cane had to be processed as quickly as possible on ripening. Wages, by contrast, could be deferred.

Despite the large numbers of workers and their bargaining power during the harvest season, wages were not high. There were 15,583 workers in the sugar industry in 1912 of whom 14,926 were day laborers; 390 were skilled or semiskilled Egyptian workers; and 267 were skilled European workers or employees, that is, professionals or managers. At the refinery at Hawamdiyyah, where cane was processed and raw sugar purified, about 90 percent of the work force was unskilled day labor.

Adult day laborers earned between 5 and 8 piasters a day during the crushing season. Adult males did not provide the only work force; entire families were employed; children earned between 2 and 4 piasters a day. Wages for skilled and semiskilled workers ranged from 300 to 600 piasters (3 to 6 Egyptian pounds) per month for cookers and drivers, to 450 to 900 piasters (4.5 to 9 pounds) for craftsmen and other semiskilled occupations, to 750 to 1,050 piasters (7.5 to 10.5 pounds) per month for electricians and mechanics. Wages seem to have been uniform throughout the industry before the First World War.[6]

There is some dispute about whether or not wages were adequate before the war, but there is no doubt that by the end of the war wages for skilled and unskilled workers were hit hard by inflation. Rising prices and falling real wages posed problems for sugar workers and others, especially during the postwar inflation. Hours were also a problem, for the mills routinely worked twelve-hour days. Finally, the seasonal nature of the industry meant workers regularly faced unemployment and could expect no job security.

In addition to the mass of unskilled workers, the industry employed one group that came to be especially important: that small number of skilled Egyptian workers. These were the Egyptian workers who were in the plant throughout the year, whose lives were intimately linked to the factory as full-time industrial workers.

MILITANCY IN THE 1910s AND 1920s

Strikes as a characteristic form of protest began early in the sugar industry and recurred frequently. They took typical forms and revolved around typical issues. The forms were spontaneous and therefore unorganized mass outbursts, occasionally violent, and the issues were wages, hours, and job security. The earliest reference to a strike in the sugar mills involves the plant at Hawamdiyyah, on the outskirts of Cairo (in Giza), in 1910.

> In February 1910 a strike just failed to break out regarding the length of the workday. The factory management barely managed to avoid it, by sowing dissension between workers from different villages.[7]

Workers in Europe had, of course, long since attacked the twelve-hour day, and European workers were fighting to abolish it in Egypt. Now, the struggle for shorter hours had become more general, given the pace of work at the height of the crushing season.

Strikes expressed more than trade union dissatisfactions with work at the sugar mills and those who ran them. The sugar factories were widely perceived as representative of, and even the basis of, European power in Egypt. Thus the factories themselves and their managers were perceived as legitimate targets for nationalist agitation. Village notables, for example, brought masses of peasants to protest at the mills in the countryside during the nationalist upheaval of 1919.[8]

The director of the sugar company made a tour of the Upper Egyptian countryside in response to complaints from workers. Henri Naus was not only a manager of the sugar industry; he was also a leader of the Egyptian Federation of Industry. After receiving petitions in March 1919, Naus went to the countryside to see the situation for himself. One of the petitions was addressed to the manager of the refinery at Abu Kurgas from the local notables and peasants.

> We the undersigned protest against the English occupation of Egypt and the
> atrocities committed in our quality as delegates of the nearly 5000 peaceful
> protesters assembled. . . . We ask the director to transmit our protests to the
> management of the company so that it may be communicated to the French
> Embassy in Cairo.[9]

The peasants had already accepted the idea that action against the interests of one colonial power could have an effect on the interests of
another.

It was probably the events at Hawamdiyyah that most influenced
Naus to visit Upper Egypt. On the night of March 15, 1919, a group of
Bedouin were said to have attacked the train station (that is, the ter-
minus for arriving cane) and then the mill. Of the eighteen hundred
workers

> a good part abandoned their posts and joined the rioters. . . . The destruc-
> tion of the train station accomplished, the rioters to the number of two or
> three thousand made known their intention of attacking the Refinery, but
> they were stopped at the factory gate by police officers, the head of the
> guards, diverse village notables, and a certain number of veteran factory
> workers who informed them [that the true, nonpolitical character] of the
> mill assured the prosperity of the region and of an important laboring
> population.[10]

Obviously the strikers were local peasants and workers, not Bedouin.
Nomads might have been driven off, had there still been any significant
number of them in Egypt by the 1919 revolution; only those who were
economically dependent on the mill and lived near it would be influenced by the arguments of village notables and "veteran workers."[11]

Even from this brief account it is apparent that there was considerable hostility among the local work force directed at the mill and specifically at the mill as a physical presence. The Europeans in charge of the
mill found it hard to understand why hostility should suddenly flare up
against the mill as a physical object. Yet it was at the factory that men
experienced Europeans at their worst. It was not uncommon for managers to blame outside agitators for the sudden outbursts of violence that
characterized the protest of the sugar workers for at least thirty years
rather than accept the presence of such hostility within their own workers. Who these "outside" agitators were is unclear, but it seems likely
that they were Egyptian salaried workers. Clearly there was a significant
split between those who saw the factories as a source of distress and
those who saw them as a source of well-being.

In Armant, Naus met several local spokesmen who expressed their views on the mills. The local social and political leaders saw the factories as both a source of economic advantage and a symbolic antagonist. They, like the leaders of the formal nationalist movement, the Wafd, whom they supported and to whom they were closely linked, wanted a change in the internal political situation in Egypt. Yet they hoped to profit from a continued association with the market forces represented at the mill. Thus, the local leaders asked Naus to push the British for complete independence, but nevertheless

> *the notables* assured Monsieur Naus Bey that he should remain calm regarding the interests of the Sugar Company and its lands because they considered the latter bound up with their own interests; it is understood that the company is a source of well-being for the country and for the growers of cane, without mentioning the ties of friendship and esteem which these latter have for the heads of the factory [emphasis mine].[12]

In Nagʿ Hammadi, where Naus also met village notables, he was told that only one result, complete independence, would satisfy them. They rebuffed Naus's contention that an intermediate political goal was necessary in order to bargain with the British. Despite the disagreement over how political goals should be formulated, the meeting broke up amicably, "and everyone withdrew while thanking him [Naus] profusely."[13]

After the 1919 revolution, workers focused on wages and the effects of postwar inflation. A strike was avoided at Hawamdiyyah in late 1919 by the Labour Conciliation Board by granting higher wages and "special conditions."[14] There was a "partial strike" at Nagʿ Hammadi in January 1920, with workers demanding an increased war bonus as well as protesting managerial severity and calling for the reinstatement of dismissed employees. Because this strike is described as the "second time" and because of the demand for reinstatement of dismissed employees, we can conclude that there was probably an earlier strike of some magnitude at Nagʿ Hammadi, perhaps in the wake of the 1919 uprising.[15] The peasants' situation may have been unusually desperate that year because wages were relatively low in comparison with inflated postwar prices and the price for cane had not risen.

By mid-1920 the peasant-workers in Upper Egypt seem to have been extremely willing to strike, and labor unrest, if not yet labor organization, began to spread. In the countryside, strikes were limited to the crushing season for the most part. At Shaykh Fadl a strike broke out on May 19, 1920, to protest mistreatment at the hands of management, but the company probably had the upper hand, for four days later the strike was over.

> The strike came to an end . . . and . . . the greatest harmony reigned among the workers and their head. All the workers returned to work except for six troublemakers who were fired for indiscipline after being indemnified.[16]

With the crushing season over, both skilled and unskilled workers had little leverage with the company because the plant could be left idle and maintenance carried out slowly or deferred completely until later in the season. The exception was Hawamdiyyah. Because it processed sugar from other mills, Hawamdiyyah was in operation all year and thus strikes were possible at any time, including the height of summer (when the heat must have made work nearly intolerable). In June 1920 the workers at Hawamdiyyah struck briefly and were given a 25 percent wage increase.[17]

In all these cases it is hard to avoid the conclusion that the strikes were spontaneous and poorly if at all organized. The workers had leaders, but the strikes did not lead to union organization during this period. Not a single record mentions the signing of an accord with a union, and the one mention of a union is so ambiguous that it confirms the absence of organization rooted in the plant rather than its presence.

Despite continuing contacts between workers and the Labour Conciliation Board,[18] local government authorities played an important mediating role between workers and the sugar companies. These local officials were the appointed representatives of the central government: the governors, prefects, and police chiefs. According to the fifth report from the Labour Conciliation Board, local authorities in Aswan and Qena transmitted to the board, via the Ministry of the Interior, the workers' demands regarding pay and conditions. Since this report deals with demands outside the period of the sugar harvest and differentiates between the raises received by monthly employees and those received by daily workers, we can conclude that the skilled workers, many of whom were European, pressed demands in Upper Egypt for higher pay.[19]

There is little evidence that a union in the formal sense existed. The union in Upper Egypt depended on the willingness of militant workers to lead actions rather than on an independent institutional framework. This is clear from one of the few accounts by a worker at the Hawamdiyyah plant at the time. According to his memoirs, Shaykh ʿAbd al-Qadr Hamada knew of two strikes in 1921 and participated in one strike at Hawamdiyyah in 1923.[20] Hamada said he was active in a union and that he aided those outstanding workers who led the strike in 1923. According to Hamada the workers did not strike primarily for wages, which Hamada described as having been among the best in Egypt at the time, or for social services, which he also rated as good. Hamada identified haughty treatment by supervisors and preferential treatment for white-collar workers as the key factors in arousing the anger of the workers.

The only other evidence from the early 1920s of a union organization among sugar workers is found in the final report of the Labour Conciliation Board, issued in 1922. According to this report, the Manual Laborers Union in Alexandria included the Nagᶜ Hammadi sugar workers' union.[21] An affiliation with the Manual Laborers Union in Alexandria in 1922 indicated a desire to affirm political *sentiment* rather than to create an organization to carry those feelings into action. The Manual Laborers Union was closely tied with the Watani party, which by 1920 had been superseded in Lower Egypt by the Wafd party. The uncompromising quality of national sentiment Henri Naus found in Nagᶜ Hammadi must be related to the workers' tie with the Watani party. The local notables were, as we have seen, nationalists, and the mill "organization" mentioned in the final report indicates they were bringing the peasants into the nationalist movement as workers.

Spontaneous militancy continued to be the recourse of sugar workers during the 1920s and for the next two decades. These strikes were often violent. For example, in 1923,

> during a strike that occurred at the mill in Armant during last February, M. Anache was jostled and struck by native workers and, thinking himself imperilled, he fired a revolver shot which killed a native.[22]

Given the temper of the nationalist movement just before the Wafd finally came to power in 1924, the French embassy refrained from having Anache acquitted by a French court precipitously, although that was, of course, its right under the Capitulations. The French were afraid "to overexcite the natives of Armant and to bring about problems that would put the European personnel of the mill in danger."[23]

NATIONALISTS IN THE 1930s

The 1930s ushered in a new era as the nationalist movement undertook more serious efforts to influence the workers' movement. Whether these efforts led to a greater disillusionment of the workers or to their clearer understanding of the nature of the nationalist movement depends on one's point of view, but there is no doubt that between 1931 and 1936 the sugar workers at Hawamdiyyah had a decisive encounter with the Wafd, ʿAbbas Halim, and those related to the nationalist movement, and that in the wake of (we cannot say with certainty *because of*) this encounter these workers turned toward a Muslim-oriented trade union leadership.

Hindered by the onset of economic decline in the late 1920s and repressed by Ismaʿil Sidki, the trade union movement revived in 1931. ʿAbbas Halim was already active in this movement, supplying it with funds and aiding its publication of a newspaper, *Al-Safaʾ*. According to this source, union organizers succeeded in creating a union at Hawamdiyyah in four days.[24] The union had 750 members among workers who were on an eleven-hour shift for less than one piaster a day. Unfortunately the union had no political influence and the company was able to gain the support of the government in shutting it down: the police attacked the union offices, made off with the papers, and gave the factory manager a list of the names of union members. The union—probably a political society if the names of the members were kept secret by the time it had a membership of nearly one thousand—collapsed. No organization could yet channel the energies of the sugar workers, and although the ex-prince may have supported the union "organizers," he was far from ready to help in the creation of a stable organization in the plant.

If the company believed that the absence of a union would mean an end to industrial strife, they were mistaken. In 1934 another spontaneous outbreak occurred at Hawamdiyyah, this one similar in many respects to the 1919 events there. An important difference in 1934, however, was the mere awareness of a trade union organization centered around ʿAbbas Halim, who was then still allied with the Wafd. On July 13, 1934, sugar warehouse workers on the day shift struck in protest over company refusal to adjust wages, and they were joined by the evening shift. The number of strikers swelled rapidly to three thousand. Suddenly,

> a conflict broke out between the leadership supporting the strike and those opposed and the company locked the gates so as to avoid a critical situation. The security forces became involved and the mudir of Giza, Muhammad Shiʿr Bey, came to Hawamdiyyah personally to mediate the struggle, but he accomplished nothing and a large group of workers continued the strike for several days despite the resumption of work in several departments.[25]

Clearly there was no unified organizational leadership for the strike. Because the departments seem to have struck separately, it seems most likely that the factory was "organized" along lines of the process conducted in different areas of the plant rather than in the plant as a whole. The industrial plant was probably still conceived of by the workers as an assemblage of smaller productive units working side by side rather than as a single industrial whole.[26]

During the first part of the 1930s, ʿAbbas Halim and the Wafd began to patronize the young trade union organizations, and as a consequence, workers were introduced to the features of relatively coherent, long-lasting organizations, in contrast to the loose associations that had led to the workers' spontaneous outbursts. Consequently, two years later when the workers at Hawamdiyyah struck again, their action differed in some regards from the sporadic rebellions of earlier years, although the spontaneous character of the protest was still apparent. On July 13, 1936, a former worker at Hawamdiyyah, Hamid Salim, entered the plant and "harangued" the workers about their low wages and poor working conditions until, being

> taken unawares, and worked up into a state of fury some of the men indulged in an orgy of destruction.[27]

The police were helpless before the three thousand protesting workers. A battalion of army troops was brought in and a pitched battle was fought, with guns on one side and the workers' tools on the other. Against sugar loaves, bottles, and stones, guns prevailed. One worker was killed and several injured. Many fled the plant, but others barricaded themselves in the factory. The affair lasted for several days, until July 18, 1936.

The strike resulted from demands, presented several days earlier, for rehiring several fired workers, including Salim, a 25 percent pay raise, and time off from work to observe Friday prayers. Salim had presented the demands, and was among those who fled the plant. He took refuge in ʿAbbas Halim's palace in Garden City, Cairo, although Halim did not condone the strike. According to the British informant, the strike resulted from a general belief among the workers that the Wafd government, which took office in 1936, was "theirs and sympathetic to them."[28]

Given the mass of propaganda to which the workers had been exposed, the workers' assumption was not unreasonable. In 1935 the Wafd party had sponsored a major national conference that had focused

on labor's demands. In addition, the party leaders had promised that a
Wafd government would pass a law recognizing labor unions. On assuming office, however, the Wafd was more concerned with negotiating
British withdrawal from Egypt than with keeping its promises to what it
could only see as unruly workers. Presenting a good face to the British
for negotiations was more important than aiding the workers at Hawamdiyyah.[29] The 1936 strike marked a turning point for the workers at
Hawamdiyyah, for they seem to have relied less on the nationalist movement after 1936. In fact, this year marked a turning point for the labor
movement as a whole, for (as we shall see in the textile mills) at this time
the push for unions allied with but separate from the nationalist movement as exemplified by the Wafd becomes more pronounced.

In the late 1930s and early 1940s sporadic violence declined as an
apparent solution to problems in the sugar industry. Instead, unions began to replace spontaneous violence, at least in Nagᶜ Hammadi, where,
as we have seen, there may have been an old association between
the nationalist movement and trade unions, and at Hawamdiyyah
where Muslim activists associated with the Muslim Brothers assumed
leadership.

On February 11, 1939, there was a strike and the threat of prolonged
conflict in Nagᶜ Hammadi. The strike was reported at length in the
Wafdist daily Al-Misri.

> The sugar workers were denied paychecks five days ago until a solution to
> their demands is reached, the most important of which is additional pay to
> those who work twelve hours a day during the pressing season. They had
> earlier hoped to win this just demand, but they were terribly shocked yester-
> day evening when the company informed them of the text of an agreement it
> had signed with the Labour Bureau; this not only did not contain their de-
> mands but rather confirmed the workday during the pressing season as
> twelve hours, that is, perpetuating the existing evil and giving it legal stand-
> ing. That was what roused the workers to the number of twenty-five hundred
> who struck all together at eight o'clock yesterday morning, occupied the fac-
> tory, including the warehouses, shops, and accounting sections, so as to con-
> trol them and maintain calm and order in the strike.[30]

Troops arrived shortly thereafter and the workers withdrew, but negotiations continued. On February 17, 1939, a Labour Bureau representative arrived, but apparently could not resolve the conflict because on
March 6 the former Wafdist parliamentary representative from Nagᶜ
Hammadi threatened that no cane would be delivered to the factory until a concession was made to the workers. This must have been a threat

with some force to it, for negotiations continued until a settlement was reached for a nine-hour day to be implemented the following year (in March the harvest and thus the "year" were essentially over).

Even after the threat to halt cane deliveries had forced negotiators to find a solution, the possibility of direct action by the workers appears to have remained. There seems to have been some sort of union involved, for we learn that workers planned a second strike and

> had not the head of the union intervened, calming down the workers, God alone knows what would have happened, and thus we came to the plan of ending the old schedule and putting in a new one guaranteeing rest to the workers.[31]

It is unfortunate that we know nothing more of this union at Nagᶜ Hammadi and especially of its president, but it is apparent that there was a group of local leaders who, along with the aid of political activists, could control the workers and bargain with the central authorities.

Agencies of the central government were certainly willing to sign contracts injurious to the workers' interest in the name of the workers. Thus, unions needed clear and direct ties to central ministries that could put pressure on other departments. In places like Nagᶜ Hammadi the unions clearly existed in close affiliation with the nationalist movement, whether the early parties before 1919 or the Wafd in the 1930s. Moreover, on the basis of the evidence, we must conclude that unions such as the one at Nagᶜ Hammadi could not maintain themselves without Wafdist assistance. Throughout the late 1930s the trade unions were fighting a difficult battle for official recognition and depended heavily on political allies.

MUSLIM LEADERSHIP IN THE 1940s

In 1942, the Wafd government passed a law recognizing unions, and the union at Hawamdiyyah was one of the first to register under the new law. The union was led by Shaykh Muhammad ᶜAbd al-Salam, who was a member of the Sharᶜi Cooperative Association; he was sympathetic to the Muslim Brothers, although not formally a member.[32] An imposing figure with a dark beard flecked with white, he was a man of formidable personality whose presence conveyed a feeling of strength and fortitude. One journalist suggested that ᶜAbd al-Salam had the force of character of a cabinet minister. He was, according to this account, born to be a leader.[33] ᶜAbd al-Salam was by all accounts a man driven "like those heroic fighters who struggled and suffered for the sake of a doctrine and who refused to give up until God gave them victory."[34] ʿAbd al-Salam was heroic, like a gadaʿ. He was also explicitly patriarchal and traditional. He was not urban.

The sugar workers' union at Hawamdiyyah was the first union to be granted recognition by the Ministry of Social Affairs, on October 14, 1942.[35] A copy of the union constitution is preserved, the second edition dated 1950. The document contains a preface that explicitly confronts the issue of how the workers live, their options, and their leaders. This preface dates from 1950 and refers to the period before the Wafd Egyptianization campaign that brought key industries under Egyptian ownership and the period immediately afterward. The sugar mills at Hawamdiyyah were bought by ʿAbbud Pasha in 1944 and during the next five years European administrators were, in theory, being eased out.

The preface to the constitution presents the correct Muslim response to the problems of the workers in Egypt at midcentury. In the first paragraph it asserts, on the part of the union president, that the audience to be addressed and the significant part of the work force to be organized is that of the section chiefs in the factory at Hawamdiyyah and at all crushing factories, although the "message" of the union is not only for them but for every Egyptian and every "Easterner."[36] The administration of the plant is perceived as rotten and the reason is the "distance of these section heads from the teaching of their religion, and from the high and heavenly counsels of the morals of their Prophet."[37]

In later paragraphs addressed to the workers and foremen, ʿAbd al-Salam advises the former to put themselves under their foremen, listen to them, obey them, and take their direction, so as to become a mass that is "serious, eager, and anxious to work which will bring back to our country great goodness and general benefit."[38] To the foremen, the advice was to follow good practices and to have the good of the workmen at heart, especially their problems stemming from poverty. The foremen are reminded that workers, too, have their pride and dignity, and that Egyptian foremen have a special obligation to use gentleness and mercy rather than cruelty and force.[39] At the time the union was formed, the preface asserts, getting rid of foreign domination was the main task confronting Egyptians. In the early 1940s, says the preface,

> we would proclaim in every place, Oh, you who believe, should you meet those who do not, do not treat them with timidity. . . . Thus we urged on the faithful to struggle with the colonialists.[40]

The nationalist and religious tone of the preface is unmistakable, and the constitution is an exemplar of a Muslim union as it might be defined by the Muslim Brothers. Yet the nature of this union cannot be the result of only Islamic ideology. The sugar workers' union at Hawamdiyyah survived on its own for at least eight years. The union therefore must have responded to what a significant proportion of the members, many of whom were of peasant background, expected from a union. Although we have no evidence on the expectations of members in earlier years, we can examine the goals outlined in the 1950 constitution as an expression of the areas of concern to workers during the later 1940s. The first goal of the union is to act as a "linking ring" between the company and its workers in every field of activity related to work. The second goal is to defend the material interests of the workers, individually as well as collectively. The third goal is to aid the workers materially and morally.[41]

These goals and their order clearly reflect a specifically Islamic vision, one that is still linked to the world of small production, although in this case the small producers are peasants, not craftsmen. Relying on the vocabulary of Islam, union leaders present their view of the factory as a solidary enterprise, in which workers and management (including not only the foremen but also the company administration as a whole) need to be tightly linked in order to maintain production.

Despite this measure of control, the union did not claim exclusive representation of the workers. The union made provisions in case of its later dissolution that suggest alternate organizations were a realistic possibility. The constitution provided that union funds were to be given "to the other unions of the workers of the sugar company proportionate to their memberships" unless a replacement for the current union is formed in six months.[42]

A significant part of the union's activity was social aid and support for the workers from their collective resources. The workers, in short, were a collective community inside the factory. After six months of paying dues, the worker was entitled to all union benefits; first and foremost was legal aid for any civil or criminal charges brought against the worker. Many of the other benefits were financial and accrued directly to the workers in case of need, especially posting money for security, injury and sick pay, aid to widows, severance pay for aged members (at the rate of three pounds per year of union membership), loans, and money for weddings. The union also was willing to aid workers arrested on the job as long as they had not done anything provocative. Those arrested could receive monetary aid up to fifteen piasters a day for a total of three months.[43]

The union was organized on the principle that the general meeting of the membership was the highest authority of the union. In the words of the constitution, the membership meeting was the "possessor of the highest power."[44] Anyone who had paid dues the month before the general meeting was eligible to vote. The tasks of the general meeting were to examine financial and organizational reports for the previous year and to elect a new administrative council (*majlis al-idarah*). Evidently the administrative council was elected from a restricted and preselected group of nominees. A procedure for self-nomination is given: anyone wishing to nominate himself for the administrative council must be able to read and write, have been a union member for two years, be paid up in his dues, and put up a twenty-piaster bond, which he forfeits if he does not win at least 50 percent of the votes in his shop. There were thirteen "shops" from which a total of fourteen administrative council members were elected. The skilled workers and those in administration elected half of the administrative council.[45]

Despite this formal structure, the strength and influence of the union was probably no more than that of the head of the union, who was called the *naqib* as well as the president in 1950.[46] *Naqib* was the title used by heads of *tawaʾif* in the previous century, and its use in the 1940s and 1950s reflects the perception of the union as a craft association. In fact, ʿAbd al-Salam, the union president, was a worker in the plant and according to newspaper reports made only twenty piasters a day.[47]

The president, one of two vice-presidents, the secretary, the treasurer, and the sergeant-at-arms formed an executive committee for the administrative council and decided on the agenda. To counterbalance the executive committee there was also a control committee, which could countermand the orders of the executive committee; the administrative council could take action if a deadlock ensued. The control committee could also investigate complaints and subject any member or any organ of the union to disciplinary action.[48] Besides the control committee there was also a disciplinary committee charged with examining the behavior of the membership, although its decisions were subordinate to the administrative council.[49] The union also had a propaganda committee and could retain attorneys, although these, as is clear from other parts of the constitution, could not themselves become union officials.[50]

If the formal organization seems to be secular and cast in a Western mold, the membership of the administration clarifies the nature of this union as Islamic. In 1950, when the revised constitution was printed, two members of the executive committee carried the title *shaykh* and two carried the title *hajj*. Two, in sum, had made the pilgrimage to Mecca and two others were considered religious leaders in some way.[51] The newspaper of the Muslim Brothers, moreover, identified ʿAbd al-Salam as a *shaykh*.[52] This newspaper also favorably reported on the activities of this union for several years. Thus the leadership of the union at Hawamdiyyah was considerably more religious in orientation than that of any other large union in a major industry, at least in the mid-1940s.[53]

The conservative nature of the sugar workers' union clearly pleased the membership, for the leadership at the Hawamdiyyah plant remained stable despite severe struggles, including lengthy strikes and retaliatory firings, at the end of World War II. There were strikes, each lasting about a week, in February and March 1945. The protests included occupying the factory.[54] The conflict was finally ended by referring the matter to a state conciliation committee, which does not seem to have reached a conclusion satisfactory to the workers.

In 1947, union activity reached a new high point at the Hawamdiyyah plant. During contract negotiations, the company decided to no longer allow workers' wages to be garnisheed, although living on credit until the pay envelope comes may be the only universal experience of proletarians.[55] The union threatened to strike in April 1947 and the company agreed not to fire those whose wages were subject to garnishment. But contract negotiations continued to drag on and a new strike deadline was set for October. The strike was never called and the newspaper of the Muslim Brothers, which had closely followed the earlier strike, turned to other issues. The union then began to deal in earnest with the situation of the workers under the new Egyptian ownership of the company, and even though this was a concern of the Muslim Brothers, the union became progressively more distant from this organization.

Until 1947 the union leadership considered the newspaper of the Muslim Brothers an important, and perhaps the most important, way to reach the general public and perhaps even the workers in the factory. Clearly publication of detailed information about the sugar workers, their grievances, and their contracts in the society's newspaper gave a certain legitimacy to the union. Even if the leaders at Hawamdiyyah were not formally members of the Muslim Brothers, they were so closely allied to the society that the lack of formal affiliation meant little. Now with their growing concern over the Palestine War, the Muslim Brothers had less attention for the union and the union now faced a double challenge: holding the support of workers while challenging the company for the workers.

The 1947 strike and the agreement stemming from it were not decisive at Hawamdiyyah. In December 1949 there was another strike and by 1950 the situation had become a national concern because of the bad relations between workers and management. The 1949 strike concerned the centrifuge workers, and the question of their situation was referred to a conciliation committee that met in Cairo rather than at the plant, as had been the case previously.[56]

In December 1950, the company refused to pay a cost-of-living increase mandated under martial law. The workers struck again and the Wafd government imprisoned ʿAbd al-Salam, even though the government had ordered the increase. In addition, the company fired the union's secretary as well as one hundred other workers. Despite several meetings held in the Social Affairs Ministry, the Interior Ministry (the national police), and the Giza governorate (the local police), the situation continued to degenerate, and the workers at Hawamdiyyah continued to gather national support through the daily press. Sugar workers in other areas, who looked to Hawamdiyyah as a standard for workers' contracts, also began to protest.   ·

The underlying issue was wages. The state set the price of sugar (which included production costs and excise taxes) and shared in the company's profits. This meant that high sugar prices for the large estate owners and high tax revenues for the state were largely maintained by low wages for workers. The wage agreement in dispute between the sugar workers' union and the company covered about 2,800 of Hawamdiyyah's 4,000 regular day workers.[57] In 1947 these workers were grouped into five categories:

(1) supergrade workers

(2) expert skilled workers

(3) skilled workers

(4) trained workers

(5) ordinary workers

There were 1,613 ordinary workers; 579 trained workers; 608 skilled workers (of whom 408 were "expert"); and 28 supergrade workers. Their pay scales ranged from 25 to 60 piasters a day for supergrade workers on salary to 5 to 19 piasters a day for ordinary workers. The supergrade workers seem to have been a small group with benefits similar to, if not identical with, those of European workers. Each classification was broken into subclasses, which created a set of "ladders" from the entry-level wage to the top. It took three to four years to climb one ladder and enter a new category.

In statements given to the newspaper of the Muslim Brothers, the union made a detailed criticism of the wage scale. The union pointed to the lack of clarity about raises, including cost-of-living adjustments; problems of who is included; the question of whether the wage scale is retroactive to 1945; and the position of workers during a probationary period. The union had other, related criticisms that reflected problems peculiar, not so much to Egypt, as to any work force made up of peasants in an uncertain economy. The workers wanted an assurance that the director, who had the right to choose new workers, would agree to pick them from among the families of those who already worked at Hawamdiyyah. They also wanted all skilled workers to be on salary rather than on wage, that is, to have their earnings protected by being given the status of "employees" or "clerks." The workers also wanted no more than a ten-piaster spread in each pay group.

The workers were obviously worried about the level of their wages, but they saw the solution to their problem, not in unemployment insurance, but rather in winning a guarantee of job security, just as an apprentice or craftsman might expect to be cared for by an owner or master craftsman. These sugar workers clearly had in mind the kind of personal bond between master and worker that all peasants rely on but can only enforce by the kind of spontaneous violence that was common in the sugar industry between 1915 and 1940.

Despite the perception of the conflict according to the peasant experience, the demands of the union seem to have been formulated with an eye to the needs of the educated or skilled workers rather than to those of the base. The key issues for the union over time seem to have been wages, equality of Egyptians with foreign employees, the eight-hour day, end-of-service compensation, which may refer to compensation for a layoff, firing, or retirement, and the end of benefits for foreigners that adversely reflected on the status of Egyptians, such as wash basins for foreign employees rather than the taps made available for Egyptians.

These demands do not seem designed to enhance the life of the peasants, the ordinary workers, yet the union at Hawamdiyyah, under the control of the Muslim Brothers, lasted at least until 1950 and probably until 1954, when the state took control of the trade union movement.

Clearly the union and the brotherhood served more than just the immediate economic needs of some members of the community, a community
then (even more so than now) made up of peasants and rural workers.
The success of this union can be attributed without question to certain
factors. For example, the union fought for some interests that clearly
concerned workers. The brotherhood complained about train schedules
that made it difficult for workers to arrive or leave on time. It undertook
the task of building a mosque by the train station, and also probably
attempted to persuade the company to provide a restaurant at Hawamdiyyah, a demand that had become popular in some industries (tobacco)
but not in others (textile).[58] On an economic level, the union appealed
more strictly to the foremen, who were in essence the skilled workers,
the literate, the leaders; they were the key constituency in a factory made
largely of those unable to chart their own course, for the foremen were
the individuals most likely to have the respect and allegiance of the ordinary workers. Thus the union and the Muslim Brothers sought the support of large numbers of workers from two directions—from the perspective of Islamic life and from that of the foremen of these workers. To
reinforce this strategy, the Muslim Brothers relied on its newspaper, influence in the palace, and empathy with the workers' oppression. Finally, the union and the Muslim Brothers used Islamic ideology to give
workers a clear sense of identity, thereby raising the issue in part above
economics. By giving the workers something to fight for and by showing
them how Islamic ideology could provide a constituency for winning
equality with the Europeans, the Muslim activists established their cre-
dentials as nationalists. The appeal to equity, which was a standard
element of the broad Islamic movement and especially of the Muslim
Brothers, furnished a rallying point for skilled and unskilled workers.

The Egyptian owners found Muslim activists more tolerant than
other union workers. A Muslim-oriented union was more committed to
production at Hawamdiyyah than a Communist-led union would have
been and in fact was more concerned with tightening the link between
workers and the factory than even a nationalist or social-democratic
leadership would be. Moreover, since the Muslim-oriented union saw
itself as a "transmission belt" between administration and worker, it
could be relied upon in contract negotiations; and its political orientations, against the British and in support of Arab Palestine, did nothing
to hinder the working of the sugar mills themselves.

THE LIMITS OF MUSLIM
TRADE UNION ACTIVITY

There are specific patterns in the role of Islamic groups in trade union activity. Generally Muslim leadership appeared in areas where unskilled workers were drawn from the peasantry and especially where the ownership of the industry had been or remained foreign. The key problem for the Muslim activists was maintaining the unity of the Muslim community in the face of challenges from foreign intervention or social stratification. Their influence was felt wherever pay, status, or working conditions tended to divide Muslims, although these activists were most successful in social situations like those found among the sugar workers. The Muslim Brothers' newspaper, unlike the left and even nationalist newspapers read by workers and trade union members, spent considerable time defining the nature of colonialism as a cultural assault and a matter of personal antagonism, and then proposing remedies based on cultural cohesiveness and personal dignity.

Islam as an ideology in the trade union movement was not too different from what was called nationalist ideology among American blacks in the 1960s: Islam provided a way for an educated elite to further its own personal interests by giving it a vocabulary likely to appeal to a mass political base. The Muslim Brothers attempted to mobilize workers against colonialism in Egypt and in so doing it had to define colonialism. Almost invariably, colonialism is that which makes it difficult for skilled or educated Egyptians to step into the positions of Europeans. Thus, in an article entitled "Sugar from Blood," the wage differential between Egyptian workers and European staff personnel in Egypt (rather than between factory wage rates in Egypt and those in Europe) is explained as the economic basis of imperialism.[59] In another article, colonialism is described as causing the split between skilled workers, who have graduated from technical schools, and clerical employees, so that such workers receive less than their due, namely, the wages and security of tenure enjoyed by employees.[60] It is, the article goes on, "the very essence of colonialism,"[61] to deny workers the possibility of advancement to higher grades such as engineer or foreman. Unskilled workers, the article continues, know nothing of culture and the "small worker" is thus like a child when he enters the factory, seeking only satisfaction of his immediate desires.[62] Thus, the article counsels, anticipating the constitution of the sugar workers, it is the duty of the owner or the shift foremen to pay attention to the needs of the workers.[63]

The paternalistic spirit urged by the Muslim Brothers in their newspaper and adopted with success by union leaders in Hawamdiyyah and
elsewhere seems to be based on creating a patron-client link between
educated, skilled workers (who were likely to become foremen if they
were not already) and the mass of men. It is an appeal described in anthropological research on peasants, and has its origins in small artisan
production, which was still the dominant form of urban production in
Egypt (in terms of employment). The heart of a patron-client relation,
however, is the personal tie in the unequal power relationship. This is,
generally, the relation most often resorted to by peasants in the countryside when they try to deal with an alien and dangerous outside
power.[64]

The Muslim Brothers are also linked to this world and thus they keep
up its political vocabulary. This is not the place for an exhaustive analysis of their political vocabulary, but one cannot avoid being struck by
how different it is from that of the Marxists. Colonialism, the immediate cause of the peasant-workers' discontent, is portrayed in personalized terms, and the nature of that discontent is presented in subjective
rather than objective ways. There is thus a heavy emphasis in Muslim
literature on *zulm* "oppression," and except in one or two cases (where
tax money is paid to a foreign state rather than to the Egyptian one),
one does not find the word *exploitation*. The point is that *exploitation*,
especially as used by Marxists and Leninists, refers to an unequal and
inequitable relation between owners and workers inherent, not in their
personalities or ethical preferences, but in their roles. *Exploitation* thus
refers to something that is inherently wrong in the very fabric of social
relations or authority relations. *Oppression* may very well refer to something that is wrong at the level of society or the state, but it occurs because of personal, moral, or ethical choices. A ruler may be oppressive,
and so may an owner, but they need not be. Moreover, in the literature
of the 1930s and 1940s, *zulm* has personal overtones; it defines how
workers are treated—with dignity or without. *Exploitation* refers to a
relation more deeply embedded in the very role of being a worker.[65] It is
not surprising then to find that much of the activity of Muslim activists
as reported in the Muslim Brothers' newspaper deals with the kind of
actions that link the educated to the broad mass of workers. All organizations of workers fight for paid holidays, and Muslim trade union activists did too, but the holidays they fought for, tenaciously, were Muslim and Egyptian holidays. Workers at the BATA shoe company as well

as in the Shell oil fields and refineries demanded the anniversary of the royal coronation and the Prophet's Birthday as paid days off.[66]

In effect, then, the Muslim Brothers and other Muslim activists were fighting to defend and extend the position of the same type of Muslims as those who had played an important role in the days before the Occupation of 1882. The peasants who flocked into factories had few on whom they could rely to press their case, and often were not in the mills long enough to gain a clear idea of their interests in opposition to those of other social groups, especially mill owners and their representatives in carrying out the discipline of the factory bureaucracy, the foremen. The Muslim Brothers and those in their orbit had, moreover, a ready vocabulary for social protest, one that was widely known and perceived as a legitimate vocabulary by the mass of Egyptians, who were, after all, Muslim. Yet we must avoid falling into the trap of seeing the appeal of the Muslim Brothers as merely linguistic or cultural: the vocabulary of Islam corresponded to that of the peasants and artisans, who became the sugar workers, oil workers, government workers, and not a few textile workers.

At the same time, given the moral, cultural, and paternal views of the Muslim Brothers and Muslim activists in general, it is unsurprising that their unions were often unable to stay intact for long periods of time, even when they were not under state attack. In the end, the Muslim activists saw trade unions as just another form of beneficial organization, like the Society for Memorizing the Quran, the Society to Aid the Muslim Poor, the Antituberculosis Society, or the Alms Society.[67] Muslim activists tended to place the problems of workers on a par with those of other oppressed groups in the Muslim political community. The workers were subjugated (*maqhurun*) in the eyes of Hasan al-Banna and it was on that basis that he agreed to cooperate at least briefly with the leftist textile workers' union in Shubra al-Khaima.[68]

Without a specific vision of workers as a distinct social group with interests in opposition to other social groups, especially owners, leaders cannot create long-lasting independent economic or political organizations. Although left organizations may, over time, be co-opted, the specific class vision of Marxism and Leninism makes the creation of an independent, interest-based (in a broad sense) organization a primary task of trade union organizers. For Muslim activists, on the contrary, maintenance of the Islamic community is primary and strengthening the Muslim educated elite is a means to keep the community together. In so doing, Muslim politics in the 1930s seemed destined to play the role of supporting the existing regime in the name of unity against colonialism and oppression. Although this appeal was couched in popular and familiar language, it did not lead to significant victories for those who were promised assistance, and its audience, although well defined, was limited in the industrial sector of the economy.

It would be a mistake, and a naive one at that, not to touch on a last aspect of the appeal of the Muslim Brothers, one they probably share with other groups of Islamic activists. As the leadership of the brotherhood turned toward open, if right-wing, political positions in the 1940s that allied them with the king, they developed a certain fund of political influence with which they could ameliorate the situation of certain groups of workers. The meetings with government officials, publicity in their newspaper, and contacts with the palace were part of the patronage apparatus that, along with the familiarity of their vocabulary, made the Muslim Brothers acceptable to many workers. These elements represented an organizational resource as opposed to the personal resource of patronage of many members of the brotherhood, such as the foremen, who could alter work assignments, disallow sick leave, and so on. In the end, though, the Muslim activists needed help in maintaining their organizations precisely because independence is not a necessary condition of their existence. When they fell into disfavor with the state, the appeals alone, no matter how popular and familiar, no longer worked very well.

CHAPTER SEVEN

Labor Aristocrats:
Tobacco and Oil

In the tobacco industry and the petroleum industry, the unions that emerged were stable organizations conceived as distinctly different from the social associations found in other industries. Among these unions there was less emphasis on union independence from the state. In the case of the oil industry, the workers made a specific decision to form a union rather than a *jamᶜiyyah* but the union leadership nevertheless saw itself as an ally of the state. This leadership was Islamic, but its orientation differed from that of the Islamic leaders at Hawamdiyyah: it was more instrumental. By contrast, the leaders of the tobacco workers offered them an instrumental version of left secularism in social-democratic terms. The leaders of these unions, Anwar Salamah of the oil workers and Fathi Kamil of the tobacco workers, represented the future of the Egyptian trade union organization. Government policy rested on the relatively privileged position of these two industries and thus made possible approaches to union leadership that otherwise would not have been successful.

State policies determine in part what strategies union leaders can adopt, but leaders must also consider the nature of the men who are to be induced to follow them. The social origins of the work force in the tobacco and oil industries are not dissimilar to those of the workers in the sugar industries and craftsmen. In the cigarette and petroleum industries workers were initially drawn from the urban artisans and the peasants, respectively. In this chapter, however, unlike the previous ones, we shall be looking at workers whose long-term commitment was to industrial labor rather than to urban artisanship or rural occupations. There is also a significant difference in how these two industries created a work force committed to factory careers. In the tobacco industry, the owners transformed the nature of the production process itself within a fairly short time (about ten years), which destroyed the power of the artisans who had previously rolled cigarettes and turned the industry into one made up largely of skilled and unskilled workers on machines. In the petroleum industry we see peasants who retain affective links to their geographical areas of origin but who are drawn away from them for such long periods of time that they become completely oriented to factory careers. We shall look at these two cases together partly because they provide a bridge from the more traditional or premodern forms of production to modern industrial forms, partly because they provide a chance to look at how industrial enterprises do change the long-term commitments of workers (sometimes by getting new workers), and partly because the two industries were, in the 1940s, similar in wages, working conditions, and political orientations of the leadership. Workers in both industries had relatively high wages, and the Communists especially often pointed to them as an aristocracy of labor created by employers able to pay more than other sectors. In calling them "yellow" or company unions, the Communists saw a significant similarity between the two essentially business-union-oriented leaderships, but misunderstood their differences over an issue that would become crucial to the political future of the unions, the workers, and the Communists themselves—independence.[1]

The major cigarette firms and the oil production industry (although not distribution, as we saw in chapter 5) were foreign owned and made regular contributions to the state budget, although the contribution of the tobacco industry was greater than that of the oil industry in the period under discussion.[2] Other areas of state policy such as Egyptian independence in energy production and employment for Egyptian workers and technicians are also important factors in understanding the oil industry, for they made the workers potential allies of the state in its negotiations with the companies.

In both industries the leaders developed a successful business-oriented unionism that can be associated with nationalist and social-democratic orientations, but the figures most associated with the success of these unions ended in opposite positions. The leader of the oil workers was

Anwar Salamah, a member of the Muslim Brothers who left the brother-hood after 1952 to become head of the state-dominated trade union movement. The leader of the tobacco workers during the same period (1942–1952) was a social democrat with ties to the British labor move-ment and ʿAbbas Halim. Fathi Kamil of the Matossian tobacco workers was marginalized because he was unwilling to participate in the loss of trade union independence.[3] In the early years Salamah and Kamil clearly had similar ideas about the role of unions and the relation of unions to production; they differed mainly in their view of the state as a means to obtaining social services and higher wages for the workers. Kamil, moreover, may have been fatally compromised by his international links in the years before 1954. Not only had he been to England after World War II, but he seems to have had close ties with members of the British Labour party and was, along with Ibrahim Zayn al-Din, a delegate to the 1949 International Congress of Free Trade Unions.[4]

It is clear from our case studies that an ideology may attract workers but it may not necessarily lead to political action in support of the ide-ology. Leaders may still follow through alone on the logic of their in-forming ideology, however. Thus the oil workers never used their poten-tial strength in the economy for political purposes, although we might have expected them to do so during the Palestine War, for example. Salamah followed up his cultural critique by becoming a state official when foreign owners were effectively ousted from his sector of the Egyp-tian economy. Salamah's behavior is convincing evidence that (1) the con-tent of the ideology does matter to the leaders and (2) revolutionary po-litical struggle is distinct from ordinary economic (or even political) struggle. Moreover, the same ideology can be used in more than one way. Islamic motifs were meaningful to both sugar workers and oil workers, who shared a peasant background, but they were also em-ployed by both Kamil and Salamah in very different ways. Two leaders made different uses of their common cultural heritage.[5]

The close involvement of the state with the oil and tobacco industries should already be evident by now. The Egyptian state budget had been self-financing since the days of the Occupation. Besides communications and transport (rail, telephone, and telegraph), which were state enter-prises, customs duties made the most significant contribution to the state budget, and tobacco was the largest single contributor to the in-come from import duties. Even in the 1940s the customs duty on to-bacco alone constituted about 17 percent of the state's budget receipts.[6] The cigarette industry was the single most important source of state

revenues for much of this period, and unlike the other major contributor to the budget—the railways—involved no capital expenditure and a
negligible cost in wages for the state. The oil industry provided far less
than the tobacco industry to the budget, but it was similar to the tobacco industry in two respects: first, both industries depended on capital from abroad; second, just as the tobacco industry depended on the
import of its primary material, which was thus subject to state control,
so the petroleum companies relied on a contractual agreement with the
state, involving royalty, price, and stock concessions.[7] In these two industries, the role of the state as a financially interested party—and
therefore as one able to intervene for or against the work force—was
greater than in many other sectors of the Egyptian economy.

THE TOBACCO INDUSTRY: FROM PROFESSION TO TRADE

The tobacco industry underwent rapid and great technological change
between 1919 and 1930 that transformed cigarette making from a
skilled profession into an industrial trade. Until the 1920s the structure
of the tobacco industry was that of a relatively large number of medium-
sized firms (that is, several dozen employees), largely owned by Greeks
and Armenians. We know from contemporary descriptions that the
cigarettes were rolled, stuffed, trimmed, and packed by hand in factories that employed men, women, and children.[8] Greeks, Armenians, and
Egyptians were employed in the plants, and the first unions seem to have
been mainly of the foreign workers. Craft organizations emerged during
the first decade of the twentieth century, and were organized according
to either ethnic or craft distinctions (or both). In 1908 a union was established at the Matossian factory, organized according to these traditional lines. The union had approximately two hundred members.[9]

Making cigarettes was a highly skilled and essentially artisan form of
production. As long as such skills are genuinely critical for production,
those who possess them have an extremely favorable bargaining position. They may also have a tendency to believe that the methods of production that give them a favorable position are in some sense immu-
table. Unfortunately this is not so. The early artisan associations in
Egypt were about to suffer the same fate as cigar and cigarette makers in
other countries; moreover the process of destruction began when they
appeared to be at their peak, for one observer just after the turn of the
century commented that

machinery is not employed in any way, except for cutting the tobacco, and it is said that the workmen wield sufficient power to render the adoption of machinery for making cigarettes a step too dangerous to be contemplated.[10]

Clearly the introduction of machinery was not too dangerous to contemplate, for this step was taken by the end of World War I.

The introduction of machinery dramatically changed the nature of the work force, the structure of the industry, and the markets for which Egyptian cigarettes were made. Whereas artisan production had included a healthy export market in addition to the large domestic market, by the 1920s this was changing. Cairo before the war had had a hundred export establishments, many of which were owned by Egyptians even if they had Greek names.[11] Within less than a decade cigarette exports declined dramatically and industrial production of cigarettes for the home market by large-capitalization firms became the rule. The new firms were far more closely linked to international firms and employed far more Egyptian labor.

The change from the point of view of the workers was swift.[12] Throughout the world, cigarette and cigar rollers had had fairly strong unions until the First World War.[13] Theirs was a skilled craft, which employed relatively large numbers of workers. In addition, tobacco, like other products in the food industry, does not store easily for long periods of time. For these reasons, the workers were usually in a strong position economically. This security was first threatened when new machinery was introduced at the time of the war, especially in enterprises owned by Greeks and Armenians in Cairo and Alexandria. The workers responded by attempting to use the economic and political means at their disposal to stop the introduction of machines, and although they were probably able to slow down the mechanization of the industry, they were unable to stop it. As a consequence, in 1920 rollers and cutters struck for job security and severance pay of one month for each year of service. The rollers also attempted to introduce the principle of hourly pay in place of piece rates, until then the accepted form of remuneration in the industry. The turn to wages from piece rates is, often, a sign of the awareness by skilled workers that they will soon become semiskilled industrial workers and an attempt to save wages. This strike by the cutters and rollers was met by a lockout: the savings in mechanization were far too great for the employers to seek reconciliation with the union. One contemporary observer, Elinor Burns, claimed that the machines cut costs by almost 90 percent.[14]

As part of their initial response, workers attempted to utilize political pressure to preserve the older methods of production and the jobs of the skilled workers. The great patrons and would-be patrons of the labor movement (such as ᶜAbbas Halim and the Wafd politicians) were closely identified with this part of the labor response. Unfortunately, all of these efforts ended in failure. In Alexandria, for example, a committee was formed to "combat cigarette-rolling machines" in 1920, and the Egyptian Democratic party, led by Muhammad Husayn Haykal and ᶜAziz Mirhum, proposed founding an Egyptian factory to counter the policies of the Melkonian factory, which, by introducing machines, was laying off workers. In the provincial town of Zaqaziq a similar attempt to set up a "nationalist" competitor to Gamsargan was begun. These attempts probably ate up the severance pay given fired workers, and then rapidly dissolved.

While the workers were joining forces to fight the policies of what were still relatively small companies, the companies themselves were undergoing a process of amalgamation. The British American Tobacco Company and a local magnate named Matossian formed a holding company known officially as the Eastern Company, and casually as Matossian's. This new company had capital of over two million Egyptian pounds.[15] Thus, by the middle of the 1920s the Eastern Company owned a controlling interest in ten firms, including not only the Matossian firm in Giza but also the Gamsargan firm in Zaqaziq and the Melkonian plants. When the first Wafd government came to power in 1924, unemployed tobacco workers played a key role in calling for a demonstration to seek relief for the unemployed. Dr. Mahjub Thabit presided over this demonstration, and the president of the tobacco workers' union called for the creation of a labor bureau.[16]

In general political action to reverse the flow of capital investment bore little fruit. The 1924 demonstration brought no action from the Wafd, which was in the process of trying to rein in the workers' movement. In 1927, petitions from the tobacco workers to persuade the state to tax the new machines in order to provide a welfare fund for laid-off workers were rejected by the minister of finance, Muhammad Mahmud. Mahmud was a wealthy landowner who had been educated in Britain, and one of the early leaders of the Wafd. Mahmud's cabinet, formed a year later when he dissolved parliament, would include leading members of the Egyptian Federation of Industry.[17]

Even when workers were successful in the political sphere, they were defeated in the economic sphere. In Zaqaziq the workers persuaded the local council to tax the Gamsargan factory 9 percent on the value of its output, but the factory, strengthened by its improved capital position, simply moved. It had once employed 1,200 workers, but when it left Zaqaziq employment was down to 85.[18] The idea of a nationalist cigarette factory did not die, however. It limped on for several more years and provided the basis for political and ideological conflict that echoed through the 1940s. In 1935, at the height of cooperation between Halim and the Wafd, the "Union" cigarette company was formed.[19] Shares were sold to such presumably interested parties as the tobacco workers themselves, Mustafa al-Nahas (the leader of the Wafd, and their prime minister whenever in office), Makram ʿUbayd (an attorney who defended many trade unionists in legal battles), and Halim himself.[20]

In 1934, it was still easy to view the old crafts as an ideal form of production whose material basis had been destroyed by colonialism. This was the position taken by Amin al-Husayni Ghanim in his book *The Workers' Movement in Egypt and Its Downfall* (*Al-Harakah al-ʿummaliyah fi misr wa sirr tadahwuriha*) (Cairo, 1934). Since the subject of the book is the state of the workers' movement in the early 1930s, and since the book is dedicated not only to Halim but also to Ahmad Husayn, founder of the fascist Misr al-Fatah, it is clear that there was still an audience—not only of displaced craftsmen—who sought to solve the social problems created by Egypt's growing involvement in the world market by returning to older forms of production and urban association. Husayn was, after all, also a believer in forming "national" craft enterprises, such as the popular project for a *tarbush* factory then under way. These ideas corresponded to those of certain British officials who believed such organizations would make control of the working class easier.

Despite the apparent appeal of such "safe" forms of working-class association, they failed to acknowledge the pace and direction of Egyptian capitalism itself. Halim's factory was essentially a political device rather than an economically viable venture, and it was Halim's factory despite its claim to be financed by workers who share in the profits. Like the model plants established a decade later by the Muslim Brothers, Halim's plant failed to achieve its economic ends. Workers in crafts could hardly pay dues, as we have seen, let alone buy shares. Halim "loaned" the company L. E. 30,000, and after a brief initial success, the company foundered because of competition from firms such as Matossian and harassment from the Wafd government, which made it difficult to sell shares. Capital declined and the firm went out of business in 1936.[21] Halim did have some genuine popularity among the tobacco workers,

most probably among those who had worked in the hand-rolling establishments. In his memoirs ᶜAbd al-Munᶜim ᶜIsawi of the Mechanized
Textile Workers Union mentions this period as the height of Halim's
popularity and suggests his base at this time was among hand-loom
weavers and employees of various tobacco companies.[22]

EARLY EFFORTS AT UNIONIZATION

The earliest attempts to form unions retained elements of a craft-
artisan association: unions were formed shop by shop, as it were, even
when all the shops were in the same large factory. The workers in the
industrial sector of the tobacco industry no longer attempted to challenge an industrial firm with an archaic form of craft production, but
they were not yet ready to relinquish a craft conception of how production was organized. For example, in November 1932 the packing section of the Bustani firm went on record to protest long hours and low
wages.[23] This complaint came from the workers in one section of the
plant, rather than from an industrial union.

An early call to form a general union of tobacco workers came in
1935 from the employees of a small company. The executive committee
of the union at the Mahmud Fahmi Cigarette Company placed an appeal in the Wafdist newspaper *Al-Jihad*, calling for a union of all workers in the industry under the Wafd General Federation, to be formed at a
public meeting to be held in January. The influence of the craft association on the union is evident in the decision of the executive committee
to remind workers that they have the right to mutual support (*taᶜawun*)
from union funds under its rule and to set up a committee to visit sick
members.[24] A tendency to organize *as if* the industrial plant were an assemblage of small shops is not unknown in other parts of the country or
the world—in Britain this tendency accounts at least in part for the
strength of the shop stewards. Nor is it completely false to the nature of
production in the tobacco industry, where the different processes can be
undertaken relatively separately. It did, however, run counter to the
physical layout of the plant, because all of the processes were carried out
in a single building.[25]

Like the sugar workers at Hawamdiyyah, the tobacco workers at the
Matossian plant also had to confront the disadvantages of relying on the
patronage system assumed by craft associations. In late 1935 there was
a strike-lockout at the Matossian plant. The strike apparently resulted
from the transfer of men from one section to another—always a prob-

lem where wages differ sharply according to the machines used and, in particular, where craft mores were involved. Although not mentioned in the daily press, the strike must have been a major affair because Richard Graves of the Labour Bureau visited the plant.[26] While Graves was in the plant, ʿAziz Mirhum arrived, a sign not only of the relative laxity of plant discipline compared to that in Europe but also of the links— friendly or unfriendly—the Wafd and other politicians had with even British members of the administration. Mirhum alleged that there had been instances of overseer brutality during the strike, which Joseph Matossian denied.

Mirhum's intervention with the Labour Bureau was evidently not limited to public disputes with Graves. He also visited Jacques Azoulai and asked him to be "on the side of the workers against the employers in the case of the Matossian factory . . . [and] explained that if Matossian will not take back all the workers without any distinction, those who go to work will sabotage the factory." Although incidents of damaging the machines were not unknown, as we have seen from the history of the Hawamdiyyah plant, the labor movement was beginning to move away from this tactic. Mirhum's threat makes more sense if it is understood as the traditional position of the patron. The Wafd politicians chose to act as brokers for the state (especially the colonial state) and the rich, to serve as the only force able to restrain the "impetuous" and dangerous masses. The Wafd did not support the workers at the Matossian plant or any other plant, and the party did not even support the workers in 1919. Instead, the Wafd party hoped to gain by being able to influence the workers and the state.

Blackmail is a handy technique, but it is not the same thing as organized mass struggle and indeed goes in the opposite direction. When it fails, as it usually does, it leaves those in whose name the blackmail was committed as resentful as those who were blackmailed. In late 1935 Mirhum sought a quick victory in order to promote the Higher Council for Trade Unions over Halim's General Federation, but both Mirhum and Halim failed to resolve the workers' problems and instead left them with new reservations about the Wafd party. A party that had promised support had instead tried to use the workers to settle an internal dispute between political factions. Although the union formed in 1942 would have good relations with ʿAbbas Halim, it would not rely on him to bargain with the company, and there would be antagonism as well as cooperation in the relation. In the factories the years 1935–1936 were crucial for determining how the workers looked at the Wafd and sec-

ondarily at Halim. If they were disappointed in the Wafd as a nationalist
political force, their disappointment was based on more than the treaty
signed with Britain and on more than ideology. The workers' view was
pragmatic. The Wafd failed to deliver.[27]

The tendency to fragment that is also found in craft associations and
undermines the workers' ability to unite was reinforced during the
1930s by the manner in which tobacco workers were organized and by
the intense competition between the Higher Council for Trade Unions
led by such Wafd officials as ʿAziz Mirhum and the General Federation
allied to ʿAbbas Halim, which included men such as Sayyid Qandil
and Muhammad ʿImara. Many organizations were torn apart in the
struggle, and the final outcome left many workers wary of relying on
either group for support in union organization. At the same time, the
Wafd press was filled with statements of support from those supporting
the Wafd. This conflict obscures an important stage in the development
of workers' organizations, one that is necessary to explain the appear-
ance of unions in the 1940s.

The Matossian factory in Giza was organized by shop as if it were an
assembly of small craft enterprises. This becomes clear if we look at *Al-
Jihad* in the spring of 1935.[28] There we find unions with names representing different sections of the plant; we also find indications that the
shops had separate leaders, since different people appear as officials of
these separate "unions." For example, the Giza Matossian Plant Cutting
Machine Workers Union appealed to Mirhum to enforce a 1919 decree
(*qanun*). The appeal was signed by Hamid Ibrahim Affendi, president,
and pledged support for Mirhum's Higher Council.[29] Two weeks later
two other unions at Matossian indicated their support for the Wafd
against Halim: the unions for checking workers and the workers of the
Matossian companies (*sic*) at Giza, the latter led by Muhammad Mustafa
al-Dahawi, as well as the packing workers indicated their pro-Wafd sentiments.[30] After another week, more unions at Matossian declared their
support for the Wafd: the Tuscan, Honied, and Good Smoking workers
union at Matossian and the cutting workers (the second time since mid-
April) are mentioned.[31] This support was confirmed later by groups of
workers (this time called committees) from checking, packing, the three
cigarette brands mentioned above, cutting, as well as the "Filtu" committee and the "Baku" machines.[32] The packing workers sent another
letter of support.[33]

The groups that declared their position were not organizations in
name only but rather small unions engaged in a power struggle. Evi-

dently Mustafa al-Dahawi had managed to expel an older leadership that supported Halim and was now consolidating his power. The expulsion makes clear that there was some sort of leadership in the plant as a whole but little organizational unity among the workers, apart from any political differences. Thus, according to newspaper reports, the workers and the branch treasurers are warned not to pay dues to leaders related to Halim, and the workers are warned not to negotiate with the ousted leadership. Finally, the new leadership suggests that the police investigate the activities of what it implied had been a nest of agents.[34]

It is clear from these reports that the workers and the leadership had a weak sense of class and a correspondingly high sense of craft forms of association. We can also draw three conclusions on how these associations functioned. First, there was a significant and understandable desire to benefit from decisions favoring craft production and to insist that such norms be applied to industrial workers (rather than demanding new laws, for example, from a presumably friendly government). Second, there was a tendency to organize by distinct units based on different locales in the plant; each unit had its own leadership. These were not sections as such but small unions. Third, the leadership of each union was financially separate, which accords with a conception of each shop as a separate work place rather than as part of an overarching whole. The tobacco workers at Matossian thus had officially given up craft associations without creating unions. Instead, they had developed a form of organization that drew more on older forms and only slightly acknowledged a new work environment.

THE BIRTH OF AN INDUSTRIAL UNION

When the Wafd legalized unions in 1942, an industrial union was quickly formed at the Giza plant.[35] In the mid-1940s, there were several thousand workers at the Matossian plant in Giza. According to the 1947 census, there were about three thousand tobacco workers in Giza; according to other evidence, there may have been about twice that many.[36] There were approximately eight hundred workers in the packing section and a larger number in the cigarette-making section (equivalent to the Honied and other cigarette workers mentioned above). There were also a variety of craftsmen including carpenters and maintenance workers. The bulk of the workers were drawn from nearby Giza through family connections.[37]

A key figure in the founding of the industrial union was an ex-government official, Fathi Kamil. Kamil had worked in a small Italian-owned enterprise making telephones in the late 1920s, then for the Ministry of Health, and finally in several cotton gins in the late 1930s before coming to Matossian. He was employed at the Giza plant of Matossian in 1939 as a salaried assistant clerk. Because he had a secondary education (which included some English), Kamil was promoted and eventually became head of the welfare department of the company. He had also been a member of the circle of trade unionists around Muhammad ʿImara (see chapter 5). At Matossian, Kamil was friendly with Ismaʿil Sayyid Salamah, who had been a member of the Mixed Tobacco Workers Union, which had gone out of existence with the completion of mechanization in 1927. It was Salamah who suggested that Kamil spearhead the formation of a union at Matossian in the early 1940s and become its president. Kamil was in a good position to do this. He spoke English, knew the workers, and understood what sort of union could meet the needs of a large company for labor peace. In addition, he had a strong personality that could attract enthusiastic supporters to his position.

In addition to Kamil's personal assets, the success of the union can be attributed to two other factors. First, Kamil was especially good at winning concessions from the company in line with the needs of his base, although not without recourse to strikes. For example, a strike broke out on May 7, 1948, over a demand for higher wages.[38] The structure of benefits obtained from the company was well thought-out and seems to have matched Kamil's generally social-democratic orientation. Second, the structure of the union—both formally and informally—was designed to ensure that the workers closely identified with it. These two facts probably explain why the internal unity of the union under Kamil's leadership was never seriously challenged before the Free Officers' coup in 1952. Let us consider each factor more closely.

First, Kamil seems to have been a moderate social democrat. In 1945 he visited England, thanks to an arrangement worked out between M. T. Audsley, labor councilor at the British Embassy in Cairo, and Ibrahim Zayn al-Din, a longtime leader of the chauffeur's union and a protégé of ʿAbbas Halim. This visit seems to have convinced Kamil of several things: that business-oriented trade unionism could bring results, that one could successfully bargain with large companies, that Egyptian workers deserved the same standard of living that British workers enjoyed, and—perhaps paradoxically from the perspectives of his hosts—that Arab workers (and the Arab world in general) must overcome Western racism. In accordance with these views, Kamil won as his first victory the provision of a company cafeteria, which replaced an older system of wandering food salesmen.[39] In addition, soon after the union was founded, Kamil won a wage increase of 20 percent, in 1943. The level of wages at Matossian seems to have been relatively high. According to *Al-Bashir*, wages at Matossian in 1950 were about 12 piasters per day for "older" workers and 6 for newer ones.[40] As a base rate for unskilled labor, this scale compares well with the rates for labor in the oil fields, where unskilled workers were paid 14 to 22 piasters per day.[41] The union also had a loan fund.

Second, Kamil developed a new form of union. The structure of the organization was based on viewing the different plant sections as component parts of the industrial whole. The sections were not full equals, as might have been the case if they were still conceived as separate entities. Rather, every three hundred workers in each section voted for a representative on the executive board, which was empowered to make decisions regarding money, hiring within the union, and complaints to be made to the company. The president was elected by direct vote of the workers and not by a vote of the executive board; this form of election gave the president a significant amount of prestige compared to that of board members. As president, moreover, Kamil used his position in a way not open to board members: every Friday, any union member with a problem could see him personally. This can be interpreted as a "traditional" practice as well as an unofficial way of running the union, and in part it undoubtedly was meant to continue a link with traditional ways: a worker could appeal directly to the president just as a member of a tribe could appeal directly to the head of the tribe in a traditional culture.[42] Kamil was also quite sensitive to the religious feelings of the members as well as to the nonmodern ways in which they viewed authority. The union had, for example, a fund to enable members to perform the pilgrimage to Mecca.[43] The union also sponsored all-night prayer meetings to celebrate the Muslim New Year.[44]

Even though the union at Giza was significantly different from a craft association or from the union at Hawamdiyyah, it did not lose all links with contemporary Egyptian reality. The members were Muslims, and many still preferred to deal with problems face to face rather than through an organization; even the industrial experience was not yet a lifelong experience for them. Nevertheless, the union at Giza under Fathi Kamil's leadership is significant for the attempt to erect an institutional structure based on organizational rather than social principles and to redefine the workers' theoretical framework to agree with significant features of their own experience rather than an ideology from their youth or a leader's personal outlook. Kamil believed that this experience would unite workers regardless of their other differences, and he wrote at length on this topic.

> Peoples, tribes, and societies differ. There is one group, however, that does not differ in any way, in its life, in its goals, in its hopes, and in its reliances. This social group is the group of workers in any country from among the wide world of God. This is because it enters life by a single path, and lives by a single path, and aims together to a single ideology, namely, to live a decent, human life untarnished by shame or injustice. I have visited several Western countries as the representative of my brothers, the Egyptian workers, and I found the spirit of the workers in any other land the same as our own spirit except in one particular: they feel strong because they are united in their ideas, demands, and goals, while we in Egypt are differentiated by parties without thinking about the bigger issues.[45]

Kamil proclaims an identity of class interests despite different national and cultural orientations, habits, and values.

When Kamil placed this identity of class in the context of national difference or religion, he was trying to appeal to what he specifically saw as a modern, class-based set of values that could unite in the work environment men who otherwise had sharp differences to overcome. For Kamil's followers the message was evocative of Surah 49 of the Qurʾan, which enjoins Muslims not to defame or insult one another even though God has created people in different national or tribal groups, which therefore represent unalterable units of human existence.[46] Kamil believed that Egyptian workers were following a path blazed by European workers, and that, despite having been created as a different people, Egyptians could nevertheless equal the material achievements of Western societies and Western workers.

> Our congress is the path we follow with the consciousness of conscience that we stand before God to witness what efforts we exert and hope to exert so that the workers and their unions will attain those rights that Western workers have only attained through their solidarity and sincerity.[47]

In Kamil's mind, Egyptian workers could obtain what European workers had obtained because they represented the same social group as workers in Europe. Aware of his base, Kamil phrased this message in an ethical-religious framework, but did so in a way that gave primacy to the experience of work over that of ideology or belief, whether in Islam or nationalism. Religion still provided the vocabulary for addressing questions of social justice and obligation. And even though his articles were written for a broader audience than the Matossian workers in Giza, Kamil accepted that he had to phrase his social-democratic ideas in the majority vocabulary—that is, a Muslim one.[48]

THE OIL WORKERS:
ISLAMIC OPPORTUNITIES
OR ISLAMIC OPPORTUNISM?

The petroleum industry is a capital-intensive industry that depends on highly skilled workers. The image of the industry is thoroughly modern, yet the most outspoken leader of the petroleum workers, and the man who would become the first head of the Egyptian trade union federation under Nasser, was a Muslim Brother, Anwar Salamah. We cannot simply dismiss this apparent paradox by saying that one leader happened to have been a Muslim Brother.[49] Rather, we must consider the history of the industry in Egypt and Salamah's philosophy and conduct as a union leader.

Several features of the oil industry are peculiar to it. First, the industry operates as a concession from the state—that is, under a grant of power from the state, which can be rescinded. The industry involves large sums of money, and this has been true throughout the history of the oil industry in Egypt. In 1911, the Shell Oil Company registered an Egyptian subsidiary, the Anglo-Egyptian Oil Company, which had a capital of one million pounds sterling, 10 percent of which was owned by the Egyptian government.[50] Shell also owned a refinery at Suez.[51] Egyptian production was not very great until the eve of World War II, when production shot up dramatically, almost quadrupling in two years, from one and one-half million barrels a year in 1938 to over six million in 1940; over thirteen million by 1948; and over sixteen million by 1950.[52] Overall investment figures do not seem to be available, but it is worth noting that the costs of exploration dwarfed the capital outlays of most of the other industries mentioned in this book: $16 million was invested between 1930 and 1945 alone.

The oil industry was not an important contributor to the state budget during this period, but it was a sector in which the Egyptian state was directly involved, for the government signed the contracts under which oil exploration and production were undertaken by foreign companies. Even though this form of state control was found in other parts of the Middle East, Egypt was careful to maintain as much control as possible.

This is especially clear if we compare Egyptian and Iraqi contracts with oil firms from the same period, 1932 to 1951.[53] We find that Iraq was far less able to bargain successfully with the companies than was Egypt. Although both countries were still monarchies, Iraqis perceived petroleum resources as belonging in part to the local communities in which they were found. Thus, in 1932 the Iraqi concession directed the companies to provide fuel to residents of the immediate area of exploitation.[54] The same contract vested in Iraqis the right to buy shares in the companies.[55] In 1938, a new agreement stipulated that measures be taken to ensure that petroleum production not pollute ground water through seepage.[56] In that year we also find the government's first attempt to persuade the companies to hire Iraqis, for they are requested to do so "to the extent possible" given the available labor.[57]

The Egyptian contracts tell a very different story. Petroleum production was in deserted areas, so some of the problems in Iraq simply never arose in Egypt. By 1937 in Egypt the companies were required to provide the government with monthly lists of employees, and Egyptians were expected to make up 90 percent of the unskilled and semiskilled labor (*ummal*) and 50 percent of the skilled and white-collar workers (*mustakhdamun*).[58] By 1948 the companies were required to abide by Egyptian labor legislation.[59] By 1951, the Iraqi government could still only request the company to teach more Iraqis to handle the jobs.[60]

Clearly the Egyptian labor force was larger, more skilled, more diversified than the Iraqi. Clearly, too, Egypt was more closely tied to the world economy. These factors enabled the state to win significant concessions from the companies, and left the state stronger rather than weaker in its bargaining position.[61] The next obvious step was Egyptian control of the industry. Not surprisingly, the Egyptianization process that spread through the sugar industry was continued in the oil industry under state auspices in the 1940s. By 1947–1948, the government was moving to assert near total control over the oil industry, probably to ensure control over an important resource. By 1948, 40 percent of the boards of directors were Egyptians, 51 percent of the shares were held by Egyptians, and 75 percent of the employees were Egyptians and received 65 percent of the salaries paid.[62]

Despite the importance of this industry to the state, the number of workers involved is relatively small; moreover, finding exact figures on the number of workers in the industry seems to be almost impossible. There were about fifty-one hundred workers in government-recognized unions in the 1940s in the "mining and oil refining sector."[63] Not only were these workers few in number, but they were spread across the relatively isolated sections of Egypt along the Gulf of Suez, where oil is located, and in the Suez Canal refineries. As a matter of record, their weight was so slight that most histories of the working class in Arabic and even many discussions of Egyptian industry hardly mention either oil workers or the petroleum industry. Obviously, too, the companies could afford relatively major wage concessions and therefore did not become a focus of labor dissatisfaction.

Most of the unskilled workers and possibly many of the semiskilled workers were originally peasants from Upper Egypt, especially from the area around Qena. This is probably only a quirk of geography: Qena is the provincial area where the Nile loops sharply east to leave a relatively short overland approach to the Gulf. Qena is therefore the part of the lengthy but narrow Nile Valley nearest to the oil fields. Qena supplied workers to Hurghada and Gemsa as early as 1912 and later to Ras Gharib.[64] The area has long been known as an important southern center for crafts, especially pottery making. Qena was one of the most heavily Muslim provinces in Egypt and Christians accounted for a much smaller part of the population than almost anywhere else (about 3 percent). It retained much of the flavor of peasant society, which is best summed up in the word *traditional*, and much of Winifred Blackman's description of traditional Upper Egyptian peasant life cited in chapter 3 is based on life in and around Qena.

This is the background of the workers Anwar Salamah organized into an industrial union.[65] Salamah's union, the first among petroleum workers in Egypt, was formed among Shell workers in 1942, the year the Wafd granted legal status to trade unions. The impetus seems to have come from a group of workers defending one of their number who was fired for making a mistake at work. A strike evidently won the man's reinstatement and gave the oil workers a sense of their potential power. An initial meeting was held at the home of one of the workers to which ninety men came; they agreed to take the organizational steps, in terms of finance and recruitment, to make their union a reality. Each agreed to pay an initial fee of five piasters and to recruit five new members. A question arose over whether the new association would be a benefit and welfare association (*jam'iyyah khayriyyah*) or a trade union ready to carry out struggle with the company. The men chose the second option, and elected Anwar Salamah as president.

The new union rapidly became active, as did other unions in the oil fields and in the Suez Canal area. The position of the union and its leadership was clearly articulated by Salamah in the newspaper of the Muslim Brothers. Salamah's argument comprised three interconnected points: (1) the oil workers are relatively poor because (2) the oil companies are exploitative monopolies that are (3) making it impossible for Egyptians to provide for themselves.[66] It is worth noting that the first point was no longer true by 1948; the second point concerned the relationship of the company to the state, not to the workers; and the third point indicates that nationalist, rather than religious, sentiment was the basis for uniting the workers.

Salamah compared the conditions of the workers in the oil fields unfavorably with those of the workers in the textile mills in Mahallah—that is, with the textile workers in the largest section of Egyptian-run enterprise in the country. Thus, oil workers are said to be so poorly paid that they (unlike the salaried employees) cannot afford meat or vegetables. Unlike the workers at Mahallah, who have housing provided by the company, the oil workers live in mud shacks, and without restaurants, mosques, and other amenities. Oil workers have had to struggle for paid holidays such as the Prophet's Birthday, the King's Birthday, and Coronation Day—a sign of the foreign imperialism in the oil fields. In addition, each oil worker has to do the work of two or three men.

Salamah argued that this state of affairs existed because an industry vital to modern development—petroleum—was in the hands of the British. This created a major fiscal problem for the state: the English government rather than the Egyptian government taxed the high profits of the oil company. As a consequence, the company was "draining the sweat of the workers into gold and silver pipelines." Thus, the main difference between the textile and petroleum industries was that in the former Egyptians used profits to help other Egyptians, which was impossible among oil workers. A more nationalist management would avoid the problems of working-class discontent and the inevitable outbursts by alleviating the causes of discontent before they became overwhelming. The state, in short, was the natural ally, if not the major weapon, of the workers in their struggle for a better life.

We find other arguments of this genre in *Al-Ikhwan al-Muslimun*. Thus, an article several months earlier accused the company of being "an exploitative company that monopolizes the critical petroleum industry and thereby gains terrific profits, and nevertheless never thinks of raising the standard of living of the Egyptian workers."[67] The writer rejected as exploitative the privileged position of the company in national economic life, not its structural relation to its own employees. The company profits from this privileged position were misspent because they were not used for the workers, who deserved a share. Again, the Shell Oil Company was attacked for acting in an imperialist fashion precisely because the workers did not share in the profits.[68] The point is not the workers' views on profit sharing in Egypt or elsewhere, although in general profit sharing is an attempt to link the interests of the workers materially to those of the company. Rather the point is the presumed *cultural* differences between the company and the workers. Egyptian companies share the profits (we are told), but colonialist companies do not. Therefore, the workers must make the company act like a national, properly Egyptian company. After all, "better a noble death in the search for a bit of bread than an ignoble submission to the colonialists in our country."[69]

Salamah's position was clearly that of the Muslim Brothers, but the constraints of being a trade union official seem to have outweighed the ideological commitments of the leader. Salamah never attempted to use the union to force the companies to act in accord with the stated prescriptions of the Muslim Brothers on the petroleum industry, or indeed on any industry. This does not mean that holding the presidency of a viable union organization "mellowed" Salamah. Rather, he adapted his Islamic orientation to fit the needs of his membership; he developed a view of how politics and religion fit together that was different from the view of leaders such as Hasan al-Banna. Salamah came to accept, certainly in practice, the idea that religion was a different sphere from politics and trade union struggle.[70] Finally, his analysis of the oil companies within an Islamic framework helped the union—workers and leaders—achieve stability and unity based on a common theoretical world view. The stable industrial organizations among the oil workers—probably unmatched in terms of commitment to industrial unionism, organizational longevity, and successful negotiations—found in an Islamic problematic an effective tool to express their goals and values to both the workers and the companies.

The analysis of the oil industry by the Muslim Brothers and Salamah meant that the struggle between the workers and the company in the postwar period would take a certain form and that the union would seek certain kinds of contracts. Ironically, the union leadership held fast to its definition of the oil company, but was unaffected by the terms of its own critique of the company when the time came to bargain with it.

After the war, workers in the Egyptian oil fields began a bitter struggle to improve working conditions. The workers do not seem to have been

concerned with saving jobs, which was a key problem for both textile workers and tobacco workers. There are no reports of widespread
layoffs, and if consumption was down slightly from wartime highs,
Egyptian consumption and world demand were beginning to pick up
the slack left by the military. The first recorded postwar strike occurred
in September 1947, when the workers occupied the Shell refineries.[71]
The unity of the Shell workers was impressive: within a couple of months
they had sent a telegram to the Ministry of Social Affairs, signed by
Salamah, claiming to represent three thousand workers.[72] This was rapidly followed by a delegation of Shell workers to the capital to meet with
relevant government officials.[73] This month included a holiday called the
ʿId al-Adha, for which the company gave holiday advances so that the
clerical employees (at any rate) could celebrate without financial strain.
In 1947 the advances were late.[74] The government organizations and
personnel were sympathetic to the workers, and this compared favorably with the chilly response of the firm. As the newspaper of the Muslim Brothers put it,

> the Egyptian workers who had been forced by poverty, penury, neglect, and
> illness, to an outburst and struck, albeit in calm, dignity, and forcefulness,
> gained the sympathy of all of the responsible government agencies, but the
> exploitative company on the other hand was not sympathetic to them at all.[75]

The original text used the Arabic word ʿatf to refer to a range of meanings from sympathy to attention. The term was widely used in the trade
union movement, and especially in the Muslim and nationalist sectors,
to refer to what was expected from state officials (or individual masters
in the crafts) as opposed to capitalist entrepreneurs.

By early 1948 strikes had broken out in almost the entire industry,
but there was never a call for a general strike. Thus, the workers at Ras
Gharib were ready to strike in early March, but were persuaded not to
do so until April 5.[76] In March the employees of the Anglo-Egyptian Oil
Company, including employees of Shell and Socony Vacuum, called for a
strike deadline in mid-March and finally struck in the last week of
March.[77] The oil fields were, in short, afire with the unrest and dis-
pleasure of the workmen. The strikes often lasted for days, with workers
occupying the worksites. The length of the strikes and the action of the
strikers indicate that the workers' anger overrode their relatively weak
financial position and their vulnerability to state interference.

The militancy of the workers might suggest that the workers received
very little from the companies, but the oil workers in fact did better

than workers in other areas. Two contracts signed by oil workers and the companies at this period, one between the workers and the Shell Oil Company and the other between the workers and the Socony Vacuum Company, describe the pay and benefits of oil workers. In addition, workers often called on government agencies for help, and the work of the Labour Bureau in the Suez region after World War II seems to have been largely (although by no means exclusively) concerned with the oil companies and their workers. The problem of dealing with the workers had already appeared to companies as one that needed constant consideration, for the companies had established positions to handle labor relations.[78] The two contracts date from after the year of the great strikes. The 1951 contract with Shell is most useful for determining wages, whereas the 1950 contract with Socony Vacuum is most useful for learning about nonwage demands.

The Shell agreement was negotiated by Salamah and is an extremely solid "business union" document, carefully detailing wage structures.[79] It enumerates seven wage categories, from a least-skilled beginning rate of 14 piasters a day to a maximum rate of 73 piasters a day for highly skilled and long-established workers; there is a provision that salaries are to be calculated on the basis of thirty times the daily rate. The contract has appended to it a set of calculations by which the government-decreed cost-of-living allowance was to be calculated on top of the existing base wage indicated above; the allowance is based on family size. The wage of the worker was supposed to cover the need of his family, and in the case of the oil workers the pay was adjusted to do so. Of course in a larger sense a worker's wage is always presumed to be sufficient for the needs of his family, but it is not usually adjusted in fact for family size. In the Egyptian oil fields and refineries, it was. The poorest wage earners received most. Thus, day laborers in the oil fields with more than three children received an adjustment of 190 percent on top of their base salary, up to a maximum of 36.6 piasters a day. Those with fewer children received smaller adjustments, and those who had a higher base received less. The minimum adjustment was 97.5 percent for single or childless monthly workers earning between 10 and 20 pounds a month.

The oil workers expected—and unlike other Egyptians received— wages to support their families regardless of the principle of equal pay for equal work. In the same way they also sought the maximum material benefits consistent with their needs. This is apparent from the nonwage demands—including those for uniforms and furnishings—made in other contracts. It is not clear that the order of the demands and concessions reflected employee preference, although those near the top of the list ought to have been the most important even if they were not the most strongly fought for. The first point in the Socony Vacuum agreement concerned vacations, and especially the right to accumulate vacation time.[80] This was important for those workers who came from Upper Egypt and wanted to spend relatively extensive periods with their families—a problem common to all migrant workers. According to this agreement, it was possible to save vacation time for the pilgrimage to Mecca; it was also possible for Nubians to save vacation time. This latter point is apparent because workers had a right to accumulate three years of vacation time—up to three months—with pay but only if the vacation was taken south of Wadi Halfa, the Egyptian-Sudanese border. The contract stated how long it took to accumulate vacation time and sick leave.

The contract indicated a refusal of the company to upgrade all workers to monthly employees and to give them clothing, but included an agreement to give them blankets and 45 piasters instead of 90 piasters for bedding. The company agreed to provide a clubhouse, but refused to undertake contractual responsibility either for an existing canteen or for cost-of-living adjustments ordered by law; in each of these two cases, the company avoided raising the value of an existing benefit. The company did agree to pay a bonus for a government-declared "Oil Month."

The union leadership in the oil industry, associated with the Muslim Brothers and guiding a work force originally drawn from the peasantry, held close to specific material goals in negotiations with the companies. In material success, the oil industry is closer to the tobacco industry than to the sugar industry. Salamah may have been a member of the Muslim Brothers, but neither he nor any of the other leaders in the oil industry identified himself religiously. No leader of the oil industry was called *shaykh* or *hajj*, as were leaders in the sugar industry. Despite a similarity in the analysis of the labor problems in the sugar industry and the oil industry, Salamah did not focus on one group, the foremen, as the key to a better future for the workers. Nor did he include a religious element in union activity, believing instead that religion and trade unionism were separate spheres of activity, with different rules governing each. Salamah's union was clearly an industrial union.

CHAPTER EIGHT

Textiles: The Proletarian Web

In this chapter I shall examine the case with which this book began: the relation of the textile workers in the northern suburbs of Cairo to the Marxist and Communist parties of Egypt.[1] The unions in these northern suburbs represented a development that was neither "historically necessary" nor yet wholly accidental: there was no absolute need for the workers in this area to be led by Communists. Yet these workers and especially the leaders who came from their ranks were *looking* for political and economic theories to define their practical roles in the unions and in the factories. They willingly and frequently engaged in what organization theory would call search behavior as earlier ways of explaining their world failed them.

Theirs was not, however, a world of intellectual debate and an abstract search for truth. Nor can we claim that hunger, misery, or shabby housing induced them to "go Communist." Misery, poverty, and hunger certainly existed among the textile workers, but we can hardly say that they were more miserable, poorer, or hungrier than the mass of peasants or the workers at Hawamdiyyah; there may have been some who were better off than their brothers at Matossian. The available statistical evidence certainly supports the contention that the textile workers earned more or less the average wages and worked the average number of hours for Egyptian workers.[2]

Again, we cannot claim that the experience of being torn from the peasant countryside and forced to work in the essentially regimented environment of the modern factory induced the workers to turn left. It is true that most (but not all) of the workers and many of their leaders were from peasant families, if they were not peasants themselves. Further, workers often objected to plant rules and regulations and how they were enforced, but there was no clash of ethos strong enough to turn workers toward the left. This sort of clash was more likely among sugar workers, petroleum workers, or tobacco workers.

We cannot blame the rapid modernization of an older production process, although textile factories were often built in certain areas to take advantage of a community of skilled hand-loom weavers as well as lower-wage peasants. If modernization were the significant factor, then the attempt by the left to move into the Matossian plant in the 1940s should have been successful. We must look elsewhere for the reason behind the textile workers' turn to the left.

The textile workers exemplified the most complete mechanization of industry in Egypt at the time.[3] Among the textile workers we find large, even extremely large, concentrations of workers in forms of production requiring heavy capital investment and up-to-date bureaucratic-technical structures.[4] It was the organizational and social environment of the plants rather than the living standards of the workers that counted.

As we look at the structure of the production process and the social origins of the workers, two things immediately stand out: first, the well-developed and widespread nature of the rationalized production process made necessary an equally efficient organizational structure to change the terms of hire; second, there was a relatively large group of skilled (and technically educated) workers who needed to protect their own position. A third factor also seems important: most of the textile mills were owned and often managed by Egyptians rather than by foreigners. Consequently the standard cultural explanation for the low wages and poor working conditions did not fit.

Egyptian ownership also conditioned the attitudes of state politicians. Since much of the textile industry was already in the hands of Egyptian capitalists, state officials (including many in the Wafd) did not need textile workers as allies in a national claim to ownership. Textile workers were thus less responsive to an appeal of the nationalist movement. But working-class organizations independent of the nationalist movement, and thus not necessarily available as relatively cheap labor, were often perceived as a distinct danger. This was especially so for the *bête noire* of the labor movement, Ismaʿil Sidki, who was prime minister between February and December 1946 as well as in 1930–1933.

Two points should be made clear at the outset. First, I am not claiming that the textile workers, taken as a mass, were class-conscious Leninists; rather, I am claiming that, for reasons similar to those that operated elsewhere, these workers were far more receptive to left leadership, based on a perspective of class and a structural critique of capitalism, than were any other industrial workers in Egypt and certainly far more so than nonindustrial workers. There were other political currents in the textile mills, including those of the Muslim Brothers and nationalists. To a certain extent there seems to have been a localization of left influence in the greater Cairo area, centered in the suburb of Shubra al-Khaima.

Second, the record is fragmentary. This is in part because of the oppositional nature of the left: much of its literature was destroyed because it was considered subversive. Some was destroyed because it was considered inconsequential. Some records were never made simply because it never occurred to the participants to record their own memories and views. As a consequence, we have no information on other areas comparable to that for Shubra, and we have little on Shubra as a community in the 1940s compared to our information on the history of the union in the area. For a variety of reasons, including the importance of Cairo as a capital, the greater visibility there, and the atmosphere of a nationalist political movement, our best evidence about textile workers is from the strongest point of the left, namely, Shubra, and I shall concentrate on this location.[5] For the sake of convenience, I have divided the textile industry into three main circles: one centered near Cairo (including Shubra); one centered in Mahallah al-Kubra (in the Delta); and one centered in Alexandria (which would include Kafr al-Dawwar).

Finally, there is one last point of introduction to be made. The industrial production of textiles was not begun at the behest of Egyptian workers or to create an Egyptian working class. Industrial production of textiles was begun and expanded in part simply to fill an available market; it was also intended by a group of nationalist-capitalists—many but not all associated with the Bank Misr group—to assert Egyptian economic independence. The new textile industry was meant to strengthen the ability of Egypt and Egyptians to act inside Egypt (a country still under English domination) and in the world market as a whole. From the point of view of these capitalists—powerful industrialists and would-be industrialists as well as their friends in the state administration—

whatever aided the textile industry was good for Egypt; whatever hindered it was bad. The growth of textile production required state aid not only in changing tariff laws, beginning in 1930, to free Egypt from purely pro-British orientations but also subsidies, subventions, and aid in finding raw materials and in keeping labor peace. In this industry, union leaders faced difficult problems. Nationalist politicians found it easy to make employers pay higher wages when those employers were foreign. What would they do about those who represented the "national" interest?

FACTORIES: THEIR GROWTH
AND OPERATION

In Lower Egypt, cotton was not only king but queen and jack as well. The daily papers, including those of the nationalists, gave spot prices for cotton in Alexandria, Liverpool, and New Orleans, and the industries of the north centered on cotton: ginning, milling, pressing, and finally weaving. The northern cities—Cairo, Alexandria, Damietta—lived in a cotton sea, or were, like Mahallah, the gift of it.

The textile industry, like the tobacco industry, underwent rapid technological and social change. Before the turn of the century Egyptian cotton was ginned locally. When it was woven on mechanized looms, they were in England. In 1899, a British group set up the Anglo-Egyptian Spinning and Weaving Company in Alexandria, which the government made into an Egyptian company.[6] Although the national or Ahliyyah (in Arabic) mill was then the most important of the "big industries," it only employed eight hundred workers as late as 1925.[7]

The Ahliyyah plant in Alexandria was the center of one of three circles of textile plants. The second circle was centered around Cairo. The first plant in this area, the Antun Shusha plant, was founded in 1885. This plant typified Cairene industry in general: it was a medium-sized company owned by a Syrian immigrant. Such people were known as "Egyptianized," and were considered neither Egyptian nor European, but were expected to treat workers better than did Europeans.[8] The third circle was based in Mahallah and dates from the rapid expansion of the Misr group textile plants in the 1930s. There was explosive growth in the industry between 1935 and 1945, when a truly national industry was created with extremely large plants. These were occasionally joint ventures with foreign capital. The Bayda Dyers, a joint venture of the English company Bradford and the Misr group and located in

Kafr al-Dawwar, is a case in point. The Bayda Dyers plant could process two hundred thousand square meters of cotton a day.[9]

Between 1930 and 1939, Egyptian output of cotton piece goods increased sixfold, largely but not entirely because of increased industrial production.[10] This large-scale production for consumers interested in relatively cheap goods was centered in Mahallah and called for relatively lower skilled workers than would be required for higher-quality production or production involving rapid changes in output. The plant at Mahallah was closely identified with the movement for the economic independence of Egypt, but ironically the "national" industry was located in the Delta because of a desire to find cheaper labor. Wages in Mahallah were roughly two-thirds those of Cairene or Alexandrian wages.[11] Employers and the government wanted to keep wages low because of the threat of foreign competition, and so stated in the 1949 contract at the Ahliyyah plant in Alexandria.[12] On the basis of quantity of goods produced, we can rank the areas in this order: Mahallah, Alexandria, and Cairo.[13]

In general, the mills in the Cairo area were in the hands of Egyptianized owners. The other textile centers were largely in Egyptian hands. It is unclear if this difference in ownership is significant because by the mid-1940s there were joint ventures involving British capital in the purely "national" sector and Egyptian participation in the Egyptianized sector.

The factories also differed in size. The factories at Kafr al-Dawwar, Mahallah, and Alexandria were extremely large not only by Egyptian standards but also by worldwide standards. The Ahliyyah plant doubled, then redoubled, its work force between 1925 and 1935 (from 800 to 3,200), and the Mahallah plant of the Misr group began with 15,000 workers in 1937 and employed over 27,000 by the end of World War II.[14] The nominal capital of the Ahliyyah plant at this time was L. E. 1.4 million, an extremely high figure by the standards of Egyptian industry.[15]

In the Cairo area, factories typically employed from 50 to 500 employees, with expansion usually connected with the building of a second plant; this was the case with the companies owned by the Syro-Lebanese families who had emigrated to Egypt—the Sibahi, Shurbagi, and Shusha families. Cairo concerns usually were capitalized at L. E. 100,000 or less per plant, and the total capital employed in Cairo was perhaps one-quarter of that employed in the Alexandrian circle.[16] Nevertheless, the capital of a single company could become fairly large, as

with the Etablissements pour la Soie et le Coton, which had seven factories with a combined capital of L. E. 600,000.[17]

The pace, productivity, and rhythm of industrial production is considerably different from that of hand production. By the end of the nineteenth century, the standard wisdom was that one power-loom weaver
could produce *at least* as much as twenty hand-loom weavers.

> A good handloom weaver of the past days would never and could never for
> any length of time together make more than fifty picks per minute, whilst the
> power-loom's capacity is from 180 to 260 picks per minute, according to the
> widths of cloth being made. . . . Thus at an easy estimate, each power-loom is
> equivalent to five hand-loom weavers and as four of these looms on an aver-
> age can be superintended by one power-loom weaver, it follows that one per-
> son with the aid of power-looms can produce as much as twenty weavers
> of the early days of the present century. . . . But even this estimate falls far be-
> low the facts because the hand-loom weaver was never a persistent worker,
> whilst the power-loom is absolutely tireless.[18]

Egyptian productivity was, in general, below even the late-nineteenth-
century norms referred to here, and there was a constant struggle over
production norms. This conflict was reflected in both rates of pay and
the *nature* of pay. Would workers be paid by the piece or by the hour?
Workers were divided over modes of payment. Trained and proficient
workers sometimes preferred piece rates; these workers called payment
by the hour anarchistic or communistic.[19] Even union militants, who
might ordinarily oppose the piece-rate system, accepted it when they believed they would benefit from it.[20]

From the point of view of individual strategies for higher earnings,
questions such as this were critical, and those familiar with the history
of so-called scientific management, or Taylorism, in the West will note
similarities here. Any particular worker has relatively little control over
all the factors that determine whether or not piece rates are in his or her
interest. The worker cannot control how quickly work stations are supplied with parts, the reliability of the source of power, or the quality
of the inputs themselves. On the other hand, given the same circumstances, more efficient workers will do better than less efficient ones if
wages are tied to effort rather than made the same for all workers, even
if most workers will do better with an hourly wage. Choosing a wage
system is clearly not a simple matter.

Without a complete knowledge of the width of the looms, the speed
of the machines, and the quality of production—things we shall never
know—we cannot compare the workers' pace of production in different

areas. These factors were equally important in terms of pay for workers in large and small factories. In Damietta, for example, wages for mechanized textile workers were essentially piece rates based on the number of machines a worker ran, the width of the looms, and the number of lines per inch of material.[21] In Shubra workers usually worked on only one or two machines.[22] This seems to suggest low levels of skill by Egyptian standards, but it more probably suggests rapid changes in production runs when we consider two other points. Wages were relatively high in Shubra for textile workers, and many of the biographies of workers suggest that they had fairly high skills.

A significant number of workers tended fewer than four machines in the Ahliyyah plant, but the company wanted more. There were three categories of workers: the "beginner," who was responsible for one loom, "half-trained" for two, and "skilled" for three, four, or more machines with the aid of an apprentice or youngster.[23] On the other hand, in some fine-weaving establishments, notably at Kafr al-Dawwar, productivity per worker was extremely high, with one worker looking after twelve to sixteen mechanical looms.[24] It might well be that the Ahliyyah plant (like that at Mahallah) represented the ordinary production line, whereas the Shubra and Kafr al-Dawwar areas represented the exceptional work and required significantly higher levels of skill. Workers in these two areas would thus have a better opportunity to make out and to determine the rules of making out.

Since Egyptian industry was competing with international firms for the domestic market (local production met only 40 percent of the demand for cotton cloth), the industry owners wanted both tariff protection and considerably higher productivity.[25] Wages, although low in international terms, were an important part of the cost of production, reaching 56 percent of the value of net output as opposed to 28 percent in the tobacco industry.[26] Egyptian output per hand in spinning and weaving was between one-half and one-third of British output at the same time.[27]

Labor was widely viewed as the key factor in the success of mechanized textile production at least in part because of the high proportion of value added through wages, something obviously true in Egypt. A standard text such as Marsden's considered "free and unobstructed access to a good supply of the best class of operatives . . . one of the primary ingredients of success" in the textile industry.[28] For precisely this reason locating mills in isolated areas in order to obtain the advantages of lower wages and rents was, by the turn of the century, already considered poor business practice.[29] In England at least, higher wages were thought to lead to faster production and a better product, and this was believed to be especially valuable for creating what we would call brand loyalty in a very uncertain market.

The factors of wages and productivity raise the issue of discipline in the work place. Mechanization did not relieve the worker of responsibility for the quality or quantity of production. Rather it meant he or she could waste considerably more material and time than a hand weaver. The discipline of the textile factory was thus the result of two factors for the workers: first, supervision and work rules and, second, the behavior of the market. Workers in the textile industry—and this is explicit in several contracts—were subject not only to supervisory control but also to market convention, which based wages on piece rates or productivity. Agreed-upon norms already existed in Britain well before large plants owned by British (or other European) investors were built in Egypt. The concept of norms was well known to factory owners in Egypt and they were used fairly widely there. Many contracts included bonuses for meeting some production quotas and penalties for falling below the norms.

Unlike other industries surveyed in this book (although not unlike some crafts), the weaver (even more than the spinner) found his wage governed by factors beyond his control: the fineness of the yarn to be worked, the humidity in the air, the size of the loom, the pattern of the cloth, and the evenness with which the machine ran. As is obvious in the contracts mentioned above from Damietta, Egyptian textile workers were aware of these factors and bargained with employers about them. Other workers found themselves penalized by a factory administration that was poorly run. In the recession following World War II workers were more than willing to work, but the factory owners could not find yarn or fabric and so either reduced earnings or let workers go. This problem became particularly acute in the Shubra area and became a part of the dialogue of the left over markets for Egyptian textiles (to which I alluded in chapter 2).

As workers became more sophisticated in their understanding of the process of mechanization, they saw clearly the factors that were tied to decisions made by others (yarn bought, machines kept up, factory size) and the factors they could only influence by the regular application of collective power, namely, the creation of sustained, independent organization.

WORKERS: THEIR SOCIAL
ROOTS AND SKILLS

The work force in the textile mills was not unlike that of other industries; the textile industry drew on the peasantry as a basic reservoir for
workers. But the textile industry did not employ agricultural workers
directly, as did the sugar industry. Working in a textile plant was a full-
time occupation and involved the opportunity to learn new skills over
time. Workers in the textile mills may have come from peasant families—although not always—but they did not remain peasants themselves, nor did their ties with the peasant world remain intact. The textile areas grew into substantial working-class quarters and continued to
grow faster than other areas. This was more true of Rud al-Farraj or
Shubra than anywhere else, but in general the textile industry brought
into existence an urban milieu.

Just as elsewhere in the world, people were pushed off the land and
pulled into the industrial sector. This is most apparent in one of the few
surveys done of Egyptian workers. In a survey taken at Mahallah on the
eve of the 1952 army coup, Ford Foundation researchers asked textile
workers if they would return to the land if given plots. The response was
mainly negative: 42 percent said they would and 54 percent said they
would not.[30] Level of skill rather than birthplace seems to have determined the degree to which workers wanted to stay in the factory. There
was little difference in response between those with rural backgrounds
and those from the cities, but there was a significant difference on the
basis of skill. The most skilled workers—those in maintenance—rejected the idea of returning to the land: 70 percent were opposed and
only 30 percent were in favor of a return to the land.

Who were these skilled workers (by Egyptian standards of the day,
highly skilled)? Many of them, especially those who became foremen,
were graduates of technical schools. Technical school attendance rose
markedly in this period, from 2,650 students in 1918 to 17,353 students in 1936–1937, and the curriculum began to emphasize the skills
needed to work in factories.[31] Given the dominance of the textile industry in the country's industrial development, the textile industry was expected to absorb a significant number of these graduates, and indeed
they had been trained to consider themselves a part of the vanguard of
Egypt's economic renaissance. The union of foremen and their assistants
at Shubra was largely made up of such men.[32]

Many Egyptians viewed the textile industry as one way to challenge

English economic power in Egypt. Egyptians had to be trained in public schools and in schools set up by the mills to ensure a national capacity to carry out the manufacture of textiles in industrial settings. This meant the creation of an Egyptian textile industry that could shake British dominance in the Egyptian market and the world market. There is some disagreement over how quickly and in what way Egyptian skilled workers were placed in the top jobs in various factories. Certainly until the 1930s most if not all skilled workers were non-Egyptian; thereafter we find increasing numbers of skilled Egyptians in the skilled jobs. The initial impetus was political, and seems to have been rooted in the policies of the Misr plant at Mahallah. The experience of Mahallah in using skilled Egyptian workers was decisive in offsetting a "planned and decisive attack on graduates of the technical and factory schools to deny them employment."[33]

In the wake of the commercial success of the Misr textile plants, smaller plants in the Cairo area were set up. These plants were ordered by the government to hire skilled Egyptian workers and to give preference not only to Egyptians over foreigners but to skilled workers over unskilled workers seeking training.[34] By the beginning of World War II, Egyptian skilled workers had replaced non-Egyptians everywhere, including at the last holdout—the Cairo Weaving Factory.

Despite these advances in employment opportunities, the skilled technical graduates believed there was a gap between what they should have and what they actually received.[35] Technical graduates would complain, worry about unemployment and poor employment, strike, and protest throughout the 1930s and 1940s. The complaints of the skilled workers were simple: they had spent time learning how to use modern machinery in hopes of getting higher wages. When they finally found work, they discovered the machines were old and their wages were consequently low. "We built high hopes and saw them dashed," wrote a group of Mahallah training school graduates to the Ministry of Education. Despite training for five years to use modern equipment, "we have seen nothing but ancient local looms which seem to date to some previous age and are slow to operate and produce little and the wage from whose employment hardly sustains life."[36]

Skilled textile workers did not want only high wages; they also wanted meaningful work: they wanted to aid in the nationalist movement. Almost a decade later another worker would write to a periodical shortly to fall under the dominance of the Muslim Brothers: "Is the struggle against unemployment limited to the provision of work that merely gathers the workers within four walls? . . . When this is done are people really satisfied that this is enough? . . . The worker in his work needs concern and guidance. . . . There is no point complaining [about unemployment] as long as we graduates of the technical schools find many burdens and terrible conditions at work hardly seen outside Egypt."[37]

Implicit in the letter is a complaint later made openly by ʿAbd al-Fattah Husayn, the labor delegate to a state committee in the 1940s. Husayn complained that technical school graduates did not get what they expected, nor were they likely to be rewarded only on the basis of their abilities and qualifications. Some made out vastly better than others because of the distinct opportunities available. Graduates of the technical schools had two career options: either into the factory or into government. The latter career was by far preferable because the workday was only six hours and the pay and benefits were stable and often higher than those available to many graduates in factory employment.[38] Technical school graduates compared themselves in terms of pay both to government employees and to French and British workers, whose productivity and pay scales were widely discussed by the 1940s in Egypt.[39]

Skills were in demand at this time and the technical school graduates were aware of just how much in demand they were and how that demand changed over time. After all, students chose their technical school curriculum at least in part to learn skills that would give them preferred careers. It is hard to say just how important to the technical school curriculum textile studies were, but they were a large and probably growing sector in the period under consideration. Almost 10 percent of the technical school graduates between 1950 and 1954 were graduates in weaving, and in other areas the percentage was higher: 12 percent in Cairo-Giza and 19 percent in Tanta and Kafr al-Shaykh. Skilled textile work was the largest single category of training in the schools.[40]

Unlike the artisans, skilled workers had chosen their lot and this had certain consequences. Skilled workers, unlike artisans, went to school and earned certificates in many cases. They did not learn their craft from a master, but rather by means of technical training, which involved (to some degree) an appreciation of the underlying principles of the machinery with which they worked and of the different ways in which such machinery could be used. These workers had an education that was rare and valuable in their society: book learning opened up career possibilities that included tremendous gains in status and power. Men who could read and write were acutely conscious of their opportunities and their positions.[41] Unlike every other group of well-educated men in the society, however, skilled workers often had to work with their hands and get dirty. Moreover, they worked in a competitive labor market, which meant they could often be replaced not only by new technical graduates but also on occasion by far less educated workers who had mastered on the job the requisite skills for advancement.

To a far greater degree than in any other industrial setting surveyed in this book, the skilled textile workers and an important subgroup of them—the foremen and assistant foremen—lived a precarious life. These men were educated and expected to be treated as educated, white-collar employees; yet they were actually engaged in the hurly-burly of production on a shop floor and were often production workers whose only real chance of advancement lay in becoming taskmasters to their fellows. When such men were given positions of responsibility in the factory, they often found themselves training men who would do their work for lower rates. Finally, the skilled workers understood that even though their skills might be in demand, their ability to realize steady high wages were limited by the condition of the market for textiles and by the condition of the factory, its equipment, and its management.

THE CASE OF SHUBRA

The union in the Cairo area was the most determinedly radical of any in Egypt and provided many (though not all) of the workers prominent in the Communist movement in Egypt. In the mid-1930s Shubra al-Khaima and the surrounding areas at the edge of Cairo were villages largely cut off from Cairo by open fields and the central terminal, workshops, and tracks of the Egyptian State Railway. What I here often call Shubra included part of Cairo itself and part of a northern suburb between the Nile and a major water channel (the Isma'iliyya Canal). This area (see Map 2) includes Damanhur Shubra, Shubra al-Khaima, Bijam, Bahtim, Musturud, Shubra itself as well as Rud al-Farraj, and parts of Al-Waily. When I refer to Shubra or Shubra al-Khaima, I am referring to this general area rather than to the specific villages within it.

The weaving industry was initially centered in the provincial capital of Qaliyub and was a handicraft industry. In fact most of Shubra was not part of Cairo at all but part of the Qaliyubiyyah governorate, a fact of some importance when it came to electoral districting and government intervention in textile affairs; the relevant officials were not officials of the capital. Given the large amount of cloth still produced by hand weaving even in the late 1940s, it should come as little surprise that

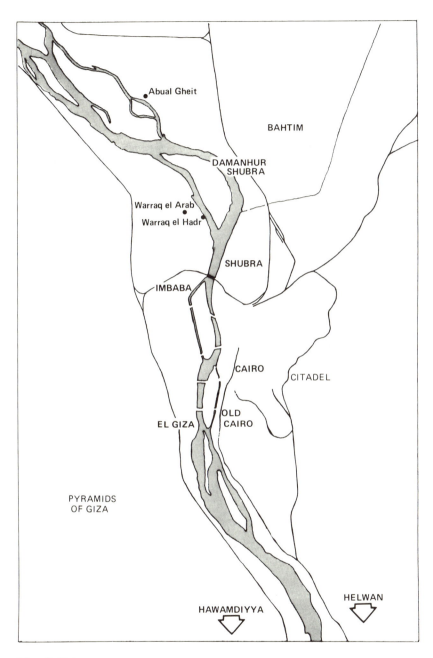

Map 2. Cairo

Qalyubiyyah province still contained quite a few handicraft weavers through this period. According to the newspaper *Al-Mustaqbal*, there were 22,000 handicraft weavers; the figure probably includes everybody who had even the most primitive loom. Nevertheless, since even the simplest shuttle could provide useful experience for mechanical looms of the period, this figure indicates that there was a significant reservoir of workers. These were by no means the skilled workers discussed above, but they did have mechanical skills that set them apart from untrained workers. Without training on even a simple loom, it was impossible to run even the most elementary weaving establishment. The poet Bayram al-Tunisi, for example, was unable to take possession of the small and primitive manufactory left him by his father because the employees—his cousins—refused to teach him the trade.[42]

Artisan workers were paid by the length of cloth and it seems probable that by the 1940s most workers made at least rough calculations comparing time and output in handicraft and mechanized industries. Some handicraft workers in the Qaliyub area (as well as those in Mahallah) are reported to have worked eighteen-hour days for 3.5 piasters a day.[43] Certainly they had a good idea of wages in different geographical areas, and by 1948 they could refer to an unauthorized reprint of the ministerial report on wages for textile workers, published by the Shubra area activist Taha Sa'd 'Uthman. This report suggested that Shubra was a relatively good place to work. Production workers in Mahallah, for example, earned an average of 15 or 16 piasters a day, whereas production workers in the Sibahi plant in Alexandria, which had left Shubra largely to escape the union, earned between 16 and 28.5 piasters a day.[44]

Social and political activity included Wafd youth organizations (a paramilitary group) and various Islamic groups. The Wafd wanted to organize the handicraft textile industry in the Cairo area, and the industry in this area was certainly large enough. The earliest mention of a general union for textile workers in the Cairo area appears in 1935 when the General Union for Textile and Associated Workers in Cairo supported the Wafd in the split with 'Abbas Halim in 1935.[45] There was also in this area a growing number of unionists who connected the factors of police repression, low wages, poor conditions, and Egyptian owned and managed enterprise. These men tended to see capitalism rather than European cultural orientations as the source of their problems. As early as 1935, workers complained about the use of local police against them without provocation in a strike at the Belgian Weaving Workshop in Shubra.[46]

Many of the plants in this area were owned in part by Egyptians or by ethnic non-Egyptians with Egyptian citizenship. By the time of World War II they had hired Egyptian skilled workers and foremen in large numbers, and no lesson struck home harder than the lesson that Egyptians or Muslims could treat other Egyptians just the way Europeans had treated them. Shaykh Abd al-Qadr Hamada, who hated foreigners all his life, especially for their conduct toward Egyptians in calling them cattle or donkeys, was amazed to discover that Egyptian foremen in the textile industry in Helwan were even haughtier to Egyptian workers than were foreigners.[47] ʿAbd al-Munʿim ʿIsawi, one of the founders of the union at Shubra, also discovered that Egyptian foremen could treat workers with the same cruelty as had foreign foremen. He wrote: "I received the same treatment [as from Europeans] but with more cruelty."[48] In 1950 a worker at the Sibahi factory in Shubra wrote that

> Sibahi is the most murderous, destructive and sweating of the factories—this very Sibahi who drinks the blood of his victims with the agreement of the government and the union.[49]

It is hard to overestimate the effects of such an experience.

THREE LEADERS

Three men emerged as left leaders of textile workers in the Cairo area in the 1940s. The first was Taha Saʿd ʿUthman, the son of poor peasants in the Middle Egyptian province of Bani Suwayf. He was one of the early members of the union at Shubra, serving in almost every official capacity including editor of the union newspaper and president of the union. Taha Saʿd attended a local Quran school at first, but later was sent to a technical secondary school by a wealthy neighbor.[50]

By the 1930s the government was anxious to assert Egyptian control, ownership, or at least influence over key areas of the economy. As part of this effort, the Ministry of Finance sent Taha Saʿd to a small textile plant in Shubra. The idea was that even if Egypt could not now run her own textile industry in every geographical area or each sector, it could at least develop a fund of skilled labor that would be available later as a political ally in a struggle with foreign owners.

Taha Saʿd at this time was less interested in organizing a union than in spreading the word of the Muslim Brothers and the Sharʿi Cooperative Association of which he was an active member. Taha Saʿd's connections with the various Muslim political groups active in the area are

unclear and as a result so too are the relations between the union, especially its leadership, and these groups. We know that prominent Muslim
religious leaders aided the union in its various struggles as late as 1945
and that such leaders were members of groups with which Taha Saʿd had
been affiliated. Thus, for example, Shaykh Zaki Zaʿtar, who was both a
local elementary school teacher and a leader of the *Jamʿiyyah sharʿiyyah
li-taʿawun al-ʿamilin bi al-kitab wa al-sunnah al-muhammadiyyah*, was
an active supporter of the union leadership in an election campaign in
1945.[51] Shaykh Zaʿtar also preached the sermon in the local mosque of
the *jamʿiyyah al-sharʿiyyah*. Further, Taha Saʿd was, at the time, a close
friend of Hasan al-Banna, Supreme Guide of the Muslim Brothers; and
the Shubra branch of the welfare association of the Muslim Brothers
was apparently an important one, for it was mentioned, among the 135
branches, in the 1943 report on the growth of the Society of Muslim
Brothers.[52]

By the mid-1940s Taha Saʿd was a skilled worker and foreman at one
of the Sibahi family factories in the Shubra al-Khaima area. In the Sibahi factories workers confronted abusive Egyptian foremen, and this
raises an obvious question about Taha Saʿd's conduct. Skilled workers in
some plants probably could decide for themselves how they treated
their subordinates, but managers for Sibahi generally could not afford to
be considerate if they wanted to keep their jobs. Taha Saʿd was probably
an exception in his relationship with subordinates.

Managers such as Ahmad Farj-allah were probably typical. As late as
1950 workers complained that Farj-allah cursed the men for not working hard enough and told them that whoever worked like a dog would
have work and whoever did not would be fired; in addition he kicked,
hit, and beat his employees.[53] Farj-allah had been active in the electoral
campaign run under the auspices of the union leadership in 1945 and
contributed five Egyptian pounds to the campaign fund.[54] It is likely that
Farj-allah simply kept pace with the times, treating his subordinates and
a union campaign according to the tenor of the times.

The second leader to emerge in the Shubra area was Muhammad ʿAli
ʿAmir, who was born in Shubra al-Khaima in 1908; his family moved to
the area across the Ismaʿiliyya Canal known as Matariyyah when he
was a young boy after a dispute with the owner of the estate on which
they had been sharecroppers. The experiences of a poor peasant family
in its various struggles with the authority of the "big house" had a pro-
found effect on the boy.[55] By 1929, young ʿAmir was accepted as a leader
of workers in a macaroni plant in Zaitun, then still a village, when he

organized a work stoppage. In part his central role at this plant was the result of his participation in the formation of a welfare association.[56] He was also recognized as a man who was as ready to fight the local police as to challenge the plant manager. If the term *gada^c* can be applied to any one leader, that leader is ʿAli ʿAmir, who took it upon himself to lead workers' struggles for better conditions, at least partly because of his temperament. At first, ʿAmir was a Wafdist, and it is even possible that his name appeared in some Wafd publicity of the Zaitun area in the 1930s.[57] There is no doubt that he was a member of the paramilitary organization of the Wafd. By 1942, however, ʿAmir had been caught up in the working-class radicalism sweeping Shubra.

The area in which ʿAmir began his union work, Zaitun and Matariyyah, was separate from Shubra al-Khaima. It was a distinct and largely autonomous section of the textile industry and of the union. The difference in leaderships in the two areas clarifies the importance of geographical proximity of factories for the success of union organization in Shubra. The Shubra factories were within walking distance of each other, as were those in the Zaitun-Matariyyah area, but the two districts were separated by the Ismaʿiliyya Canal.[58] The isolation of the separate factory areas from each other affected the fortunes of the union. Thus, the branch of the Mechanized Textile Workers Union in Matariyyah was formed separately and we do not hear of it until 1942.[59] We do not know if ʿAmir was an activist in this branch, but like Muhammad ʿAli ʿAmir the union in the area was connected with the neighborhood as well as the factories. If this tended to make the union somewhat less well integrated in good times, it also made it distinctly more able to survive in bad ones. Thus in 1948 when the union in Shubra al-Khaima was in disarray, the textile workers in the Matariyyah-Zaitun area had the basis in both membership and seasoned leadership to form a successful left-oriented textile workers' union.

The third leader to emerge in the northern suburbs of Cairo was Mahmud al-ʿAskari, a skilled worker who had been involved since the 1930s with militant and politically active trade union leaders in Cairo. He was a member of a committee that called for a hunger strike in 1938 to protest the absence of comprehensive labor legislation. This hunger strike included a significant part of the Wafd-oriented trade union leaders from the tradesmen and craftsmen and the hunger strike was explicitly modeled on the moralizing and nationalist politics of Mahatma Gandhi's hunger strikes in India.[60]

The group with which al-ʿAskari was involved included several socialists, and certainly involved him in the world of national as well as nationalist politics. None of these men was a Communist in 1939, and except for al-ʿAskari they had probably heard little of Communists and disliked what they had heard. Al-ʿAskari was affiliated with left radicalism in Shubra for so long that when the union decided in 1945 to run one of their own members for a seat in parliament, al-ʿAskari was vetted because of his background. According to Taha Saʿd, a major objection to al-ʿAskari's running was a problem of status.

> Several of the foremen had an antagonistic attitude to al-ʿAskari personally and created a storm among the foremen that they should not accept being represented by a worker in parliament, especially since he did not have a certificate and they had diplomas.[61]

Al-ʿAskari was already well known as a leftist and a good choice for a campaign designed to further "class" positions. Nevertheless, another Sibahi foreman, Faddali ʿAbd al-Jayyid, was chosen to appease the skilled workers.

In the late 1930s all of these men were still largely pro-Wafd and considered themselves nationalists. By the end of 1946 all three leaders either had joined Leninist parties or were on the verge of doing so. Al-ʿAskari and ʿUthman were also writing articles for the newspaper *Al-Damir*, a Leninist newspaper.[62] We cannot say for certain what persuaded these men to become Leninists, but we can look at the events of the early 1940s for clues.

In the 1940s Yusuf Darwish, a Communist attorney, began to represent the Shubra union. The ideas of Yusuf al-Mudarrik, a longtime trade union activist and socialist, also became important when he and al-ʿAskari and others were interned during the early days of World War II because the British feared their influence on a critical war-related industry. It was not the mere verbal skill of Darwish that enchanted the educated and activist union members such as Taha Saʿd or ʿAli ʿAmir, nor was it the effect of talking with al-Mudarrik and Greek Communists in jail that turned al-ʿAskari toward Leninism.[63] These men were engaged in search behavior: they were looking for ways to understand their situation in a comprehensive fashion. If arguments alone had been involved, other intelligent and potentially prominent political figures might have been recruited. As al-ʿAskari pointed out, Anwar Sadat was in jail with them at the same time. The key factor can only have been the degree to which Leninist ideas made sense of the situation in Shubra and for textile workers as a whole, ideas that crystallized an analysis begun earlier by these men.

I have already enumerated several of the critical arguments made by these men (in chapter 2). In the world of Shubra, arguments that the workers could depend only on themselves and not at all on the employers' benevolence or the state's consideration were certainly plausible. Further, the workers had sufficient economic and political resources to organize themselves.

THE UNION

Shubra was poised for an industrial takeoff in the 1940s because of the influx of foreign capital associated with prominent Egyptians, a need for skilled workers, and a growing estrangement of working-class leaders from the Wafd. In addition, either through interlocking directorates or through investment choices, several factories were owned by the same investors.[64] The key problem for union organizers in the textile industry—as in the other industries we have looked at—was to establish a link between skilled and unskilled workers, for the latter supplied the muscle and the former were strategic for industrial production, more so in the textile industry than elsewhere in Egypt.

Unlike industries tied to agriculture, textile production is tied to an unstable market, and in the textile industry in Egypt in the 1940s the market was especially unstable, which meant employment was unstable.[65] In Shubra where relatively small plants were the rule and where the bulk of production was of a higher grade than the articles produced at Mahallah, demand was unstable and so were jobs. As a consequence in Shubra more than elsewhere, skilled workers (as opposed to craftsmen) suffered the ups and downs of market conditions and viewed a union organization independent of the needs of the owners or the state an important way to preserve their livelihood.

The union that arose in these circumstances was the General Union of Mechanized Textile Workers of Cairo and Its Suburbs.[66] The constitution, as amended April 26, 1942, set out the goals of a radical—but not Communist—union.[67] All the goals of the union were given in terms of the worker-members and without reference to the employers. As required by law, the union constitution eschewed political or religious activity, but unlike other constitutions of the period it also had no prefatory or other material invoking Islamic motifs.

The union goals included mutual union solidarity among the workers, defense of the workers' rights, better labor legislation, and an end to illiteracy among the members. The union also sought, on behalf of the members, to improve their levels of skill. This last one must have been important for many workers, and it certainly suggests the degree to which the union wanted to be seen as the source through which workers upgraded themselves rather than allowing the employer to be that source.

The problem of skills was real, for skills were considered a capital fund belonging to the worker, who therefore was foolish to share his skills with other workers.[68] Worker antagonism on this question could be destructive for both the plant and the workers as collective bargainers. As Taha Saꞌd ꞌUthman pointed out, there was a constant danger of skilled technical school graduates being replaced by agricultural laborers the graduates had trained.[69] Only state intervention had made skilled workers the preferred employees, and their high wages were a favorite target of employers.

In order to achieve its goals and protect its members, the union had to establish and maintain an identity and its integrity. As part of this process, the union undertook the socialization of the membership, and dealt with this more seriously than had any other union in Egypt. Union membership became effective when the executive board accepted the application for membership, and the application included advance payment of a month's dues and a swearing-in ceremony. The member had to recite the union oath at the ceremony.

> By Almighty God I will be faithful to the union and its members and carry out the lawful orders of the executive committee, keep its secrets, and fulfill what is expected of me in the pursuit of the interests of the mass of workers, so help me God.

After six months the union member was allowed (and one suspects encouraged) to carry his membership card (*carnet*) and wear the union button. Nonpayment of dues was grounds for expulsion.

The union was organized on the basis of elected delegates from different plants in the area of Shubra al-Khaima. The general assembly elected the members of the executive board, with the proviso that there be three members from each factory who were known to the members there.[70]

The union was prepared to defend its members over problems at work, but reserved the right not to defend those it considered troublemakers. Specifically, the union insisted that any worker who planned to leave his job had to notify the union, which would then attempt to "put him on the right track"; if the worker refused union guidance, he was on his own.[71] In general the union leaders understood the need to maintain an organizational identity and thus considered it an entity separate from, though accountable to, its members. Thus union property was union property, not that of the members. Union funds could only be withdrawn with proper organizational signatures and seals.[72] Not until the treasury contained L.E. 20 were any personal benefits (sick benefits, death benefits) to be paid, and that sum was still large—at least half a year's gross wages for a textile worker.

The textile workers in Shubra knew they were well organized and organized on a European model. In a sense they were going Fathi Kamil one better, for if he believed working conditions and wages should be as good in Egypt as in Europe, the union leadership in Shubra believed union administration and organization should be as advanced as European models.[73]

This degree of organization was not familiar to—or even the preference of—all of the workers. Thus the pages of the union newspaper were filled with arguments about different forms of union organization. One issue of *Shubra* just after the adoption of the constitution delved explicitly into the issue of organization versus association. The occasion was a letter supposedly received from an Egyptian skilled worker who had recently returned from Europe. The author of the letter mentioned three distinct ideas of unions.

> Looking into the matter I decided to see the degree of understanding Egyptian workers have about unions. I found three different concepts exist: first, the idea of the union as a welfare and mutual-aid society; second, the idea of the union as an instrument to make the worker as powerful in his job as the owner; third—and this is the proper conception of a union as I studied it in Europe—is the union as a general school, guide, counselor, and in a sense a doctor curing ills, which pushes forward for that which is right and that only.[74]

He goes on to suggest that a night school to eradicate illiteracy be started so that the third form will prevail.

In response to this front-page letter others wrote that the leaders at Shubra were glad to be considered good unionists, they were building slowly but carefully, and they would defend the workers' rights, including the right to be literate.

The newspaper probed all of the key questions—especially those of major political orientations—openly. There was, apparently, a struggle going on in the union over what direction it should take. Since the textile factories were relatively small for Egyptian industrial plants (although not for manufacture in general), the union newspaper also carried out an unremitting struggle against anything that brought the employers' point of view into the union, and against what the writing staff saw as a variety of anticlass positions. With this exception, the newspaper managed to cover a broad range of positions. One of the newspaper's prominent writers, Taha Muhammad Fauda, took the position I have generally presented as that of the Muslim Brothers. He argued strenuously that the main problem of the workers was estrangement from purely Egyptian customs. For example, he suggested that foreign ownership was the decisive factor in the plants,[75] that the workers' conditions would be improved if there were no women working in the factories,[76] and that there should be more social and religious clubs for workers to attend.[77]

Fauda spoke only for a minority, and he generally was not echoed in the major policy statements of the newspaper. More common were attacks on the nature of the relations in the plant and on the ties that bound owners and politicians. Thus we find an anonymous columnist known as the Wronged Soldier suggesting that union members seek out other sources of news than those provided by the employers, and warning that the modern worker was not like the worker of old, for the modern worker

> is absolutely opposed to the exploiters who continue their exploitation, and everything the workers do and all the demands they put forward are only human rights of this period and are granted by other employers in other countries.[78]

In *Shubra* the union had a powerful instrument for organizing workers and for promoting the ideas of the union among the workers. It was, though apparently without the direct influence of the left as yet, near the "collective organizer" Lenin considered necessary for a revolutionary party. It was not, unlike Lenin's *Iskra*, an all-encompassing national paper, but it was certainly far more than a set of exposés on factory life or union announcements. *Shubra* gave the union a way to reach workers and involve them in the life of the union, and because of this the newspaper was not to last long. One of the peculiarities of Egypt's legal system is that newspapers are licensed and licenses are private property. The owner of the license for *Shubra* was persuaded not to let the workers continue to use it. For all intents and purposes the paper ceased publication in August 1942.

Shubra was different from other large textile areas in one other respect: the multiplicity of employers made it difficult to blacklist radicals, and repeated firings simply sent the radicals into other shops.[79] The employers may have wished to blacklist workers, but without coordinated records and closer connections they could not do so. Employers at Mahallah were far more effective. Far from hiring Communists (or other militants) in the work force, employers at Mahallah, for example, undertook systematic purges. We know that union membership of any kind was often grounds for dismissal and even the followers of ʿAbbas Halim were threatened with loss of jobs at the Misr factories in Mahallah.[80]

The union and the left benefited from the concentration of workers who lived in a two or three mile radius from the center of Shubra al-Khaima. The political support for the ideas promoted by the leading activists in the union becomes apparent when we compare the election results of the 1945 campaign of Faddali Abd-al-Jayyid for a parliamentary seat. Abd al-Jayyid had been a president of the Shubra union when he entered the 1945 campaign. He died shortly after losing the election. Faddali won more than 15 percent of the vote in Damanhur Shubra, Bahtim, Bijam, and Waily (see Table 1). He won less than one percent of

TABLE I   LEFT VOTING IN THE SHUBRA AREA, 1945

Polling Station	Faddali # of Votes	Shala-qani # of Votes	Total # of Votes	% Total Vote to Faddali	% of Faddali's Vote Won in District
Shubra al-balad	81	35	591	13.7%	9.5%
Damanhur Shubra	235	42	359	65.5%	27.7%
Nubar	81	3	512	15.8%	9.5%
Bahtim	204	232	508	40.2%	24.0%
Basus	2	1328	1330	0.2%	0.2%
Abu Ghayt # 1	2	780	806	0.2%	0.2%
Abu Ghayt # 2	6	433	866	0.7%	0.7%
Qanatir # 1	32	169	471	6.8%	3.8%
Qanatir # 2	15	209	327	4.6%	1.8%
Bijam	118	138	724	16.3%	13.9%
Minyat Sirij	23	74	442	5.2%	2.7%
Waily	50	151	270	18.5%	5.9%
Total	849	3611	7306	11.6%	~100.0%

SOURCE: Taha Saʿd ʿUthman, *Mudhakkirat wa wathaʾiq min tarikh ʿummal misr: al-ʿummal wa al-intikhabat al-barlaminiyyah* (Cairo: Maktabat Madbuli, 1982).

NOTE: There were three other candidates besides the eventual winner, Shalaqani, and Faddali ʿAbd al-Jayyid. Rounding precludes totals coming to exactly 100.0%.

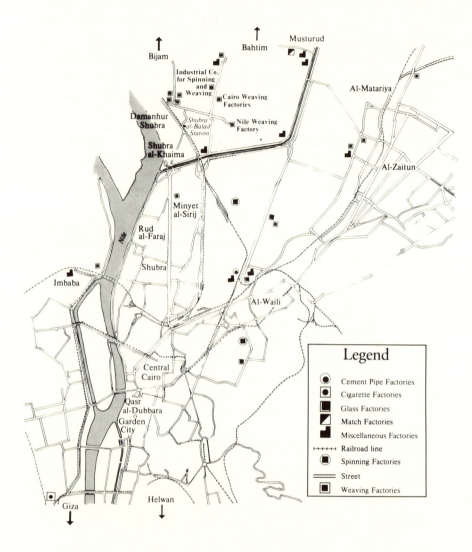

Map 3. Cairo—Shubra Area

the vote in the outlying areas of Basus and the Abu Ghayt polling areas, where presumably peasants under the direct control of landlords cast their ballots or had ballots cast for them without benefit of independent oversight of the electoral process. Indeed, the 1945 elections were corrupt, and there was no chance that ʿAbd al-Jayyid would win.

The 1945 election results conform to the political strength of the textile union in textile worker neighborhoods. If the election district had included working-class areas such as Zaitun or Matariyyah rather than such relatively distant and diverse areas as Qanatir, Abu Ghayt, and Basus, the political power of the union militants might have enabled ʿAbd al-Jayyid to win the election. It is impossible to believe that the electoral district lines were not drawn with such considerations in mind, especially since Qanatir at the head of the Nile Barrage is well outside the area of Shubra.

THE CASE OF MAHALLAH AL-KUBRA

In the large combines owned and run by Egyptians, central record keeping and thus social control undoubtedly were easier, and these factors probably prevented the combines from becoming centers of autonomous radicalism similar to Shubra. But such control could not completely safeguard them from left influence and we should not be surprised to find significant union activity in the largest combines.

There is a long tradition of union organization (at least formally) in Mahallah. Mahallah was a center for ginning cotton and for artisan activity at the turn of the century. As a consequence, the union in Mahallah had a predecessor but also had to assert its own industrial approach over the older craft norms; this was probably more difficult in Mahallah than it had been in Shubra, which was more separated from the hand-loom producers in Qaliyubiyyah and more integrated into the life of the capital. During the 1935 split between ʿAbbas Halim and the Wafd, a Mahallah trade union federation sided with the Wafd. The Mahallah federation included representatives from the tailors, cobblers, launderers, cooks, waiters, fez makers, and artisan weavers as well as representatives from the "cotton companies."[81] The delegation sent to Cairo by the Mahallah federation included a local lawyer (presumably a Wafdist official), a motor vehicle driver, a worker in a cotton gin, and a mechanic in the textile plant. Lawyers had played an important role in gathering union support for the ouster of Halim, for it was they who called the unions together.[82] The union that was part of the 1935 federation hardly lasted longer than the day's paper mentioning it. Certainly it cannot have had much impact on the conditions of workers in Mahallah, which were frankly so miserable that government reports said the workers lived in houses unfit for animals.[83]

The Mahallah workers faced a company management that was clearly antagonistic to their immediate interests, but they could expect little support from the government. In June 1938 a strike broke out in response to a cut in wages. Because the weaving workers were paid by piece rates, a cut in the length of time per shift meant a decrease in their total wages. About 1,500 workers were involved and 55 were arrested. The statement of the court reveals an official attitude different from that shown to petroleum or sugar workers.

> The Correctional Court of Mehallat el-Kubra believes that it must express its active regret and astonishment at these foolish acts by the weaving workers of the Misr Spinning and Weaving Company of Mehalla. It believes them to be ungrateful and far from accomplishing what they owe a company that has helped them, sustained them, and opened a door through which they could pass while still untutored. . . . In such a situation the workers must cooperate with the company for production, and sacrifice their own personal interests so as to serve the nation, develop its commerce, and not waste the fruit of such gigantic effort by the influence of dangerous opinions that we do not wish to see among the workers for any reason whatsoever.[84]

The court went on to suggest that strikes and the possible destruction of implements or structures were essentially un-Egyptian and ran counter to whatever religious inspiration Egyptians might have (presumably both Christian and Muslim). Suggesting the important role of the Misr firm in national economic life, the court declared it to be "one of the pillars of our present rebirth [which] has neither overtaxed the workers nor demanded more than they can do, considering that payment was by results."[85] For the workers, of course, income was the key factor, not rates by themselves. In such a situation, the workers will correctly perceive the government officials and the employers as antagonists.

There are three key differences between Mahallah and other textile areas. First is the isolation of Mahallah, and second is its character as the model for the national industry. Because of this distinction, the firm and the government were ready, even anxious, to fight the spread of radical ideas in this area. Third, Mahallah produced primarily coarse cloth for the home market.[86] As a result, Mahallah employed far more unskilled workers than did the plants at Shubra. Yet it retained greater control over any political leadership that might arise among them. The state, which subsidized the Mahallah undertaking, considered Mahallah a critical area in which to fight radicalism and was able to contain it here.[87]

Although Mahallah never developed a left political organization like that in the Shubra area, it was hardly devoid of moves in that direction. In 1942, the workers had far-reaching expectations of the Wafd when Mustafa al-Nahas again became prime minister. The return of the Wafd to power was taken by the workers—even during wartime—as a signal that they could renew the fight to improve their situation, and a strike broke out at Mahallah shortly after Nahas assumed the premiership. Part of the work force struck and was replaced with scabs, whereupon Nahas interceded with the company and the original workers returned to their jobs, with a warning from Nahas

> to keep themselves quiet, act with restraint, and distance themselves from any who would counsel dissension or incite disorder especially in such a grave situation.[88]

After the Wafd had made unions legal in 1942, there had been a rush to form one at Mahallah, and the company had attempted to gain control of it. By November 1942, 6,000 workers had joined the Mahallah union and new members continued to register at the union headquarters. The union had hoped to attract 10,000 members.[89] It succeeded beyond its dreams: it ended up with 17,000 members.[90] The new federation at Mahallah now comprised five unions: the spinning and weaving workers, the ginners, commercial employees, artisan weavers, and a nearby group of linen workers.[91] The increase in the number of workers and the growing importance of the industry gave the textile workers added influence.

The Misr union rapidly became a company union, and probably as a result a focal point for the kind of spontaneous warfare characteristic of the sugar industry in the 1920s and 1930s. In fact, the concern of the company to control the union and the nature of the ensuing struggles suggest that there might have been support for a radical union at Mahallah even if such support had been less than majoritarian.

One of the few survey-research reports from the period indicates the high degree of discontent workers had with the Misr union in 1952.[92] They must have already felt this way in 1947 when almost the entire month of September was engulfed in a bitter strike, whose path can be ascertained in part from published news accounts and in part from the later report. Workers resented work rules that included penalties for lateness, reading newspapers, smoking cigarettes, not wearing pants or shoes, and leaving a post to pray.[93] The underlying issues of the strike itself concerned structural problems of the textile industry: threats to employment, widespread layoffs, and increased workloads coupled with pay cuts. There had been threats that large numbers of skilled workers would be laid off and replaced by less-skilled workers, and these fears were aggravated by foremen who had more or less total discretion to fire.[94] Equally important was an attempt by the company to drastically change the prevailing production norms and thus the game of making out. Specifically, the company sharply cut the piece rate in April 1947 and workers feared further cuts were coming.[95]

The new pay rates were probably an attempt by the company to take advantage of the growing number of skilled and semiskilled workers in the area. As more workers sought jobs, the company could demand more output per worker, which would inevitably tighten discipline in the plant and reduce wages. The company was unilaterally trying to change the rules of making out. Muhammad Hasan al-Ghazawi, leader of a company union formed after the strike, casually defended the practice of paying only 1.75 times the old rate for men who had to tend twice the number of looms, specifically, from two to four looms.[96] Yusuf al-Mudarrik's cryptic comment that the "price" of cloth had gone from 135 to 105 piasters suggests that workers had indeed suffered a 22 percent pay cut by the change in the number of looms to be tended at the same base rate.

In response to the company changes in rules, the union first presented demands that addressed the long-term problems: the union demanded new elections, no fines, no layoffs, a 25 percent wage increase, the participation of union representatives in making up work rules, and paid vacations. The workers then struck in September 1947. Their slogans included not only Down with Yellow Unions but also Down with Colonialism, and Down with Fines as well as Down with Enslavement. Communist newspapers covered the strike extensively and stressed the anomalous situation of a low-wage industrial plant gaining mass support because it was an enterprise ostensibly run in the national interest.[97] The left, which was probably represented among the leadership, attempted to make the strike at Mahallah a national issue, and Yusuf al-Mudarrik, a trade union activist during the war who became the leading Egyptian representative at the founding convention of the World Federation of Trade Unions in 1945, published a pamphlet on the strike. He reported wages and disciplinary measures—especially fines—as the major complaints; workers especially resented a requirement that they pay for certain administrative costs of the company and union each time they were rehired after a layoff, including what was presumably a file card and union card.[98] These procedures, of course, also made it easier for the company to keep track of workers.

The workers at Mahallah had undoubtedly become used to a certain standard of output and resented unilateral company action that changed their work and rates of pay. There was little they could do and the strike

was over by the beginning of October 1947, although it evidently left an
enduring legacy of anger and bitterness. In order to make the changes
stick, the company had to maintain control of the union, and the union
officers were, within a short period, white-collar employees.[99] The foremen and other skilled workers who provided the leadership in Mahallah
were union leaders in other sectors of the economy and their leadership
in Mahallah did not by itself guarantee that the union would be a "company union." The more critical factor at Mahallah was the absence of
an ideological perspective that tied the skilled worker to the operative.
After 1947 the company and the state took special pains to ensure that
such a perspective did not develop. Ironically, the use of fines and probably the threat of suspension helped to create what appears to have been
a powerful sense of class identity among the operatives, even if they
lacked the vocabulary to express this sense.

> The worker obeys orders to avoid fines. Fear of the supervisor is less a factor
> than a conscious attempt not to deprive the family of any portion of income.
> This negative pressure has now created a feeling of solidarity and common
> cause in the labor force and antagonism toward the company. To some ex-
> tent, where there is communication between worker and assistant [foreman],
> the assistant has come to identify himself with the workers.[100]

This sense of class and of class differences (rather than status differences) was plainly apparent, and workers said openly that they "tend to
resent strongly the large differential between themselves and their supervisors and higher management whom they believe receive these salaries at their expense."[101]

The textile workers, especially the skilled workers, viewed the union
as an organization, not just as a self-help group and certainly not as
a charitable association. By 1945 Mahallah was to some extent moving toward the left centered in Shubra. The president of the union at
Mahallah donated L.E. 50 for Yusuf al-Mudarrik's flight to Paris in
1945 to attend the founding of the left-oriented World Federation of
Trade Unions.[102] He also pledged the political support of twenty-six
thousand textile workers. Nevertheless, the layoffs, the concerted activity of the company, and the general anti-Communist atmosphere prevailing after 1946 probably arrested the development of a leftist union.

POLITICAL CONFRONTATION

If the left found its stronghold among the workers in the textile industry, and especially in Shubra, its position was by no means uncon-
tested. As I pointed out earlier, the Muslim Brothers had always had

members and sympathizers active in the textile workers' unions, not least Taha Saʿd ʿUthman, who later became a leading Communist organizer. At the time he entered the union, however, Taha Saʿd's relation with Hasan al-Banna, the founder of the society, was "like that of father and son."[103] Indeed, Taha Saʿd was one of a group whose members were specifically released from their assignments there in order to build the union, for al-Banna agreed that workers should unite against oppression and colonialism. The Muslim Brothers and others who agreed with their philosophy remained active in the union throughout the period of its formation, but the leaders of the union—Taha Saʿd and al-ʿAskari—turned to the left sometime between 1943 and 1945. Taha Saʿd remained a practicing Muslim, as did many of the rank and file, even as he and other activists took another path in their work for the union.

So strong was the Shubra union that the decisive event in its history was, not its formal dissolution by the state in 1945, but the bitter battles of the postwar recession that destroyed production in the area. A series of bitter strikes occurred between late 1945 and early 1946, punctuated by repeated arrests of the top leaders. Although Shubra itself was patrolled by police and the army, militants participated in the major political events of 1946 and in several major strikes. These culminated in a major test of strength with the government and a call for a general strike in mid-1946.

The ill-conceived plan by the Egyptian Communists (who seem to have been influenced as much by Gandhian ideals here as they had been in 1938–1939) to force Britain to quit Egypt economically, politically, militarily, and culturally within a month or face a general strike of the workers had severe consequences for the workers. The strike led not only to formal orders for dissolution but to massive repression coupled with a serious attempt at supplanting the left union by its competition. At this moment the Muslim Brothers were able to assert their organizational strength in the textile industry. The society attempted to retain the formal structure of the Shubra al-Khaima union but to change the character of its organizational behavior, especially the relation of the leaders to the base. Simply put, the society attempted to reintroduce the threat of uncontrolled, spontaneous working-class action as a tool to win demands rather than to oppose unfavorable employer policies with organized and thus responsible disruption.

According to a report entitled "Decisions of the Mechanized Textile Workers Union at Shubra al-Khaima in the Matter of Kastru Factory Workers," the union called the Labour Bureau, which was responsible for looking into layoffs at the Kastru factory, and then gave a three-day notice for solving the problem.[104] If the problem of the layoffs was not ameliorated in three days, the union was "not responsible for any action to which the workers resort." As in the case of ʿAziz Mirhum and the Matossian workers, blackmail may be a useful short-term tactic, but it indicates the weakness of the organization's leadership. Unable to call a prolonged strike, the union threatened to unleash the workers on the plant. The statement was signed by eight union officials representing eight different Shubra factories, one of whom, a pasha, hardly seems to have been elected from the shop floor by his mates.

The basic problem in Shubra, which the brotherhood was aware of and concerned about, was the collapse of the wartime market for textiles produced in Egypt and the consequent collapse of Shubra-based firms. Muhammad Sharif, one of the main writers on labor affairs for the brotherhood's newspaper, alluded to this the day after the ultimatum was given when he suggested that foreign colonialism was trying to destroy both Egyptian industry and (thus) the Egyptian worker, who was despised and oppressed.[105] Because of the deep anger in Shubra, Sharif concluded, it was hardly possible to counsel restraint there, and on the third day of the ultimatum the police were called out to do something immoral, namely, to restrain the "righteous anger of the masses."[106] Sharif differentiated the union from the masses and suggested that police action was aimed at the former and not the latter.

As a tactic, union leaders often publicly deny what they condone in practice—violence by the members—and violence, especially against industrial plants, usually indicates a weak union. In reality the Muslim Brothers were far from being the clear leaders of the textile workers. A leaflet distributed by Communist trade unionists in Shubra at this period denied the Muslim Brothers' claims not only to represent the workers but even to have formed effective trade union committees.[107]

The Muslim Brothers used tactics that were effective against their enemies in the short run, but caused them significant problems in the longer term. For example, they turned over Communists to the police.[108] In the volatile and often violent situation in Alexandria at the time, the Muslim Brothers were trying to take advantage of a particularly favorable relation with the police, but this tactic made it impossible for men such as Taha Saʿd ʿUthman to continue to work with their old acquaintances and belied the claim of the society to be a religious and moral association.

The brotherhood was also hampered in its approach to the workers by its own ideology. We can see this in the clumsy strategy adopted for the Sibahi plant that was moved from Cairo to Alexandria to escape the leftist Shubra union.[109] The union elections at the Alexandria Sibahi plant had just brought to office a leadership friendly to the Muslim Brothers.[110] The new union leadership had been elected during a round of fierce strikes, and with the hope that the organization would mediate with the Labour Bureau. The leadership itself issued a statement that they were "only honest workers who did not allow outside agitators among them."[111] Yet when it came to criticizing the owner Sibahi for his labor policies, the Muslim Brothers were ineffective as leaders, except perhaps in terms of what we would call media events. One thousand Sibahi workers went on strike March 6, 1948, after the firing of fourteen new union members, and at least one man was killed by police, but despite a sit-in the workers gained nothing from the firm and remained besieged in the factory until at least March 19 when they sent a telegram to the king, asking for support and vowing to stay put until justice was done.[112] The outcome of the strike is unrecorded.

In dealing with this bitter enemy of workers whose leaders were close to the Muslim Brothers, their newspaper was restrained. One of the few complaints in the newspaper about Sibahi was that he had a chief accountant who was Jewish; as someone of Syrian origins, Sibahi should have been one of the first to chase out the Zionists instead of giving them the opportunity "to suck the blood of the workers."[113] Such an ethnoreligious analysis made sense when it was applied to British and French interests in the large transformation industries such as sugar or perhaps even tobacco. There foreign capital profited and foreign troops remained on Egyptian soil to back up the profit taking. Despite the influence of the Palestine war on popular feeling, however, such ideas did not go far enough in explaining how to win gains in the textile industry. Relying on Sibahi's Muslim and Arab background was not a certain way to win benefits, especially since the Muslim Brothers were not hard on Egyptian owners, who were often more oppressive than the large European firms because they operated closer to the margin. Even in attacking Europeans the Muslim Brothers were selective, for as we saw in the sugar industry foreigners also collaborated with Muslim Egyptians.[114]

It should not be surprising then that the Muslim Brothers were unable to maintain a position of superiority in the textile industry. Even with considerable support from the state and the employers, the Muslim Brothers could not prevent the left from making a comeback. Within a year and a half, the left was clearly on the offensive again in the greater Cairo area. This time, the geographical center of the left was in the Matariyyah-Zaitun area. In the fall of 1947, the left made an attempt to bring together textile worker representatives from Shubra, Mahallah, Cairo, Damietta, and Alexandria to form a national union of textile workers with an eye toward immediately resolving the strike in Mahallah favorably and reopening closed plants.[115] The left as a whole had staying power, and its individual supporters continued to work for trade unions. Muhammad Zahran of Damietta, for example, secretary of the union at the Lozy silk works in that town, reappeared to work with this group of leftists as he had earlier worked with al-Mudarrik. In fact, for many Egyptian workers (unlike the intellectuals perhaps), doctrinal disputes were less important than the continuation of a functioning trade union.

THE WORKERS' GAINS

There were definite affinities between the most advanced section of the industrial work force and the most modern section of the political spectrum in Egypt. Nevertheless, the joint struggle of the textile workers and the left did not result in a true Communist union. If we look at the unified textile workers' contract of 1949, we can see that the situation of the workers themselves made it difficult to achieve the goals of the Shubra militants, who maintained the highest level of wage rates throughout this period.

Workers obviously preferred to celebrate the holidays of their society, and thus fought tenaciously and won such paid holidays as the ʿId al-Adha, the Prophet's Birthday, the Muslim New Year, Coronation Day, Constitution Day, Jihad Day (commemorating the founding of the Wafd), and the particularly Egyptian Sham al-Nissim.[116] They also sought and won preferential hiring of workers' children and official notice that although wages would be based on output, minimum productivity bonuses would be paid to all workers because "family cares" could reduce production below minimum productivity norms.[117]

The textile workers, especially those in Shubra, stand out for their tenacious and often successful struggle to create an independent organization. The textile unions functioned without significant financial or other aid from outside patrons. The Shubra union, for example, was able to collect dues and motivate the members consistently in ways that (as we have seen) were not available to craft workers or sugar workers. The union published its own newspaper rather than relying on the

Wafdist or other press. The textile unions were able to negotiate effectively with a number of owners, and found allies among state officials without sacrificing their own independence. Unlike the tobacco workers and oil workers, the textile workers often faced a hostile state that supported local owners—both Egyptians and non-Egyptian Arabs.

Leninist ideology came to the textile workers in Shubra relatively late in their development of a union and was recognized as a sympathetic ideology rather than adopted as a blueprint. It is apparent from the progress of the Shubra workers before the Communist intellectuals appeared on the scene that local radicalism was open to some form of Marxian orientation and was moving in the direction of organizational behavior based on class lines, which Leninist ideology may systematize but cannot create. The Marxist-Leninist paradigm made less headway outside Shubra for a variety of reasons. In Mahallah and other Delta cities (except Alexandria), the textile industry was too important a part of the state economic strategy for the state to allow leadership of the workers to pass into the probably hostile hands of the Communists. In those cities the work force was often drawn directly from artisan backgrounds (recall the description of Damietta in chapter 3) and was therefore far more enmeshed in a union movement whose tone was initially set by artisan and Wafdist orientations. In Alexandria there was intense conflict between the left and other forces in the union allied with the Muslim Brothers. Here the left more often lost, perhaps for no other reason than that the quality of the leadership was not as high as at Shubra. It is, after all, an argument of this study that organizations are not created independently of real political struggles in which the quality of leadership, the accidents of history, or even chance play a role. The challenges by the left were most successfully articulated in Shubra. In addition to the many factors that have been singled out there was one more: the very instability of production. When the plants were in full swing, owners and managers had to make the best of their situation and produce to the maximum for a highly variable and unstable market. In such moments the skilled and semiskilled workers, who formed the core of the Shubra militants, had far greater bargaining power than their numbers might lead one to expect, even as the Communists in the Egyptian political scene often had influence beyond their numbers.

CHAPTER NINE

Conclusion

An analysis of unions in several industries in Egypt has yielded insights into the world of workers and their relationship with owners and the state that merit greater discussion in order to uncover the implications of these insights. First, the Communists were strong in the textile area north of Cairo and weak elsewhere. This limited influence of the Communists had an important impact on Egyptian politics because it was real enough to threaten other political actors, but it remained too limited to be decisive. Our discoveries about the unions in Egypt have more than a historical importance, for the political problems posed by the Communists in Shubra have again arisen in Egypt.

I began this work with a question rooted in Egyptian empirical reality, but no issue exists in isolation. In the second part of this chapter I shall place Egypt's Communists and industrial politics in a broader perspective than the empirical focus of this book has hitherto allowed. Inevitably this part will have more of the spirit of an agenda for further research than of a completed argument.

COMMUNISM AND EGYPTIAN POLITICS

The Cairene textile industry strongly resembled the world described by Leninist theory. Textile workers in Cairo (and in Kafr al-Dawwar) possessed critically needed skills for an industry that competed in an uncertain environment. These workers therefore lived in that part of Egypt's society and economy in which the most direct and intense struggle between worker and owner occurred. The most highly skilled textile work-ers, many of whom were foremen, had formal education as well as skills learned on the job. Both the education and the skills were in relatively short supply in an industry in which labor in general accounted for a high proportion of the value of the product. For Shubra workers unem-ployment meant little more than seeking work elsewhere. There was a clear and evidently accurate belief that they could get other jobs if fired for insubordination as long as the general economy was strong.

Employers had a different perspective. Employers felt a constant need to drive down wages and use the available skills as fully as possible in order to compete with foreign producers for the top of the textile mar-ket. The textile industry itself was, moreover, widely seen as the cutting edge of important national policies designed to change Egypt's status in the world and in the international market. The textile manufacturers could therefore count on the acquiescence if not active support of state officials when it was necessary to limit the economic gains of workers.

The conflict between workers and owners became intense because even though the textile industry was profitable, it never had the reserves of the large monopoly or quasi-monopoly firms in the tobacco or oil industries that allowed companies to make significant concessions to the workers. The instability of the market for fine textiles also gave the struggles over wages and conditions a sharper tone. From the point of view of the owners, skilled workers were in an enviable position, but all concessions given workers at the height of the demand for woven goods might mean ruin for the owners at a lower point in the cycle. From the point of view of the workers, concessions given up in low periods were unlikely to be easily won back later.

In addition to the struggles over economic issues, workers and owners struggled over political issues in the plant and the nature of the author-ity exercised in the factories. Everywhere the workers—especially the skilled workers—opposed the unrestricted rule of the owners. In so doing, the workers opposed, by means of distinct ideological formula-tions, physical and verbal abuse from the owners or their immediate agents. Workers also attempted to create alternate forms of authority in the plant to ensure that some workers would not be used against others. Thus, the skilled workers were always aware that they might be training their own replacements not only in the long term but also in the short term of an upcoming strike or lockout. In the textile industry, lead-ers such as Taha Sa'd 'Uthman were acutely aware of such problems early on.

In most of the industries examined, workers faced with such challenges were able to find significant (and inexpensive) resources in the social framework of the community from which they were drawn. In the sugar communities, in the oil fields, and even in the tobacco industry as well as among the artisan communities, already existing dense social networks sustained outside the factory nourished the unions. The textile workers were the exception. The growth of the towns in the Shubra area, for example, was quite recent, and though there were undoubtedly young communities of immigrants (Taha Saʿd and Faddali ʿAbd al-Jayyid were probably of such a community), they lacked easy access to a network that offered both solidarity and sanctions. Only a stable bureaucratic organization could provide the necessary social cohesion. But such organizations, unlike those of Halim or the Wafd, had no easy access to funds that would allow them to provide economic incentives to join the union. Rather textile workers were forced to discover methods that could convince workers to provide resources for the union on a regular basis.

Many of the unions created in the 1940s were thus stable, bureaucratic organizations. The workers of the Shubra area were not the only ones to recognize the need for a stable bureaucratic organization: the oil workers, led by a member of the Muslim Brothers, created such an organization. What was unique to Shubra was the ability of the workers and leaders to create such an organization without recourse to other resources and thus independent of other commitments. The Shubra union was independent of the political parties and of the need for stable employment. It was highly dependent, however, on the conscious support of the members. Yet only this type of political commitment could have nourished a union in Shubra: owners were not only antagonistic to unions in general but could see no way in which they could gain by cooperating with each other or procompany unions. Thus no union organization predicated on an alliance with the owners could survive.

The Shubra workers had to create their own union, and Leninist ideology provided the tool by which that impossible feat could be accomplished. By explaining why workers had to rely on themselves and by providing a supreme example of what workers could do when they did rely on themselves (making a revolution), Leninism tapped spontaneous political energy and channeled it directly into an organization rather than a charismatic leader or a government party, which was the case with the other political organizations in Shubra. The Muslim Brothers also tapped such energies, but were uncertain how to use them as well as against whom when the antagonists were not clearly identifiable as alien.

I have not discussed whether or not the textile workers' leaders were good Leninists. It might be argued that they were not good Leninists by contemporary standards: they were certainly not apt followers of the Zhdanovite Stalinist theories of a world completely split between socialism and imperialism in the 1946–1948 period. It might be suggested that they were more akin to left nationalists than to "true" Leninists. To so argue, I believe, misses the point. These men were the embodiment of Leninism as it existed in Egypt. They had a well-developed sense of Egypt as a world of antagonistic social classes that were not necessarily bound together in national union; they also clearly viewed the political independence of workers' organizations as critical to their success, and saw the transformation of the state as a necessary goal. Finally, they had been invited to the founding of the World Federation of Trade Unions in Paris in 1945, certainly an instance of an international cachet. Unless Leninism is to be reduced to the expressed policy of the Soviet Union or unless Western analysts wish to administer tests of orthodoxy (a paradoxical situation), we must accept as Leninists those who call themselves so, especially when they are accepted as such by the Communist movement.

Outside the textile industry, conditions were never very favorable to the extension of Leninist leadership. In instrumental or in normative terms, few other workers were likely to be attracted to Leninist movements. The artisans, owners of tools and possessors of expertise, might have been attracted to radical ideologies, but their resources were extremely limited. Even if European penetration of the Egyptian market did not destroy craft production, as has sometimes been alleged, it did push it into successively less-skilled and less-profitable activities. Egyptian metalworkers were more likely to be tinkers or smiths in light metals than the skilled blacksmiths who formed the basis for production of large engineering industries such as steel or vehicles. This was not the result of artisan choices, but probably simply a response to the relative weakness of the Egyptian state in relation to imports of foreign goods.

In other situations, workers may have confronted that important character in any economic history—the capitalist system—but they often did so with the state as a potential ally. The oil workers did not lack militancy but Leninist ideology would have been of little instrumental value, for it would have antagonized friendly state officials, and the capitalist company they faced was more easily conceptualized as a culturally alien entity than as an institution structurally similar to an Egyptian-owned firm, especially when most of these firms were, as I have shown, extremely small.

Clearly what counts in determining the political orientations of workers and their organizations is not simply the organization of the productive process itself or the attitude of the state toward "workers" as a category. Rather what counts is the orientation of the state to the particular industry or even firm and especially toward the "rules of the game" in the plant. For example, oil workers were never, it seems, favorably disposed toward the left in Egypt, but this is not true in other countries. It may be that where oil workers are favorably disposed toward Leninist leadership, as in Iran or Iraq, the state does not seek the workers as an ally against the firm, but rather is an ally of the firm against the workers. The Iraqi state, in its contracts with the oil companies, did not make strong demands in the mid-1940s comparable to those of the Egyptian government.

Clearly there were not many areas in which we might expect Leninist unions to develop. And even among groups most supportive of the Communists, their numbers were not large. There were probably not more than several hundred Communist textile workers among 125,000 men, women, and children in the industry about 1947, and these thousands were in turn a tiny minority among the millions of economically active Egyptians. Nevertheless, the Communists are important for two reasons. First, the textile mills were often situated in the fast-growing industrial suburbs, where Egyptian-owned industry was also growing. In this instance, Shubra (on the outskirts of Cairo) or Ramlah (in Alexandria) might have been similar in the concentrations of workers to the Vyborg suburbs of Saint Petersburg: the Communists' influence as trend setters was greater than their influence at any single moment. Rather like borrowers on a margin, the Communists in moments of crisis had tremendous leverage on the capital or Alexandria far beyond their numbers. One example was during the shocking government failure in the aftermath of the Palestine War when the whole state was in disarray. In fact in the mid-1940s, from the first massive left-led demonstration of workers in 1942 until the confrontation of students and workers with the police and troops in February 1946, this is how urban mass politics actually worked in Cairo.[1]

The Communists were a steady influence in the trade union movement over several years. They participated in and even on occasion called together larger numbers of unions. The union in Shubra attempted, with some success, to organize other workers in their geographical area. Certainly union leaders expected these unions, which depended on the textile union for support, to remain politically allied with the Shubra union and they expected the members of such unions to be available for political action in support of the leaders of the Shubra union. Damanhur Shubra, one of the strongholds of Faddali ʿAbd al-Jayyid in the 1945 election, was not only an area in which textile workers lived but also the area of the boatmen's union.

Perhaps more important for Egypt than the strength of the Leninists (which appeared worrisome but not overwhelming to opponents in the postwar period) was their weakness. The Communists were far too weak between 1945 and 1952 to have contended directly for the power to remake the state. Certainly wherever the working class gained any power under Leninist leadership, the leaders have insisted that the government recognize the demands of skilled workers in critical sectors of national industrial life, especially demands related to stable employment. The Communists were also too weak to maintain an identifiable and distinct political party in an open political arena. The different Communist groups with a base in various textile areas had no strategy to form a single united political party. After the Free Officers' coup in 1952 the tendency of the government was to eliminate independent groups and the various institutions that supported them. If the left had represented a stronger and more politicized base, the government might not have destroyed open political conflict in Egypt. And this step was a critical factor in the breakdown of the Egyptian economy and polity today.

Between 1952 and 1954 when the Egyptian parliamentary regime was finally destroyed, the Free Officers under Gamal Abdel Nasser attempted to assert their control over the entire Egyptian political arena. In the final showdown in 1954, Nasser won over significant sections of the trade union movement, especially those based in the transport unions, which historically had been open to nationalist leadership. A general strike in support of Nasser sealed not only the fate of parliament but of an independent trade union federation, and the entire workers' movement became what parts of it had been before: an instrument of state policy against foreign-owned firms.[2]

The loss of independence had an economic as well as a political price: the ability to bargain over making out disappeared. The loss of trade union independence seems to have been compensated for in two ways: rising incomes and what can only be called tenure. Real wages rose from 1954 until well into the 1960s.[3] This was in part because of actual raises given workers, in part because of subsidies, and in part because of increased fringe benefits. More importantly, workers gained a firm hold on their jobs and it became difficult (if not impossible) to fire them for economic (as opposed to political) reasons. Guaranteeing the job is one of the few functions of the unions today, along with channeling benefits and preempting an independent workers' movement. This right of the workers not just to a job but to the position they currently hold, at least in the public sector, is considered one of the most important steps of the workers under the post-1952 regime by activists such as Jamal al-Banna and is fully in accord with their understanding of how a truly ethical and Islamic national economy should work.[4]

This situation probably developed in part because the Free Officers never changed the personnel of the various state offices, but rather attempted to use them for their own policy ends; and in part because the Free Officers were carrying out a policy that generations of nationalists had wanted. Before 1952, the companies had complained bitterly about the personnel of the state administration.

> With the conciliation commissions under Fuʾad Cherine, the owners were at the mercy of the officials whose principal shortcoming was pro-Egyptian demagogy, but after the reform of the conciliation and arbitration commissions [under the Free Officers] we have seen some of them animated by a desire to judge justly.[5]

Fuʾad Shirin was a Wafdist official who often intervened favorably for the workers' movement, and he is mentioned favorably by al-ʿAskari, who called him an "honest nationalist."[6]

The army officers streamlined the labor conciliation process, and though it benefited industrial managers, it did not improve relations with foreign owners. Whatever the intentions of the Free Officers may have been, those relations were rapidly to get worse. The government was soon to nationalize broad sections of Egyptian industry, and the old officials, not the politicians, would help. Although men like Shirin were removed from high office, many administrative personnel of a slightly lower rank remained in place and provided continuity, such as Sawi Ahmad Sawi, who had been a labor department inspector before 1952 and became a trade union official afterward, or Ibrahim Nusayr, a policeman who was fired in 1951 for being too prolabor but later returned to the police (it seems) with responsibilities for the trade union movement.[7] These administrative officials seem to have been of two types: those who honestly wanted to help the workers and those who were simply out to feather their own nests. It is apparent that both tendencies were widespread by the mid-1960s, for we have allegations that the tremendous quantities of money being passed through the trade union movement for a variety of reasons had already drained it of its original purpose and certainly of much of its former vitality in defending the workers.[8]

Personally I believe workers should get the greatest possible benefits. Unfortunately, as most observers have noted, the Egyptian economy is now extremely inefficient. This is because the Free Officers chose, in essence, to buy off the independence of the trade unions along with a minimum of repression. The leaders seem to have been given good positions and the circumstances of the bulk of the urban work force undeniably improved. Most important, it seems to me, is that the workers were guaranteed an income and seen as having the right to a specific job, as if the job itself were their property just as the workshop of the artisan or the plot of the peasant may be his property.[9] If the worker is perceived and perceives himself as "owning" a job, then it will be difficult to utilize labor efficiently. Of course, there is a more efficient arrangement followed in many East Asian countries, where there are minimum benefits, relatively great repression, and unions control workers for the needs of production. There is also a heavy political price.

It might make more sense to recognize that an independent trade union movement, likely to have significant but by no means total Leninist leadership, could have an important economic as well as political function. The Leninists would not be likely to lead the entire trade union federation; social democracy and, depending on the mix of investment sources and state policies, nationalism (even of a religious orientation) would be strong contenders. This form of trade union independence would not be free, of course; it would have its own price. It would raise the level of overt conflict in society, certainly. Unlike several of the analysts to whom I alluded in the Introduction, who view conflict as inherently unhealthy (a view they share with traditional political philosophers), I hold that raising the level of overt, public, and mass conflict might be healthy. This would make clear, at long last, the true costs of the present (or any) system. As more people know who pays for what and who benefits, there is likely to be more open conflict about who should pay and who ought to benefit. To say that, however, is only to say that politics—not just policies—is the way we resolve problems about ethics, resources, and power. It is self-evident, but it is also—for those who wish a world where the ruling elites decide everything without reference to the institutional and organizational strength of the mass of the population—often difficult to accept.

POLITICS AND THE POLITICS OF WORKERS

I began this book by asserting that it was not a book about Egypt although the empirical material of the book was entirely Egyptian. There is no need to justify this choice, but I should perhaps make explicit an argument that is implicit in many similar books. Can a study of any one country or even two or three yield important information about a topic such as workers and politics? Put so baldly, the question seems unfair.

We routinely grant a wider validity to studies of important issues rooted in the experience of one country. There is a curious degree of fashion involved here if we look at what countries or which periods count for which kinds of questions. England, Brazil, and China, for example, have been the basis for countless studies on capitalism and democracy, dependent development, and revolution, respectively. Researchers rarely probe the realities outside the charmed circle of exemplary cases. This study is an attempt to ask some old questions in a new setting in the hope of learning more about the setting and the questions. In the Introduction I suggested that the standard theories about workers and Communists did not apply to the leaders of unions in one sector of the Egyptian economy. These theories did not explain why these workers became Communists or why they were able to lead an important organization of workers.

The standard theories and explanations tended to see "workers" as a somewhat undifferentiated category and suggested as well that the politics of class was tightly linked to the politics of revolution among workers. This study of Communists and workers in Egypt suggests instead that workers are not an undifferentiated group, which has important implications for analyses drawn from either a Marxist or a liberal tradition. The former tradition suggests that the power relations between worker and owner, at the most abstract level of analysis, over time annuls distinctions between workers unless an effort is made to recreate them. Thus, the argument runs, workers may not be an undifferentiated group, but they ought to be and tend in that direction.

The anti-Marxist tradition reaches the same conclusion in a different way: workers are so highly differentiated in terms of occupation, wages, skills, and the like that the differences cease to be important, especially at the level of politics. Workers—at the most abstract level of analysis— are only economic and political individuals in a world of markets and polls. They are undifferentiated except insofar as the state denies them economic or political rights, that is, integration into the comity and polity.

In both views, workers cannot change the terms of a social contract set by others and have no positive views of their own. Moreover, in the case that implicitly dominates the thinking in both camps, namely, the Russian Revolution, consciousness of social and economic antagonism is seen as leading directly to a desire to remake the state itself. Class consciousness is, in short, presumed to be revolutionary. Yet consciousness of class and even of class antagonism need not logically lead to a desire to remake the state, even if such a progression is ideologically desirable for party leaders. What the Shubra case suggests, in fact, is that groups of workers may become convinced of the reality of class antagonism and thus become conscious of class (as well as status) differences without becoming convinced of the need to transform the state.

What if the workers are conscious of social and class antagonism but do not wish to transform the state? For Leninists and for those influenced by the Leninist theory of revolution or the Russian case material, this is a problem that can be resolved by suggesting either that class-conscious workers (who are *ipso facto* revolutionaries) do not have sufficient consciousness or that the time is not yet right for them to make a fundamental change in the state. This problem of "false" consciousness is, I believe, a nonproblem, and so too are analyses that suggest that workers (in Europe or the third world) have insufficient awareness of class because the colonial experience has made them only too aware of their national identity. It is equally reasonable to suggest that workers can be conscious of class, can see the owners and the state as antagonists, and yet wish to strengthen the formal structure of authority in the plant and in the state rather than trying to change the structure entirely. Viewed in this way, the workers in Egypt (and perhaps elsewhere in the third world) appear to be more interested in the strengthening of formal and legal authority than are the owners or managers who strenuously insist on retaining their personal prerogatives.

If this is so, then it suggests that the historical causality asserted by Edwards in *Contested Terrain* is inverted. Rather than seeing new types of formal authority in the plant and in the polity emerging as the result of the challenges of workers to the owners, we should see them as the very essence of the challenges themselves. I shall not pursue this argument here; I wish merely to leave open for investigation the question of which social group actually pursues the strengthening of what Max Weber called legal-rational authority. Paradoxically, this means that the

Communists themselves (or other working-class radicals) may be forces for the stability of formal patterns of authority in the plant and outside it.

Another question pursued in this analysis concerns the nature of the markets for labor in Egypt. Much of the literature on labor market segmentation has been concerned with why and how labor markets are segmented: are ascriptive criteria used to exclude some workers, or are some markets inherently imperfect, or does what is called labor market segmentation really reflect significant differences in the ability of some groups to gain desirable skills? Certainly all three options appeared in Egypt (and probably did and still do in other parts of the world). At some periods Egyptians were excluded from some positions; at other times and probably quite commonly the labor markets were extremely thin at best and operated within restricted sets of employers and potential employees; at other times it was almost impossible to conceive of Egyptians (or some Egyptians) learning the skills needed for some jobs.

If Egyptian workers and especially the skilled textile workers were interested in expanding the role of formal authority in the factories and the state, they seem to have been less uniformly interested in changing the labor markets. Certainly the skilled workers wished to end any formal prohibition on what positions could be held by Egyptians; certainly, too, less-skilled workers were interested in acquiring skills. There was less unanimity, however, on increasing the supply of skilled labor or even on opening up recruitment for some positions to other workers. In fact, the workers seem to have used whatever social or political instruments they had to limit the openness of the labor markets. If Qena supplied workers to the oil industry, for example, there seem to have been no demands to open up recruitment to communities in Aswan or Asyut. The skilled workers wished to control the entry of other skilled workers into the market, and even the less-skilled workers who had privileged entry to an industry often wished to restrict the market.

Clearly skilled workers especially (but others in settings such as Egypt) had ambivalent and even contradictory perceptions of capitalism. The workers wished to limit the power of owners inside and outside the factory. The struggle to limit the power of the owners in the factory and outside it in the political arena led to a desire to strengthen the formal apparatus of authority. The struggle to limit the power of the owners also, however, entailed an attempt to limit the spread of formal markets for labor. Certainly the Egyptian workers and perhaps those in the third world at large have an ambivalent view of the formal behavior associated with capitalism: they welcome the extension of formal patterns of authority that limit the power of the owner, whereas they wish to retain less developed patterns in terms of markets, which also limit the power of the owner. If we combine the way workers look at the extension of formal authority in and outside the plant with the way they look at markets, we can see more clearly the evolution not only of Nasser but of other third-world regimes.

In the heyday of modernization theory it seemed plausible that societies developed in a more or less unilinear fashion with greater and greater weight on formal, rule-governed authority and with greater and greater economic efficiency. One persistent line of attack on modernization theory grew out of studies of Latin America (and perhaps secondarily South Asia) and suggested that such easy and unilinear patterns of development were not valid descriptions of the real experience of real countries. The proliferation of dependency theories and their transformation into more sophisticated perceptions of the relation between ex-colonial countries and the colonial metropoles have certainly expanded our understanding of political change in the third world.

Today in our attempt to understand how industrial growth occurs and its relation to politics, our attention turns either to the countries of the Pacific Rim or to the largest of the Latin American countries, Brazil and Mexico. If Egypt is not an advanced industrial society today, then it counts merely as one of the losers in the race for economic and political power. But if Egypt is not an advanced industrial society or even a moderately industrialized one, it is not for lack of trying. The Wafd, Isma'il Sidki, the Communists, and a large number of investors wanted Egypt to become far more of an industrial society than it was or is.

But this is not a book about industrialization or economic policy or even development. It is a book about the politics of workers. And viewed from the perspective of the thirty years since the end of the parliamentary regime and the Free Officers' coup, we must conclude that the politics of workers count even in policy areas where they have no direct say. Insofar as states can satisfy the demands of workers by changing the rules of discipline in the factory and outside it, they can also destroy the independent organizations of workers. In the case of the Nasser regime, ending both internal and external forms of discipline by essentially guaranteeing jobs had negative effects on the economy as a whole. What happened under Nasser was by no means peculiar to Egypt, but rather endemic to the third world.

The workers did not themselves propose the solutions to the problem of class struggle that Nasser's regime developed. Nevertheless, those so-lutions created tremendous support for his regime. Even those workers who explicitly connected issues of authority in the plant with the politi-cal arrangements of the system as a whole supported Nasser in the end. Those for whom the nature of authority in the plant and in society as a whole was less clear, or more highly personalized, supported him ear-lier. What may well be worth further investigation is the degree to which the bargains struck by workers to gain victories in a limited and imme-diate sense over their class antagonists also limit any eventual exit into the world of industrial power so desired by elites and nonelites.

Notes

CHAPTER 1

1. Regarding Egypt, there are several arguments along this line, notably Mahmoud Hussein, *Class Conflict in Egypt, 1945–1970* (New York: Monthly Review Press, 1973), and Anouar Abdel Malek, *Egypt: Military Society* (New York: Random House, 1968). Amin ʿIzz-al-Din follows a similar approach in his extremely important three volumes on the history of the Egyptian urban working class, *Tarikh al-tabaqah al-ʿamilah al-misriyyah mundhu nashaʾatiha hattah sanat 1919* (Cairo: Dar al-ʿarabi li al-kitab, n.d.), *Tarikh al-tabaqah al-ʿamilah al-misriyyah min sanat 1919 ila sanat 1929* (Cairo: Dar al-shaʿb, 1970), and *Tarikh al-tabaqah al-ʿamilah al-misriyyah fi al-thalathinat* (1929–1939) (Cairo: Dar al-Shaʿb, 1971). See also the somewhat less sophisticated and complete work by ʿAbd-al-munʿim Al-Ghazzali, *Tarikh al-harakah al-niqabiyyah al-misriyyah min sanat 1899 ila sanat 1952* (Cairo: Dar al-thaqafah al-jadidah, 1968). In general I shall not refer to these works, not because they are without value, but because I have referred to original sources wherever possible and because for much of the analysis that follows their coverage simply does not conform to the demands of this study. A variant of this argument is that time alone is the decisive factor in how workers develop a sense of class. See Jacques Couland's "Regards sur l'histoire syndicale et ouvrière égyptienne (1899–1952)," in *Mouvement ouvrier, communisme, et nationalismes dans le monde Arabe*, ed. René Gallisot (Paris: Editions Ouvrières, 1978). A sustained argument in this vein may be found in Robin Cohen and Richard Sandbrook (eds.), *The Development of an African Working Class* (London: Longman, 1975), which considers workers in other parts of the third world.

2. Of contemporary Egyptian analysts and historians, Nawal ʿAbd al-ʿAziz Radi certainly makes a good case for such an approach in her study of the workers at the workshops of the Egyptian State Railway; she argues, with consider-

able merit, that these workers were tightly linked to the nationalist movement. The problem for her is the opposite of the one I pose for myself: Why were other workers not so tightly linked? See her *Adwaʾ jadidah ʿala al-harakah al-niqabiyyah* (Cairo: Dar al-nahdah al-ʿarabiyyah, 1977). Raʾuf ʿAbbas seems to have changed his position somewhat between *Al-harakah al-ʿummaliyyah fi misr min sanat 1899 ila sanat 1952* (Cairo: Dar al-katib al-ʿarabi, 1968) and his more recent *Al-harakah al-ʿummaliyyah al-misriyyah fi dauʾ al-wathaʾiq al-britaniyyah min sanat 1924 ila sanat 1927* (Cairo: ʿAlam al-kutub, 1975), and now seems more inclined to see workers gravitate toward nationalism than to Marxism, although this may be so only because the second study is of British documents from a period when the Wafdist national movement was far more important in British eyes than the recently smashed Communist movement. There are also books in English on Egypt specifically and on this phenomenon generally. Let me limit these remarks to a few. See, for example, Willard Beling, *Modernization and African Labor* (New York: Praeger Publishers, 1965), as well as his earlier *Pan-Arabism and Labor* (Cambridge, Mass.: Harvard University Press, 1961). More general sources along this line are Ukandi Godwin Damachi, *The Role of Trade Unions in the Development Process* (New York: Praeger Publishers, 1974), and Jacques Berque's article "Classes Sociales," in *De l'Euphrate à l'Atlas* (Paris: Editions Sindbad, 1978). Of course, any of the numerous studies of the labor movements in Latin America, especially Peronist Argentina, would make a point similar to Radi's with equal force.

3. This is the argument provided in general terms by Chalmers Johnson, *Revolutionary Change* (Boston: Little, Brown, 1966). Johnson suggests peasants are most likely to be affected by such a process and his earlier work, *Peasant Nationalism and Communist Power* (Stanford: Stanford University Press, 1962), makes such an argument in depth. According to this analysis, we should expect peasants in factories to be most amenable to Communist leadership because they would experience the greatest disruption of their living patterns. A similar argument is that of Samuel Huntington in *Political Order in Changing Societies* (New Haven: Yale University Press, 1969) and of Ervand Abrahamian in *Iran between Two Revolutions* (Princeton: Princeton University Press, 1982). The argument here is that modernization did not so much destroy a previously stable society by tearing it apart as by creating new forms of power through social mobilization. In each case political unrest develops, not because of conflicting interests arising from inherent social conflict, but because of a lack of "balance," an analytically vague concept. I do not believe any Egyptian scholars have adopted a framework like this for writing about the development of the Egyptian working class. Discussion of the problem of loss of "balance" and of the ways in which Western colonial practices disrupted a previously stable society was not uncommon in Egyptian literature of the period. See, for example, Hasan al-Banna's *Mudhakkirat fi al-daʿwah wa al-daʿiyyah* (Cairo: Dar al-shabab, 1977), or the extremely popular story by Yahya Haqqi, *Qindil Umm Hashim*, or any of several early novels by Tawfiq al-Hakim.

4. One of the earliest and still best analyses linking millenarian appeals and revolutionary theories is Eric Hobsbawm's *Primitive Rebels* (New York: Norton, 1959); elements of this approach may be found in studies of Arab societies

and revolutionary movements. Although there are no scholarly works in this framework on the Egyptian working class, the framework was considered a plausible explanation by observers at the time. See for example Salih Mikhail's *Al-siyasiyat al-qawmiyyah wa al-duwaliyyah bayna al-shuyuʻiyyah wa al-ishtirakiyyah wa hurriyyat al-tabaddul* (Cairo: Maktabat al-nahdah al-misriyyah, 1948). As the English translation of the title indicates (National and international policies between Communism, socialism, and the free market), the work represents an avowedly capitalist defense of the workings of the market. For workers' expectations on wages and for the degree to which workers turned a favorable situation during World War II into a moral expectation, see Salih Mikhail, pp. 22–23. A similar approach in English is found in Manfred Halpern's *The Politics of Social Change in the Middle East and North Africa* (Princeton: Princeton University Press, 1963). An earlier form of this approach occurs in Bernard Lewis's article "Communism and Islam," in *The Middle East in Transition*, ed. Walter Z. Laqueur (New York: Frederick A. Praeger, 1958).

5. Walter Laqueur suggests this approach in *Communism and Nationalism in the Middle East* (London: Routledge, Kegan Paul, 1961).

6. See Michael Burawoy, *Manufacturing Consent* (Chicago: University of Chicago Press, 1979), p. 51. There is a ceiling of 140 percent, "imposed and recognized by all participants."

7. Ibid., p. 64.

8. There are only hints of this in Burawoy, but it clearly is important in establishing to whom he turned for support. See ibid., p. 88.

9. Ibid., pp. 98–99.

10. Ibid., p. 98.

11. Richard Edwards, *Contested Terrain* (New York: Basic Books, 1979).

12. Ibid., p. 131.

13. Ibid., especially pp. 57–58. Edwards cites "increasing costs" of direct methods of control as well as "day-to-day resistance" to "oppressive jobs."

14. Ibid., p. 63.

15. Ibid., especially p. 132.

16. In this regard an ancillary question raised but left unanswered by Burawoy, Edwards, and Sabel remains: To what degree is the shaping of discipline in the plant the result of initiatives by the workers as well as the result of decisions by the owners whether for reasons of "worker resistance" or for reasons of economizing on control costs? In my view, the evidence shows that the world of the factory and its administrative discipline is to an important degree the result of workers' efforts to rationalize the work place in the face of opposition from owners. This question would be worth pursuing from a comparative framework if we had more studies on the various types of work administration and the forms of worker politics.

17. Edwards, *Contested Terrain*, p. 179.

18. Charles Sabel, *Work and Politics* (Cambridge: Cambridge University Press, 1982), p. 1.

19. Ibid., p. 78.

20. Ibid., pp. 102–103.

21. A "career at work [is] a series of remunerative tasks that successively

challenge and require the development of whatever powers one takes as the measure of human worth." Ibid., p. 80. Sabel suggests that different groups measure
worth differently. I suggest that what is also important is the perceived length of
the series and the perceived difficulties involved in moving along the chain.

CHAPTER 2

1. Some male city dwellers who got their hands dirty were not Egyptian.
Most of them were Greeks or Italians, and a few were of other nationalities.
Although these men were part of the working class in the classical Marxist
framework, they were not usually considered workers by Egyptians. Their
wages were usually higher and they often had more responsible positions; as
long as foreigners could claim extraterritorial privileges, these men were subject, not to Egyptian law, but to the law of their home country. They may, in one
sense, have shared the class situation of Egyptians, but they were of a different
social status. It is therefore important to understand who was regularly considered part of the Egyptian working class, for even though European Marxists
played a role in the formation of unions and political parties, they were not routinely thought of as an organic part of the Egyptian proletariat.

2. Cairo streets often empty on Friday afternoons, but by the time of the national championships, especially if the Ahli and Zamalik clubs are in contention, they can be as deserted as American streets on Superbowl Sunday. This
now common national orientation to sports did not come about without significantly altering social habits.

3. *Dalil Dumyat*. See pp. 161–163 for descriptions of the various clubs and
their proprietors.

4. See *Mu'tammar al-niqabiyyin*. *Al-'Amal* even claimed that Halim became
active in the labor movement because he wanted the workers to be able to have
the free time to enjoy sports. While this is an absurd reason for Halim's support
of the labor movement, it is an interesting illustration of what some trade union
leaders considered plausible. See *Al-'Amal*, November 24, 1947. I shall refer
again to Halim, for he was on the scene of the trade union movement for a fairly
long time. He was interested in the trade unions for reasons of his own, and was
certainly in no way even a committed reformer of the aristocracy, let alone something on the order of a Red Prince. He may have entertained ambitions for the
throne.

5. See *Al-Ikhwan al-Muslimun*, November 30, 1947.

6. Ibid., September 15, 1946.

7. Ibid., November 26, 1947. The popularity of the matches between union
teams should not be underestimated. The leftist *Al-Damir* congratulated the
players on a successful team fielded by the Shubra boatmen's union on a cup
match. See *Al-Damir*, November 28, 1945.

8. Regardless of whether or not this story is true, it was extremely popular.
Both Muhammad 'Ali 'Amir and Hasan 'Abd al-Rahman told me about this incident. 'Ali 'Amir recounted with some relish Halim's use of the heavy Egyptian
police whip, the *kurbaj*, in the event. Personal communications.

9. Muhammad 'Ali 'Amir was, and remains, a moving and eloquent speaker

for whom *balagha* ("eloquence") is important. Personal interview, Cairo, January 1981. For other working-class figures, such as Taha Saʿd ʿUthman, however, it is more important to speak "in plain Arabic."

10. *Al-Jamahir*, May 26, 1947.

11. The workers occasionally wrote in a more elevated form, *qasidah*, and were often deluged with poems in this form from educated persons outside their ranks, but clearly it was not their preferred form. See, for example, the poem written in the form of a *qasidah* and published in honor of Makram ʿUbayd, one of the most important Wafdist politicians associated with the unions; it included the verse "to the great fighter and pride of the bar / how great is the honor of the unions in your hands!" *Al-Misri*, December 12, 1938. The April 26, 1942, general meeting of the textile workers' union had Maghrabi give a poem immediately after the main report. *Shubra*, April 30, 1942.

12. *Al-Damir*, November 14, 1945.

13. For Bayram al-Tunisi's poem *Al-ʿamil al-misri* (The Egyptian worker) see *Turath Bayram al-Tunisi* (Beirut: Manshurat al-maktabah al-ʿarabiyyah, n.d.), pp. 64–65.

14. See Taha Saʿd ʿUthman, *Mudhakkirat wa wathaʾiq min tarikh ʿummal misr: al-kitab al-thani* (Cairo: Maktabat Madbuli, 1982[?]), pp. 124–125.

15. There is some quantitative evidence for this speculation. According to Hasan al-Saʿati, *Al-Tasniʿ wa al-ʿumran* (Cairo: Dar al-Maʿarif, 1958), one sample of Alexandrian workers indicated that about 31 percent spent daily time off in cafés, 49 percent at home, and only about 6 percent in religious observances. The figures are not appreciably different for the weekly day off. See pp. 267–270. This has probably been the case since coffee was introduced in medieval times. See Roger S. Hattox, *Coffee and Coffeehouses* (Seattle: University of Washington Press, 1985), pp. 122–124.

16. See Kamal ʿIzz al-Din's memoirs as reported in *Al-ʿAmal* of the 1932 union demonstration: "On a night in *Tuba* [a Coptic month name] in 1932, it was so cold the blood almost froze and the message came to quickly assemble a meeting of the federation of unions, and it being forbidden among the workers to meet publicly . . . we assembled in a café on Falaki Square." *Al-ʿAmal*, October 5, 1946. Again, in ʿIsawi's memoirs, the workers "return" to the cafés after they no longer have their offices in which to conduct meetings. Unpublished memoirs of ʿAbd al-Munʿim ʿIsawi.

17. See al-ʿAskari's memoirs, in *Al-ʿUmmal*, August 29, 1977, on celebrating a successful strike and cementing unity by drinking black coffee together in a café.

18. See Hasan al-Saʿati, *Al-tasniʿ wa al-ʿumran* (Alexandria: Dar al-maʿarif, 1958), pp. 248–249.

19. See *Al-Iʿtisam*, July 22, 1943, for a condemnation. Hasan al-Banna visited cafés to preach to the patrons about the evils of their ways, not to discuss religion. This is not the place to discuss the meaning of Quranic verses regarding alcohol, but it is apparent from the public press and movies at the time that drinking was not uncommon. Among taxicab drivers, for example, drinking and sex were fairly common recreational activities. Hasan ʿAbd al-Rahman, Personal interview, Cairo, February 1980.

20. It would be interesting to know what Copts did about holidays; companies that recognized Christian holidays for European employees must have done so according to the contemporary calendar, which is not the one used by the Coptic church. Coptic Easter, for example, does not coincide with Roman Easter. I have found no discussion of this question.

21. *Al-Jihad*, April 6, 1935.

22. Personal interview, Cairo, February 6, 1981.

23. For a discussion of the term in contemporary colloquial Arabic in Cairo, see Dilworth Blain Parkinson, "Terms of Address in Egyptian Arabic" (Ph.D. diss., University of Michigan, 1982), pp. 377–379. "Being a gadaᶜ has both positive and negative implications. It implies strength, vitality, and ability to control (rather than be controlled by) women, karam 'generosity,' sagaaᶜa 'courage,' and a host of other virtues associated with wiladd ilbalad 'the local boys,' i.e., those who adhere to the local, traditional customs and values. On the other hand, it also implies a certain coarseness, lack of refinement, bullheadedness, and other traits that educated people associate with the term baladi 'local, non-westernized, uneducated.'" Ibid., p. 378.

24. Personal interview, Cairo, March 28, 1981. This discussion lasted for well over an hour and a considerable part of it had to do with defining the word *gadaᶜ*, which I had already heard from other trade unionists.

25. It is remarkable how close personal ties between members of the political elite are, and how small a group it is, even when the people involved take quite dissimilar party positions. For a fictional account of the tightness of the networks involved, see Najib Mahfuz, *Al-Summan wa al-kharif* (Beirut: Dar al-qalam, 1972), p. 48.

26. See *Al-Ikhwan al-Muslimun*, November 30, 1947. The word for "clerk," *muwazzaf*, refers to any level of official position involving literacy.

27. For further argument in this direction see my "Bases of Traditional Reaction: A Look at the Muslim Brothers," *Peuples Méditerranéens/Mediterranean Peoples*, January–March 1981.

28. The author of the book to which I refer, Husni al-ᶜUrabi, had been a leading member of the Egyptian Communists in the 1920s; he left Egypt after the debacle of 1924–1925 and traveled extensively in Europe. His exact political affiliations in the late 1930s are in doubt; but as quotations from his book make clear, he was still in the Marxist orbit in the early 1930s. As I have pointed out before, this is not a study of the history of the left as such.

29. Husni al-ᶜUrabi, *Ma hiya al-niqabah?* (Cairo, 1931). I am indebted to Jamal al-Banna for lending me a copy of this pamphlet.

30. The publisher says in a note that "the working class" is the majority in the Arab East, something clearly not true if *working class* refers to industrial workers, but certainly correct if it includes agricultural laborers and small peasants, as indicated in chapter 3. Al-ᶜUrabi limits his discussion to urban workers.

31. Al-ᶜUrabi, *Ma hiya al-niqabah?*, p. 11.

32. Until now I have used *jamᶜiyyah* to refer to any loosely arranged mutual-aid association. It is perhaps time to point out that the word in the Egyptian dialect can refer to those who regularly contribute to a particular kind of fund. Each member in a group of, say, ten members will give a certain amount, from

piasters to pounds, to a common fund each month and the fund as a whole will be given to a different member each month. It is not clear from the context when this precise meaning comes into play—or even if it does—although al-ʿUrabi may have something like this in mind.

33. *Al-Yaraʿ*, June 15, 1942. The diary entry is said to date from February 1934.

34. Al-ʿUrabi, *Ma hiya al-niqabah?*, pp. 14–15.

35. Ibid.

36. Titled *Niqabat al-ʿummal*, or *Workers' Unions*, the booklet was published in Beirut, and significant sections of the text have been translated in Jacques Couland, *Le Mouvement Syndical au Liban, 1919–1946* (Paris: Editions Sociales avec le concours de CNRS, 1970), pp. 151–161. This translation is from Couland. Shamali may have been influenced by his experience in Egypt in the early 1920s. See Hanna Batatu, *The Old Social Classes and the Revolutionary Movements of Iraq* (Princeton: Princeton University Press, 1982), pp. 382–386.

37. Couland, *Le Mouvement Syndical au Liban, 1919–1946*, p. 155. What I have rendered as "unhealthy" is presumably *ghayr-shaʿbiyyah* in the original or *non-populaire* in Couland's translation.

38. "Al-niqabah fi misr wa kayfa takun," *Al-Yaraʿ*, May 6, 1942.

39. "Al-huquq al-mashruʿah," *Al-Yaraʿ*, July 5, 1942.

40. *Al-Bashir*, October 7, 1950. Jamal is the brother of Hasan al-Banna, Supreme Guide of the Muslim Brothers. Although not himself a member, he lived, as he put it, "in an atmosphere of religion" and is probably typical of intellectuals in what I have called the *mouvance* of the brotherhood.

41. *Al-Jihad*, April 5, 1935.

42. *Al-Ikhwan al-Muslimun*, November 2, 1946.

43. Ibid., November 3, 1947. In chapter 8 I shall indicate more fully left objections to behavior of the Muslim Brothers at this period. Given contemporary Communist views of Sibahi, it is simply impossible to conceive of the left union in Shubra phrasing demands in this way.

44. Ibid., January 29, 1948. The workers are described as poor—*masakin*—analogous to the way Hasan al-Banna described the workers as oppressed.

45. *Al-Yaraʿ*, May 18, 1942. "Due" is my translation for *haqq*. The original reads: *iʿtaʾ kull dhi haqq haqqahi bi-taqsim ʿadil wa tawziʿ sharif*.

46. Muhammad Sharif, former labor editor for *Al-Ikhwan al-Muslimun* and an attorney, used this formulation to discuss *insaf*. Personal interview, Cairo, February 1981.

47. Bernard Lewis, et al., *The Encyclopedia of Islam*, vol. 3 (Leiden: E. J. Brill, 1972), p. 551.

48. Ibid., p. 1236.

49. See *Al-Damir*, November 28, 1945. *Individuals*, as Taha Saʿd uses the word, refers to particular members of the propertied classes. It should be remembered that Taha Saʿd had been a member of the Muslim Brothers as late as the early 1940s. Technically the members of the Shubra union who were part of the group that published *Al-Damir* were not yet actually members of the Communist organization. They were all members of the Workers Committee for

National Liberation, the "national liberation committee." This committee was not a Communist organization, but those who constituted it were clearly well within the Leninist orbit. It was, as a point of unity, specifically not "the preparatory committee for the political party of the working class," that is, a Leninist party, but might have been thought of as a preparty formation. Of course, if people are thinking in such terms they are already close to becoming Leninists, no matter which particular group they finally join. See "Mudhakkirat Taha Saᶜd ᶜUthman," *Al-Katib*, July 1971, p. 175.

50. Interestingly enough Taha Saᶜd uses the word *kufr* for this abjuration, which is similar to an abjuration in Islam.

51. Taha Saᶜd and *Al-Damir* were speaking from the Leninist perspective as it existed in Egypt at the time. If this perspective seems to have similarities to our own, that should not seem too strange to us. In Vietnam at this time Ho Chi Minh was modeling the Vietnamese declaration of independence from France on that of the United States.

52. "Unemployment" appeared in *Al-Damir* for July 8, 1946, and "Nationalism" in the issue of November 7, 1945. The original titles are "*Al-batalah . . . mushkilat al-saᶜah wa al-istiᶜmar al-iqtisadi*" and "*Wataniyyat al-ᶜummal*." "Nationalism" was written by Mahmud al-ᶜAskari and "Unemployment" is unsigned.

53. This is not simply the result of my reading one Leninist article as a guide to policy. Taha Saᶜd ᶜUthman suggests that this was the basic policy line of his particular group. See his memoirs in *Al-Katib*, September 1971, pp. 172–173.

54. *Al-Bashir*, September 2, 1950.

55. Questions on the nature of the capitalists in Egypt and their relation to foreign investors are more fully explored on the political level in Joel Beinin, "Class Conflict and National Struggle: Labor and Politics in Egypt, 1936–1954," (Ph.D. diss., University of Michigan, 1982), and Eric Davis, *Challenging Colonialism* (Princeton: Princeton University Press, 1983).

56. Parenthetically I suspect the reason American concepts of labor management often seemed to be taken up by Egyptians was that pluralist and corporate conceptions of group behavior focused on occupational groups rather than on social classes.

CHAPTER 3

1. Karl W. Butzer, *Early Hydraulic Civilization in Egypt* (Chicago: University of Chicago Press, 1976), p. 109.

2. R. M. Barbour, *The Growth, Location, and Structure of Industry in Egypt* (Washington, D.C.: Praeger Publishers, 1972), p. 57.

3. A. I. Gritly, *The Structure of Modern Industry in Egypt* (Cairo: Government Press, 1948), pp. 366–367.

4. Alan Richards, *Egypt's Agricultural Development, 1800–1980* (Boulder, Colo.: Westview Press, 1982), pp. 162–163.

5. Ibid., p. 159.

6. Annis Dosse, "Modern Egypt Economically Treated" (Ministère de l'Economie et des Finances, Dossier No. F30 687, Archives Economiques and Finan-

ciers, EGYPTE, Typescript). A copy of this report, prepared for British use, was obtained by French sources in Cairo. It probably represents the earliest critical view of Egypt's economic situation by an Egyptian economist. Dosse was a professor at the Ecole de Commerce du Caire.

7. Barbour, *Growth, Location, and Structure*, p. 54.

8. See Harold B. Butler, *Report on Labour Conditions in Egypt with Suggestions for Future Social Legislation* (Cairo: Government Press, 1932), p. 20. Hereafter cited as the Butler Report.

9. Samir Radwan and Robert Mabro, *The Industrialization of Egypt* (Oxford: Clarendon Press, 1976), p. 28.

10. Charles Sabel's remarks in *Work and Politics* (Cambridge: Cambridge University Press, 1982), pp. 83–84, are entirely apposite:

> One implication . . . for the young worker is that his new craft collectively possesses a huge store of concrete knowledge. . . . He [therefore] cancels his past insofar as he now accepts his craft and not the occupation of his parents or schoolmates as the legitimate field in which to demonstrate his capacities.

11. Janet Abu-Lughod, "Varieties of Urban Experience: Contrast, Coexistence, and Coalescence in Cairo," in *Middle Eastern Cities*, ed. Ira Lapidus (Berkeley: University of California Press, 1969), p. 161.

12. S. D. Goitein, *A Mediterranean Society*, vol. 1, *Economic Foundations* (Berkeley: University of California Press, 1967), p. 93. I cite this not so much to show that nothing changed, although vocabulary remained the same for a while, as to show how rapidly the very concept of labor and laborers changed with the introduction of new forms of production in the 1930s.

13. Ibid.

14. André Raymond, *Artisans et Commerçants au Caire pendant le XVIIIe siècle* (Damascus: Institut Français de Damas, 1973), pp. 215–218.

15. Ibid.

16. Gabriel Baer, *Studies in the Social History of Modern Egypt* (Chicago: University of Chicago Press, 1969), pp. 150–151.

17. Mancur Olson, *The Logic of Collective Action*, Harvard Economic Series, 124 (Cambridge, Mass.: Harvard University Press, 1971), p. 68. See especially, "Coercion in Labor Unions," pp. 66–75.

18. The description here is drawn from the 1916 *Report of the Commission on Commerce and Industry* (Cairo, 1922). An English translation of the relevant sections is available in Charles Issawi, *The Economic History of the Middle East, 1800–1914* (Chicago: University of Chicago Press, 1966). My citations therefore will be to Issawi, except in a few instances where the language of the Arabic version is important for the way it implicitly defines workers, work, and industry as late as 1916. In those instances I will use my own translations from the Arabic version: Egypt, *Taqrir lajnat al-tijarah wa al-sinaʿah* (Cairo: Al-Matbaʿah al-amiriyyah, 1925), p. 455.

19. Issawi, *Economic History*, p. 456.

20. Ibid., p. 457. Does the congruence of this outlook with the nonbureaucratic norms that characterize "traditional" society need to be stressed?

21. See Yusuf al-Sibaʿi, "A Contented Fellow," in *The Cobbler and Other Stories* (Cairo: Atlas Press, 1973), pp. 209–232. Several of Sibaʿi's novels deal

with this environment in a similar manner. While Siba'i was by no means a great writer, he was popular and an important political figure under Nasser.

22. See Gritly, *The Structure of Modern Industry*, p. 488.

23. Perhaps the most honest account of this duality of our view of peasants is presented by Robert Redfield in his comments about his work and that of Oscar Lewis in his book *The Little Community*. Unfortunately, although Redfield recognized the duality, he attributed it to idiosyncratic differences between himself and Lewis. For those of us who live in capitalist industrial societies, however, the Fall dates from the destruction of rural society in the eighteenth century, and we are as ambivalent about it as any older divines were about Adam and Eve's ouster from the Garden.

24. Jacques Berque, *Egypt: Imperialism and Revolution* (Washington, D.C.: Praeger Publishers, 1972), p. 54.

25. Ibid., p. 56.

26. The situation of the peasants throughout this period was by no means easy. The village was a means of defense against taxes and the military draft. See Richards, *Egypt's Agricultural Development*, pp. 20–24, for a review of the extreme difficulties under which peasants lived even when overall production was improving.

27. Ibid., p. 65. Richards is referring specifically to workers on the estates known as *izbah*, which include many of those engaged in growing sugar cane.

28. Afaf Al-Sayyid Marsot, *Egypt's Liberal Experiment, 1922–36* (Berkeley: University of California Press, 1977), p. 15.

29. Winifred S. Blackman, *The Fellahin of Upper Egypt* (London: Frank Cass, 1968 [first ed. 1927]), p. 24. Unfortunately anthropology came late to Egypt so we have few descriptions of the peasant world just at the time of the Occupation. Clearly, however, peasant society did not become demonetized over time, and as Eugen Weber points out in *Peasants into Frenchmen* (Stanford: Stanford University Press, 1976), p. 131, peasants are always "avaricious" because they have few coins.

30. Blackman, *The Fellahin of Upper Egypt*, p. 174.

31. Ibid., p. 168.

32. Henry Habib Ayrout, *The Egyptian Peasant* (Boston: Beacon Press, 1963), p. 100.

33. Ibid., p. 108.

34. Ibid., p. 54.

35. Ibid., pp. 96 and 111.

36. See *La Bourse Egyptienne*, February 26, 1934.

37. Butler Report, p. 20.

38. Egypt, *Taqrir*, p. 53.

39. Martin Briggs, *Through Egypt in War Time* (London: Fisher Unwin, 1918), p. 101. The town referred to is Damietta (or Dumyat in Arabic).

40. Unfortunately, although the problem was widely known, there was a tendency in some of the literature of the time to make the autocracy of the foreman a more limited problem than it really was. Thus I shall cite two studies dealing with this problem in the textile industry. It is necessary to do this because the first set of authors cited, Harbison and Ibrahim, saw differences where apparently none existed.

41. William Morris Carson, "The Mehallah Report" (Badr al-Shayn: Ford Foundation, 1953), mimeographed.

42. Gritly, *The Structure of Modern Industry*, p. 484.

43. Frederick H. Harbison and Ibrahim Abdelkader Ibrahim, *Human Resources for Egyptian Enterprise* (New York: McGraw-Hill, 1958), p. 74.

44. Ibid., p. 54.

CHAPTER 4

1. Max Weber, *From Max Weber* (New York: Oxford University Press, 1972), pp. 77–78.

2. Katharine Chorley, *Armies and the Art of Revolution* (Boston: Beacon Press, 1969), p. 19.

3. See Moshe Ma'oz, *Ottoman Reform in Syria and Palestine* (Oxford: Clarendon Press, 1968).

4. See Gabriel Baer, "The Village Shaykh, 1850–1950," in *Studies in the Social History of Modern Egypt* (Chicago: University of Chicago Press, 1969), especially p. 32. As Baer points out, the *shaykhs* and ʿ*umdas* are the agents of the state: *al-ʿumad wa-l-mashayikh hum nuwwab al-hukumah*. Nevertheless, the state had all but lost the capacity to appoint them by the time of the Occupation, the position being subject instead to state ratification of village decisions.

5. Baer, "Submissiveness and Revolt of the Fellah," in *Social History*, p. 101.

6. Robert Tignor, *Modernization and British Colonial Rule in Egypt, 1882–1914* (Princeton: Princeton University Press, 1966), p. 384. Tignor's discussion makes clear that what occurred in 1894 was an opportunity long awaited by both sides to settle the question of who controlled the army and thus who controlled the Egyptian state—the Egyptian dynasty or the British. Not until 1952 would control of the army pass to Egyptians, and this change led to a different political system.

7. Ibid., p. 115.

8. This issue is too complex to go into here, but it seems useful to suggest that the problem was not the nature of the law but who gave legal decisions. In essence Egyptian law had been enough concerned with problems of equity (as had English common law in the eighteenth century when it was still traditional law rendered by justices of the peace); the problem for Europeans was that those who dispensed it were unreliable as far as the likely content of their decisions.

9. Tignor, *Modernization*, p. 126.

10. Herbert Liebesny, *The Law of the Near and Middle East* (Albany: State University of New York Press, 1975), p. 74.

11. Jacques Berque, *Egypt: Imperialism and Revolution* (Washington, D.C.: Praeger Publishers, 1972), p. 130.

12. The reasoning was simply that the company's capital was wholly raised in France in French francs and there was not even a market for its debentures in Egypt when issued. It was thus subject only to French law.

13. It may be difficult to realize today just how completely even the most ordinary governmental functions had been taken from Arabic during the colonial period. Law 62/1942, a measure passed by the nationalist Wafd, is illustrative. The law mandates the use of Arabic for any public documents presented to

state officials or posted. The law provided for fines for heads of companies that did not comply. This was not a purely Wafdist measure. Isma⁽il Sidki, prime minister in 1946 and an early splitter from the Wafd, whose career was closely linked to the palace and Britain, issued an amendment extending the law, so that posted documents in languages other than Arabic could not be larger than the Arabic-language posters. See Egypt, *Majmu⁽at qawanin al-⁽amal fi misr* (Cairo: Al-Matba⁽ah al-amiriyyah, 1954), pp. 49–51 (Laws 62/1942 and 132/1946).

14. Marius Deeb, *Party Politics in Egypt: The Wafd and Its Rivals, 1919–1939* (London: Ithaca Press, 1979), pp. 22–29.

15. There is nothing particularly Egyptian or Middle Eastern about this, and, in fact, it was the peasants who provided the force while the urban working class and middle classes provided the fuse in most modern peasant uprisings. See J. Craig Jenkins, "Why Do Peasants Rebel? Structural and Historical Theories of Modern Peasant Rebellions," *American Journal of Sociology* 88 (1982): 487–514, especially the conclusion on p. 512 that "peasant rebellion might provide the 'dynamite,' but other groups must provide an organizational basis before rebellions become sufficiently large in scale to usher in major political and economic change."

16. See Baer, *Social History*, p. 101, but also ⁽Abd-al-⁽azim Ramadan, *Tatawwur al-harakah al-wataniyyah fi misr min sanat 1918 ila sanat 1936* (Cairo: Dar al-katib al-⁽arabi), p. 66.

17. Material from the archives of the French Foreign Ministry will be referred to with the form M[inistère des] A[ffaires] E[trangères], followed by a volume number, a carton number, and a sheet number. All references are to the K series. MAE K–56–1, Sheet 70. Although one can only wonder at the reports of an official who believes peasants need to be taught to dig holes, one can admire the greater awareness that colonialism could be defeated and had specific weak points.

18. Ibid., Sheet 5.

19. See Baer, *Social History*, p. 101, and Berque, *Egypt*, pp. 307–308. The case mentioned by Baer involves peasant discontent with a leading nationalist landlord, a member of the Wafd national leadership.

20. See Amin ⁽Izz-al-Din, *Al-harakah al-⁽ummaliyyah fi misr min sanat 1919 ila sanat 1929* (Cairo: Dar al-sha⁽b, 1968). The word *jahiliyya* "ignorance" evokes a sense of the unintegrated life among the Arabs before Islam and a consequent need now to incorporate the workers into civil society.

21. Muhammad Anis, *Dirasat fi watha⁾iq thawrat sanat 1919 (Part One)* (Cairo: Al-Maktabah al-anglu al-misriyyah, 1963), pp. 10–11.

22. See, for example, Eric Davis, *Challenging Colonialism* (Princeton: Princeton University Press, 1983). Marius Deeb's chronology of the period in *Party Politics* also generally supports my presentation here, for he divides the years 1919–1939 among an emerging national movement, a constitutional system (1923–1930), a dictatorship of the king and Isma⁽il Sidki, and the decomposition of the Wafd, from 1935 to 1939. In fact this chronology is the basis for his chapters on the Wafd.

23. See Deeb, *Party Politics*, pp. 154–161. Deeb does not seem to have a clear grasp of the links between the labor movement and the Wafd, and thus the reason for the relatively greater Wafd strength in urban areas escapes him.

24. Saʿd Zaghlul, *Athar al-zaʿim Saʿd Zaghlul: ʿAhd wizarat al-shaʿb* (Cairo: Matbaʿat dar al-kutub, 1927), pp. 242–243.

25. The Wafd leadership was primarily composed of large landowners: of twenty-seven members of its "high command" eleven were large landowners. See Deeb, *Party Politics*, p. 69.

26. *Al-Jihad*, January 10, 1935. All references in this section to Mirhum's report are drawn from *Al-Jihad*'s publication of it in this issue.

27. *Al-Jihad*, January 3, 1935. In the state-owned industry firing was an especially common form of retribution for workers who supported the Wafd when it was out of power. The news account, titled "The Workers Fired for Political Reasons," describes a report delivered by ʿAziz Mirhum to the prime minister regarding an incident at the Tursanah in May 1931. The workers not only refused to vote as directed by the then prime minister Ismaʿil Sidki but rioted to boot. The plant was closed for two months and only pro-Sidki workers were later rehired. What Mirhum made explicit to the workers was that "their state" would now give them their much promised due: *waqt al-insaf al-ladhi waʿadatkum bihi dawlatukum fi akthar min tasrih*.

28. *Al-Jihad*, March 30, 1937. Ramlah is a district in Alexandria.

29. ʿAbd al-ʿAziz Bayyumi, a worker at the Matbaʿah ʿAmiriyyah who was interviewed by Nawal Radi for her *Adwaʾ jadidah ʿala al-harakah al-niqabiyyah*, viewed 1935–1936 in just those terms. Given the precarious legal situation of workers in the previous years and Sidki's preference for capital development at the expense of workers' benefits, Bayyumi's viewpoint seems to have a good deal of merit if by *revolution* one means an unexpected and significant change. This view should not be considered unusual in the labor movement at this time. Bayyumi was a well-known figure whose judgment was not disparaged in the trade union movement even by leftists who were critical of the Wafd. Yusuf al-Mudarrik, a prominent activist associated with the Communists and a delegate to the 1945 meeting of the World Federation of Trade Unions in Paris, congratulated such old-line activists as Bayyumi in *Al-Yaraʿ* for May 6, 1942, for having stuck it out for so long in the movement.

30. See ʿAbbas Halim, *Al-ʿUmmal al-misriyyun* (Cairo: Matbaʿat al-abbassiyyah al-hadithah, 1934), p. 13. Halim specifically asserts that this kind of action helped to preserve the crafts in Egypt (p. 19), and was therefore valuable. There is certainly no doubt that the butchers and other craftsmen needed help. For example, in 1935 the butchers in Alexandria asked the municipality to distribute their pay rather than allowing the masters (*muʿallimun*) to do it, so as to ensure that all were paid equally for equal work. See *Al-Jihad*, March 3, 1935.

31. See, for example, Taha Saʿd ʿUthman, "Mudhakkirat Taha Saʿd ʿUthman," *Al-Katib*, September 1971, p. 188.

32. Not all workers blamed Halim, however, not even those who did not particularly care for his leadership in later years. Some unpublished memoirs blame the Wafd.

33. ʿAbd-al-ʿazim Ramadan, *Al-Siraʿ bayna al-wafd wa al-ʿarsh, 1936–1939* (Beirut: Al-muʾ assasah al-ʿarabiyyah li al-dirasat wa al-nashr, 1979), p. 131.

34. *Al-Jihad*, January 3, 1935.

35. *Al-Yara*, June 25, 1942.

36. Unpublished memoir of ʿAbd al-Munʿim ʿIsawi, for example.

37. See Robert Tignor, *State, Private Enterprise, and Economic Change in Egypt, 1918–1952* (Princeton: Princeton University Press, 1984), pp. 130–132.

38. Letter from the French consul Gaillard to the Ministry of Foreign Affairs, dated June 7, 1922 *Ministère de l'Economie et des Finances*, Dossier No. F30 687, Archives Economiques et Financières, EGYPTE.

39. Note from the Ministry of Foreign Affairs to the Ministry of Finance, dated July 6, 1925 *Ministère de l'Economie et des Finances*, Dossier No. F30 687, Archives Economiques et Financières, EGYPTE, item no. 2082.

40. See International Labor Organization Publication, *Informations Sociales*, February 16, 1931. In fact, it was specifically a part of the Office of Public Security. This meant that the unions were essentially subject to the police. Records of the British Foreign Office will be cited in the form F[oreign] O[ffice], with a following record number. FO 371/16125.

41. *Informations Sociales*, February 16, 1931.

42. Butler Report, pp. 22–23.

43. FO 371/17978. The reference here is to a mass rally in front of Halim's palatial residence in downtown Cairo, quite near the British barracks, after the authorities had declared this home off-limits to union members. Two to three hundred workers attempted to enter the house while Halim was in Alexandria and the police attempted to force them out; in the end, twenty-six were arrested and two killed. Halim was arrested later and spent a month in jail, during which he engaged in a hunger strike.

44. FO 371/19070.

45. Bayram al-Tunisi, *Turath Bayram al-Tunisi* (Beirut: Manshurat al-maktabah al-ʿarabiyyah, n.d.). See pp. 214–216 for "Al-Qarn al-ʿishrin" (The twentieth century).

46. This and the following narrative are contained in FO 371/19071 and FO 371/19072 and cover the period between April 29, 1935, and May 3, 1935. Graves distanced himself from the security apparatus in both intramural and outside discussions. He publicly denied aiding the police in their crackdowns on Halim's unions. See *Al-Balagh*, March 4, 1935.

47. See FO 371/17978 for the comment of one official: "It is of course ridiculous to tell Egyptian workmen to lay their complaints before the police. A beating up is all they will get in that quarter." In England, "prima facie Mr. Graves' attitude is preferable to Mr. Keown-Boyd's" because of the known Egyptian antipathy to "unions on the line of U.S. company unions." See FO 371/19069, minutes signed by Somers-Cocks.

48. See Tignor, *State, Private Enterprise, and Economic Change*, pp. 160–161.

49. See, for example, Finance Ministry, Egypt, *Annuaire Statistique de l'Egypte, 1921* (Cairo: Imprimerie Nationale, 1922), pp. 203–222.

CHAPTER 5

1. There was and remains in Egypt a wide range of workers who can be classified under the categories "artisans" and "servants." In the former category

I would include hand weavers, makers of fezzes, and basket weavers (among others); in the latter I would include cooks, barbers, gardeners, launderers, and even the *sufragis*, who still exist in government offices. Although those in the second category often work for wages, their work is so closely linked in a social sense to their employer that I chose here to call them servants rather than service workers. The term *servant* also gives a better flavor of their existence.

2. Gabriel Baer, *Egyptian Guilds in Modern Times* (Jerusalem: Israeli Oriental Society, 1964).

3. Ibid., p. 18.

4. Ibid., pp. 78–93.

5. Charles Issawi, *The Economic History of the Middle East, 1800–1914* (Chicago: University of Chicago, 1966), p. 454.

6. Malikah ʿIryan, *Kitab markaz misr al-iqtisadi* (Cairo: Matbaʿ at Raʿmsis, 1923), p. 77.

7. For a complete list of such crafts and trades see Baer, *Guilds*, pp. 166–176.

8. Baer considers this to have been a feature of guild life. Ibid., p. 27. Even Western craft unions are not organized on less-than-citywide scales.

9. *Nahdat al-ʿummal*, July 25, 1937.

10. Ibid. The leader of the taxi drivers in the late 1940s, Hasan ʿAbd al-Rahman, is still called a *shaykh*. Interview, Cairo, February 6, 1981.

11. *Nahdat al-ʿummal*, August 1, 1937.

12. *Al-Jihad*, January 16, 1935.

13. *Nahdat al-ʿummal*, July 25, 1937.

14. *Al-Jihad*, May 3, 1935.

15. *Al-Ahram*, December 15, 1920. It seems that about two-thirds of these workers were not Egyptian.

16. *Al-Jihad*, April 9, 1935.

17. Mahmoud Amin Anis, *A Study of the National Income of Egypt* (Cairo: Société Orientale de Publicité, 1950), pp. 898–900.

18. Ministry of Finance, Egypt, *Population Census of Egypt, 1947* (Cairo: Government Press, 1954). See pp. 318–324 for figures on duration of employment in the crafts and professions.

19. *Al-Yaraʿ*, March 4, 1943. This newspaper interviewed several union leaders at this time; all of the narrative on Hussayn is drawn from this interview.

20. *Al-Jihad*, March 19, 1935.

21. *Al-Yaraʿ*, November 19, 1942.

22. Thabit is listed as a representative of the workers of the Egyptian State Railway workshops in the seventh report of the Labour Conciliation Board in 1922.

23. *Al-ʿAmil al-Misri*, May 19, 1930. The following narrative is drawn from this source unless otherwise indicated.

24. *La Bourse Egyptienne*, January 5, 1934. ʿAbbas Halim also specifically mentions widespread unemployment among upholsterers. See also ʿAbbas Halim, *Al-ʿUmmal al-misriyyun* (Cairo: Matbaʿat al-ʿabassiyyah al-hadithah, 1934), p. 21.

25. *Al-Wafd al-Misri*, October 2, 1938, and October 25, 1938.

26. *Al-Jihad*, January 9, 1936.

27. Ibid., April 9, 1935.

28. Ibid., May 1, 1935.

29. See note 19.

30. *Al-Wafd al-Misri*, October 26, 1938.

31. *La Bourse Egyptienne*, June 20, 1934.

32. Ministry of Labor and Training, United Arab Republic, *Maslahat al-ʿamal: Idarat al-buhuth al-fanniyyah wa al-ihsaʾ*, Dossier No. 4/6/4/11, items no. 21–26. The dossier contains the court report from the Cairo appeals court regarding disposition of the suit in 1952. The following discussion of the Socony Vacuum oil vendors is taken from this dossier.

33. Many vendors were poor, but not all were. As with any group of tradesmen, routes, connections, and subcontracting all influenced income. Those who sold thousands of cans a month made incomes of well over L.E. 100 a month. The main point is not that many artisans or tradesmen were poor, although many were, but rather that they were self-employed yet dependent on a stronger partner for supplies and on the state for the rules on prices, hours for selling, and the cost of the commodities.

34. See note 32.

35. *Al-Wafd al-Misri*, October 2, 1938.

36. Ministry of Labor and Training, United Arab Republic, *Idarat al-buhuth al-fanniyyah wa al-ihsaʾ: Qism al-tasjil*, Dossier 12/6/4/11.

37. *Al-Thaqafah al-ʿUmmaliyyah*, December 1, 1975.

38. Between 1930 and 1934, according to ʿImara, Halim paid out at least L.E. 7,000 of his own money as "loans" for the various union federations he headed. See Amin ʿIzz-al-Din, *Tarikh al-tabaqah al-ʿamilah al-misriyyah fi al-thalathinat (1929–1939)* (Cairo: Dar al-shaʿb, 1971), p. 104.

CHAPTER 6

1. See, for example, V. I. Lenin, *The Development of Capitalism in Russia*, in *Selected Works*, vol. 3 (Moscow: Progress Publishers, 1967), pp. 541–547, but especially p. 547:

> By destroying the patriarchal isolation of these categories of the population who formerly never emerged from the narrow circle of domestic, family relationships, by drawing them into direct participation in social production, large-scale industry stimulates their development and increases their independence, in other words, creates conditions of life that are incomparably superior to the patriarchal immobility of pre-capitalist relations.

See also Alex Inkeles and David Smith, *Becoming Modern: Individual Change in Six Developing Countries* (Cambridge, Mass.: Harvard University Press, 1974), pp. 155–174.

2. Karl Baedeker, *Egypt* (Leipzig: Karl Baedeker Publisher, 1902), p. 194.

3. Jean Vallet, *Contribution à l'étude de la condition des ouvriers de la grande industrie au Caire* (Valence: Imprimerie Valencienne, 1911), pp. 83–84.

4. C. J. Robertson, *World Sugar Production and Consumption* (London: John Bale, Sons & Danielson, 1934), pp. 83–84.

5. Jean Mazuel, *Le Sucre en Egypte* (Cairo: E. & R. Schindler, 1937), p. 82.

6. Vallet, *Contribution*, pp. 75–78.

7. Ibid., p. 85.

8. See MAE K–56–12 and MAE K–56–13.

9. MAE K–56–12, Sheet 119 verso and 120.

10. MAE K–56–13, Sheet 129.

11. Gabriel Baer, "The Settlement of the Beduins," in *Studies in the Social History of Modern Egypt* (Chicago: University of Chicago Press, 1969). Baer discusses the settling of the Egyptian Bedouin at length. They were almost completely settled before the turn of the century.

12. MAE K–56–13, Sheet 127.

13. MAE K–56–13, Sheet 124.

14. Labour Conciliation Board, *Premier Report* (*August to November 1919*) (Cairo: Government Press, 1919), pp. 6–7.

15. Labour Conciliation Board, *Second Report* (Cairo: Government Press, 1920), pp. 6–7.

16. Labour Conciliation Board, *Third Report* (*March to June 1920*) (Cairo: Government Press, 1920), p. 4. There was also a strike at Kom Ombo.

17. Ibid.

18. Labour Conciliation Board, *Fourth Report* (*July to September 1920*) (Alexandria: Imprimerie Arturo Serafini, 1920), p. 7. A member of the board went to Hawamdiyyah in July 1920 to discuss the interpretation of a cost-of-living adjustment.

19. Labour Conciliation Board, *Fifth Report* (*October to December 1920*) (Alexandria: Imprimerie Arturo Serafini, 1920), pp. 5–6. Some increases were tied to family size.

20. This is drawn from an unpublished memoir written at the Silk Workers Club in Helwan. I presume the manuscript was not written by Hamada and was done in the late 1960s or early 1970s. Jamal al-Banna kindly provided me with a photocopy.

21. Labour Conciliation Board, *Seventh Report* (*July 1921 to March 1922*) (Alexandria: C. Molco and Co., 1920), p. 19.

22. MAE K–63–79.

23. Ibid.

24. *Al-Safaʾ*, April 19, 1931.

25. Amin ʿIzz-al-Din, *Tarikh al-tabaqah al-ʿamilah al-misriyyah fi al-thalathinat (1929–1939)* (Cairo: Dar al-shaʿb, 1971), p. 72. But see also Nawal ʿAbd al-ʿAziz Radi, *Adwaʾ jadidah ʿala al-harakah al-niqabiyyah* (Cairo: Dar al-nahdah al-ʿarabiyyah, 1972), p. 60.

26. In chapter 7 I discuss the same conception among tobacco workers during this period.

27. Sulayman al-Nukhayli, *Al-harakah al-ʿummaliyyah fi misr wa mawqif al-sihafah wa al-sultah al-misriyyah minha min sanat 1882 ila sanat 1952* (Cairo: Ruz-al-yusuf Press, 1968), pp. 160–166.

28. FO 371/2 0115.

29. The few documents of the Suez Canal Company that survive in Paris and bear on the labor movement are enlightening. In the estimate of one anonymous correspondent for the company, the Wafd, as soon as it took office, made clear that it would by no means assist the workers involved in the 1936 affair. Having

helped to bring the Wafd to power, the workers would not benefit, and if the Suez Canal Company authorities knew it, so presumably did the sugar workers. Specifically, "the Wafdists, having come to power and having good relations with the English are not, in what they are involved in, going to exploit the situation." According to the same source, 78 workers were tried; of these, 46 were acquitted and 32 received jail terms of two months to two years. See Archives of the Compagnie Universelle de Suez, File 146, undated typescript.

30. *Al-Misri*, February 16, 1939.

31. Ibid., March 17, 1939.

32. Interview with Jamal al-Banna, Cairo, December 22, 1980. Jamal is the brother of Hasan al-Banna, the founder of the Muslim Brothers and its Supreme Guide until his murder. Jamal was also a trade union activist at this time, and is still involved in promoting Islamic trade union concepts. During the course of the interview Jamal observed that there were many who saw in Islamic ideology a motivating force for trade union leadership and who were, like himself, personally close to members of the Muslim Brothers though not in it. Obviously there was what the French would call a *mouvance* of the brotherhood beyond its actual membership.

33. Sulayman al-Nukhayli, *Al-harakah al-ʿummaliyyah fi misr*, p. 256. The journalist was from the periodical *Al-Zaman*.

34. Ibid., p. 257.

35. Niqabat ʿUmmal masnaʿ takrir al-sukkar bi al-hawamdiyyah (Union of the workers of the sugar factory at Hawamdiyyah), *Al-Laʾihah al-asasiyyah al-muʿaddalah* (Revised Constitution) (Cairo, 1950 [A. H. 1369]), p. 11. Hereafter cited as the Revised Constitution.

36. Ibid., p. 2.

37. Ibid.

38. Ibid., pp. 8–9.

39. Ibid., p. 9.

40. Ibid., p. 8.

41. Ibid., p. 16.

42. Ibid., p. 17.

43. Ibid., pp. 18–21. Section 4 is on the rights of members.

44. Ibid., p. 23. Other points on the subject of the general meeting are from the same page.

45. Ibid., pp. 24–48. Section 7 is on the Administrative Council.

46. Ibid., p. 10.

47. *Al-Ikhwan al-Muslimun*, December 30, 1947.

48. Revised Constitution, p. 32.

49. Ibid., p. 32.

50. Ibid., pp. 33–34.

51. Ibid., p. 35.

52. *Al-Ikhwan al-Muslimun*, October 5, 1946.

53. The newspaper of the Muslim Brothers had a much broader influence among activists than the society itself, perhaps because reporters could travel more easily than recruiters could recruit and because exposure of conditions is a necessity for those organizing unions. Interview with Jamal al-Banna, Cairo, January 3, 1981.

54. Sulayman al-Nukhayli, *Al-harakah al-ʿummaliyah fi misr*, p. 253.

55. *Al-Jamahir*, May 19, 1947.

56. See note 54.

57. *Al-Ikhwan al-Muslimun*, January 9, 1947.

58. Khairya Khairy mentions that she personally spoke to unnamed union leaders from Hawamdiyyah who had tried to establish a restaurant by asking the company; when turned down, they appealed to the Labour Bureau. Given the date of her thesis and the generalized repression against the left, it seems likely that she is referring to the Muslim Brothers–oriented union. Parenthetically, workers seem to have preferred company restaurants when they felt they got good value and opposed them when they did not. See Khairya Khairy, "The Nutritive Aspect of Egyptian Labour," (B.A. thesis, American University of Cairo, March 1946).

59. *Al-Ikhwan al-Muslimun*, December 30, 1947.

60. "Behind the Smoke of the Factories," *Al-Ikhwan al-Muslimun*, November 30, 1947.

61. *Hadha al-istiʿmar bi-shahmihi wa lahmihi*. This is by no means an isolated example. See also "British Monopolies and Egyptian Workers," part of a group of articles on the oil industry, which castigates the British for using cheap Egyptian labor. The article asserts that the solutions are first to allow Egyptians to become employees and second to make wages equal to those of Europeans working in Egypt. *Al-Ikhwan al-Muslimun*, February 6, 1948. A similar commentary appeared November 11, 1947.

62. "Only his bit of bread, and no more," to be exact.

63. Given the similarity between the sugar workers' constitution and this article, for example, it seems plausible to assert that although the leaders at Hawamdiyyah may not have been formally enrolled in the Muslim Brothers organization, they clearly were so close as to be ideologically indistinguishable on issues such as these.

64. See, for example, Joel Migdal's *Peasants, Politics, and Revolution* (Princeton: Princeton University Press, 1974). Migdal discusses at length the ties that make peasants seek protection against the intrusion of the outside world—whether the state or the market—from a powerful local official. In this analysis, the foreman substitutes for the lord of the manor.

65. Those familiar with Barrington Moore's use of the word *exploitation* in *Social Origins of Dictatorship and Democracy* (Boston: Beacon Press, 1967) will notice that I am using the word *oppression* to refer to the kind of extortionate economic exaction as well as the personal humiliation he refers to as exploitation. See pp. 470–471. *Exploitation*, as used by Marx, is a perfectly useful word to suggest a structural mechanism by which a social surplus is created.

66. I mention this because winning such holidays was considered a significant victory by union activists affiliated with the brotherhood; recognition of these holidays represented a victory for Egyptian culture over Christian culture, as well as parity for those in the private sector with those in government service. Coronation Day and the King's Birthday do not, however, appear to have been as important for organizers in the textile industry. See *Al-Ikhwan al-Muslimun*, January 25, 1948, February 8, 1948, February 12, 1948.

67. For one direct and cogent presentation of this view, see "Beneficial Societies" in *Al-Ikhwan al-Muslimun*, January 9, 1948, where precisely this case is argued, using these particular examples.

68. See the memoirs of Mahmud al-ʿAskari in *Al-ʿAmal*, November 8, 1976, for a description of the ties between Muslim activists and leftists there. Al-ʿAskari notes that oppression and injustice rather than a specifically class perspective linked the Muslim Brothers, even briefly, with the left.

CHAPTER 7

1. See, for example, the transcript of an interview with Ahmad Sadiq Saʿd, a leader of the *Al-Fajr al-Jadid* group in the 1940s, in ʿAbd-al-azim Ramadan, *ʿAbd-al-nasir wa azmat maris sanat 1954* (Cairo: Matabiʿ ruz al-yusuf, 1976), pp. 299–300. Sadiq Saʿd argues that the high profits of the "monopolistic companies" such as the tobacco company, the Shell company, the tram company, the electric company, and the Kom Ombo company allowed them to pay high wages and thereby to create "yellow" or company unions. I think the relatively capital-intensive production in these companies and the cost of disruption made them likely to pay high wages.

2. This is no longer true of course. For a more comprehensive view of oil and the Egyptian state today see Marie Christine Aulas, "Sadat's Egypt: A Balance Sheet," *MERIP Reports*, July–August 1982, especially p. 8. Aulas develops an account of what she calls a "rentier" state, which may apply to several other countries where the state budget depends on remittances, tourism, services, or exports of products such as petroleum. These would include countries as diverse as Turkey and Nigeria. Aulas's article originally appeared in French. "Anatomie d'une dépendance: Egypte," *Peuples Méditerranéens/Mediterranean Peoples*, April–June 1982.

3. Salamah became head of the trade union federation and minister of labor in 1957. In the interim the Muslim Brothers had been jailed by the Nasser regime. Fathi Kamil lost government-influenced elections at the Matossian plant in 1954 and became active in pan-Arab and other international aspects of the Egyptian labor movement; that is, he was kicked upstairs. Like many leaders or potential leaders who oppose government policy, Kamil was put in a position where he could do little, but was not forced into active opposition.

4. See Sayyid Qandil, *Al-ʿAmil wa al-niqabah* (Cairo: Dar al-tibaʿah al-misriyyah al-hadithah, 1949), pp. 3 and 18, for information regarding Kamil's role and praise for him as an "antiextremist" and viable trade union leader able to work with members of parliament. In the aggressively nationalist political atmosphere of Egypt in the early 1950s, affiliation with the pro-Western ICFTU cannot have helped Kamil's career at a moment when all trade union careers were becoming only another track in the state administration.

5. I intend to examine this point more closely, using these materials, in a forthcoming article.

6. See Egypt, *Annuaire Statistique de Poche, 1948* (Cairo: Government Press, n.d.). State receipts are given as varying between about L.E. 77 million in 1943–1944 and L.E. 101 million in 1947–1948, with tobacco duties in the

same period varying between L.E. 13 million and L.E. 18 million, which is between 16 and 18 percent. See pp. 323 and 336.

7. See Benjamin Shwadran, *The Middle East, Oil, and the Great Powers, 1959* (New York: Council for Middle Eastern Affairs, 1959), pp. 425–431. Egypt also owned shares in the Anglo-Egyptian Oil Company.

8. See Jean Vallet, *Contribution a l'étude de la condition des ouvriers dans la grande industrie au Caire* (Valence: Imprimerie Valencienne, 1911), pp. 96–100.

9. Ibid., pp. 142–143.

10. Frederick Courtland Penfield, *Present-Day Egypt* (New York: Century Company, 1912), p. 76. Penfield had been the U.S. consul general to Egypt.

11. Ibid.

12. The following narrative is largely condensed from the history of the trade union movement in Amin ʿIzz-al-Din, *Tarikh al-tabaqah al-ʿamilah al-misriyyah min sanat 1919 ila sanat 1929* (Cairo: Dar al-shaʿb, 1970). See especially pp. 74–79.

13. Samuel Gompers, for example, was a product of the cigar rollers union. So were important Cuban trade union leaders of the same period. See, for example, Maurice Zeitlin, *Revolutionary Politics and the Cuban Working Class* (Princeton: Princeton University Press, 1967). In Cuba, brewery workers and cigarette makers thought themselves "privileged" in terms of pay.

14. See Elinor Burns, *British Imperialism in Egypt* (London: Labour Research Department, 1928), p. 51. Burns estimated the cost of production went from four shillings sixpence per thousand to fourpence, and that twelve main firms that had employed 1,519 workers in 1920 employed only 318 in 1921. Although Burns was writing for the British Communist party and wanted to show the situation at its bleakest, it was undoubtedly quite bleak. Her own sources are British Commercial Office reports. The decline in employment resulting from the introduction of machines may be overstated. The postwar recession probably also played a part. Employment would go up later.

15. See R. M. Barbour, *The Growth, Location, and Structure of Industry in Eygpt* (Washington, D.C.: Praeger Publishers, 1972), p. 66, and Samir Radwan, *Capital Formation in Egyptian Industry and Agriculture, 1882–1967* (London: Ithaca Press, 1974), pp. 170–171, for details on capital of various firms in this sector and Matossian, which adjusted its paid-up capital at several points in the 1920s in the process of buying up other firms.

16. See Amin ʿIzz-al-Din, *Tarikh al-tabaqah al-ʿamilah al-misriyyah min sanat 1919 ila sanat 1929* (Cairo: Dar al-shaʿb, 1970), p. 153.

17. Marcel Colombe, *L'Evolution de L'Egypte, 1924–1950* (Paris: G. P. Maisonneuve, 1951), pp. 333–334, contains a list of the personnel of various cabinets at this time. For a list of officials of the EFI see Egyptian Federation of Industry, *Livre d'Or de la Fédération Egyptienne de l'Industrie* (Cairo: Imprimerie Schindler, 1948), pp. 42–43. Light on the liberal political views—in economic matters at any rate—of Mahmud and the men around him may be found in Afaf Al-Sayyid Marsot, *Egypt's Liberal Experiment, 1922–36* (Berkeley: University of California Press, 1977), pp. 111–113, and Jacques Berque, *Egypt: Imperialism and Revolution* (Washington, D.C.: Praeger Publishers, 1972), pp. 404–409.

18. See Amin ʿIzz-al-Din, *1919–1929*, pp. 183–184.

19. It may be worthwhile to point out that the word used is the equivalent of the English *union* in the sense of "federation" and is related to the word for *unity* or *unit*, rather than to the word for an association. In Arabic, the name was *ittihad* rather than *niqabah*.

20. See Kamal ʿIzz al-Din's memoirs in *Al-ʿAmil*, November 14, 1946, where he claims the first two shares in the company went to Nahas and Makram. Regarding Halim and the attempt to get tobacco workers to buy company shares, see Nawal ʿAbd al-ʿAziz Radi, *Adwaʾ jadidah ʿala al-harakah al-ʿummaliyyah al-misriyyah min sanat 1930 ila sanat 1945* (Cairo: Dar al-nahdah, 1977), p. 231.

21. See Raʾuf ʿAbbas, *Al-harakah al-ʿummaliyyah fi misr min sanat 1899 ila sanat 1952* (Cairo: Dar al-katib al-ʿarabi, 1968), p. 101. It is difficult to accept ʿAbbas's belief that founding the factory was a commercial venture in which Halim hoped to profit from a tie to the nationalist and class sentiment of the cigarette-buying public. Halim showed little interest in commercial deals in general (he didn't need the income); and his behavior is far more easily explained by personal motives: Halim wished to make himself the patron of a dependent workers' movement—something the leaders of that movement sought equally strenuously to avoid.

22. ʿAbd al-Munʿim ʿIsawi, "Safhah matwiyyah min tarikh niqabat ʿummal al-nasij," in *Al-Thaqafah al-ʿummaliyyah*, June 1969. ʿIsawi was an official of the union and participated in some important conflicts in the union, but his comments here do not appear to be self-serving. Interestingly, ʿIsawi ascribes Halim's influence to his "use of violence with the employers."

23. See Aziz al-Maraghi, *La législation du travail en Egypte* (Paris: Librairie Technique et Economique, 1937), p. 204.

24. *Al-Jihad*, January 2, 1935. The committee was formed, in part at least, to determine the nature of the sickness as well as to cheer up members. Tuberculosis was a common problem of tobacco workers.

25. Fathi Kamil, Personal communication.

26. FO 371/19072. This is a report from Graves, including an attachment from Jacques Azoulai. The report is dated November 5, 1935, and forms the basis for the account in this section.

27. Fathi Kamil, president of the union at Matossian between 1942 and 1954, was emphatic on this point. Interview, Cairo, February 20, 1981.

28. I shall present this evidence in some depth for two reasons. First, it is important to my general argument that the creation of industrial unions is itself an artifice and that unions do not spring "naturally" from craft associations. Second, this particular bit of history is little known and deserves wider publicity. In addition to examining the relevant documents, I had a lengthy discussion with Fathi Kamil over whether such a situation ever existed; the documentary record seems to support the assertion of a transitional—if ineffective—form such as I describe.

29. *Al-Jihad*, April 13, 1935. The Arabic name of the union is *niqabat makan al-farm bi-fabriqat Matossian bi al-Jiza*.

30. *Al-Jihad*, April 27, 1935.

31. Ibid., May 1, 1935. Tuscan, Honied, and Good Smoking were brands of cigarettes produced in the cigarette department at Giza.

32. Ibid., May 6, 1935.

33. Ibid., May 8, 1935.

34. Ibid., May 6, 1935.

35. This seems an appropriate place to acknowledge two debts. The first is to Fathi Kamil, who spent well over a dozen hours with me and Joel Beinin in an effort to help us understand his union, the Egyptian trade union movement, and his not inconsiderable role in it. As the following presentation makes clear, I do not agree with Fathi Kamil on all points, but I do wish to underscore my gratitude for his generosity and for the valuable insights we gained from talking to him. I also wish to thank Joel Beinin (see chap. 2, n. 55) for introducing me to Fathi Kamil and for generously sharing tapes of interviews he recorded in 1979.

36. See Ministry of Finance, Egypt, *Population Census of Egypt, 1947* (Cairo: Government Press, 1954), p. 231. *Al-Bashir*, August 12, 1950, suggests a figure of 6,000 before layoffs of about 1,300, which might mean a 1947 figure of 4,700.

37. This narrative is largely a résumé of an interview with Fathi Kamil, February 20, 1981.

38. See Sulayman al-Nukhayli, *Al-harakah al-ʿummaliyyah fi misr wa mawqif al-sihafah wa al-sultah al-misriyyah minha min sanat 1882 ila sanat 1952* (Cairo: Ruz al-Yusuf Press, 1968), pp. 252–253. As al-Nukhayli points out, the press was not always good on following up strikes, and domestic news was crowded out with the intensification of the Palestine War that month.

39. The roots of this system of provisioning industrial workers in Egypt went back at least to the turn of the century. It is described by Vallet in his account of the sugar workers.

40. *Al-Bashir*, August 12, 1950.

41. See *Idarat al-buhuth al-fanniyyah wa al-ihsaʾ, qism al-tasjil*, Dossier 11/4/3/5 & 1, (Box 2) which contains the Suez Canal area contracts including those of the Shell workers. Wage comparisons are tricky at best, but especially so in this period of Egyptian history because there was a base rate, to which was added a cost-of-living allowance, family supplements, and bonuses. It is never clear, and this is especially true of the popular press, whether *wages* refers to base rates or take-home pay. It would hardly seem possible that take-home wages were on the order of 12 piasters a day when the average for the tobacco industry in 1936 was already over 11. See ʿAbd al-munʿim Nasr al-Shafiʿi, *Baʿd mashakil al-ʿamal fi misr* (Cairo: Dar al-nahdah al-ʿarabiyyah, 1939), p. 11. For all workers the average is actually 10.6 piasters, but if children are excluded it rises to over 11. Parenthetically, it should be noted that the complexity of the contracts did not inhibit the workers' organizations from fighting over them. And to refer to yet another Weberian basic, if the contract meant anything in Egypt at this time, it was viewed in Egyptian basic industry as the preferred form for regulating relations between employer and employee.

42. This right of personal appeal survives in the regular royal audiences for the public held in Saudi Arabia.

43. See *Mu'tammar al-niqabiyyin,* September 9, 1950, p. 5.

44. Ibid., October 20, 1950, p. 15.

45. Ibid., September 7, 1950, p. 2.

46. In numerous conversations with Kamil he insisted on the importance in his life's work of fighting against "bigotry." Unfortunately, as with many trade unionists, his focus on successfully achieving unity tended to make him unwilling to discuss either outright failures or the real difficulties in the path of success. Quran 49:13.

47. See note 45.

48. In fairness to Fathi Kamil as an individual, let me underline my contention that he was, in many ways, pouring new wine into old bottles by introducing new meanings to a dominant vocabulary. I do not mean to suggest that he was personally insincere in using Muslim vocabulary or that he was simply caving in to Islamic populist pressures.

49. Unfortunately there is not enough data to compare oil workers in Muslim countries over a variety of periods and conditions in the manner of this study because other authors are generally more concerned with the political ideologies of the workers to the exclusion of the forms of organization they preferred. It is interesting to speculate on the split between the different nationalities representing different sections of the work force in a predominantly Muslim area such as Baku between 1900 and 1917. Since shop-floor associations seem to have been stronger than union organizations, there was evidently a link between organizational approach and political outlook. Moreover, Muslim peasants performing unskilled or semiskilled labor in the oil fields seem to have been more influenced by cultural than by political critiques of their situation as well as being satisfied with relatively smaller gains, perhaps because they had so little to start with. See Ronald G. Suny, *The Baku Commune, 1917–1918* (Princeton: Princeton University Press, 1972), especially pp. 48, 56, and 348.

50. Shwadran, *The Middle East,* p. 425.

51. Ibid., p. 427.

52. Ibid., pp. 428–429.

53. See Muhammad Labib Shuqayr and Sahib Dhahab (eds.), *Ittifaqiyyat wa 'uqud al-batrul fi al-bilad al-'arabiyyah* (Petroleum agreements and contracts in the Arab countries), Part I (Cairo: Institute of Higher Arab Studies, the Arab League, 1959). This is a useful resource: contracts are given chronologically for the major countries.

54. Ibid., p. 251.

55. Ibid., p. 265.

56. Ibid., p. 278.

57. Ibid., pp. 299–300. Workers are referred to somewhat archaically as *ahl al-sina'ah wa al-kitabah,* almost as craftsmen were in Egypt.

58. Ibid., pp. 389 and 399.

59. Ibid., p. 421.

60. Ibid., p. 311.

61. In a global sense, however, Egypt was ahead of its day and the companies seem to have withdrawn rather than submit. In a test of strength Egypt could not

best the companies, not because of absolute incapacity, but because of relative weakness in the world market.

62. Shwadran, *The Middle East*, p. 427.

63. A. I. Gritly, *The Structure of Modern Industry in Egypt* (Cairo: Government Press, 1948), p. 550. It seems unlikely that there were more than ten thousand workers in the oil industry.

64. See also Fuad Abd al-Massih, "The Labor Policy of the Anglo-Egyptian Oilfields" (M. A. thesis, American University at Cairo, May 1952). The bulk of the 1,070 workers at Ras Gharib came from Qena; there may have been as many as 3,000 people living there (p. 32).

65. This account is taken from Muhammad ʿAbd Allah Abu ʿAli. *Al-Tanzim al-ijtimaʿi li al-sinaʿah* (Alexandria: Al-Hayʾah al-ʿammah al-misriyyah li al-kitab, 1972), p. 151. Dr. Abu ʿAli's study is of social theory of industry, illustrated with examples from Egyptian industry. His own source for this account is not given, but it may well be Anwar Salamah or another union leader. To my knowledge there are no published accounts of the founding of this union, and, as mentioned in the Introduction, Salamah is unwilling to talk to researchers—or at any rate to foreign ones.

66. *Al-Ikhwan al-Muslimun*, April 20, 1948.

67. Ibid., November 10, 1947.

68. Ibid., March 1, 1948.

69. Ibid., March 5, 1948. This, it should be pointed out, is from a story on the oil workers in Ras Gharib.

70. Salamah told one American scholar that "the Supreme Guide [of the Muslim Brothers] took care of religion and I took care of the oil workers." This separation of spheres would probably have surprised Hasan al-Banna, who probably did not consider the possibility that Salamah thought of him as a spiritual but not a temporal leader.

71. *Al-Ikhwan al-Muslimun*, April 20, 1948. Salamah mentioned this strike in this article, discussed above. The May-October 1947 copies of this journal are missing from the Dar al-Kutub.

72. Ibid., November 4, 1947.

73. Ibid., November 10, 1947.

74. Ibid., November 5, 1947. These advances ought to be seen in the light of Christmas bonuses, which, once achieved and depended upon, become not only a difficult material benefit to give up but also a particularly galling social problem. Ebenezer Scrooge may not be a character of Arabic folklore or literature, but he represents a type who has become, in the contemporary capitalist world, universal.

75. Ibid., November 10, 1947.

76. For their readiness see *Al-Ikhwan al-Muslimun*, March 5, 1948, where the news indicates they were convinced by the union leadership not to strike when the company refused to implement a conciliation commission decision. News of the strike appeared in *Al-Ahram*, April 5, 1948.

77. *Al-Ikhwan al-Muslimun* reported the strike on March 20, 1948; *Al-Ahram* on March 24.

78. These included both Egyptians and Europeans. Fuad Abd al-Massih, "Labor Policy," p. 24, mentions an Egyptian labor relations specialist working for the Anglo-Egyptian firm and clearly there were English officials also.

79. *Wizarat al-quwah al-ʿamilah: Idarat al-buhuth al-fanniyyah*, Dossier 11/4/3/5 & 1 (Box 2).

80. *Wizarat al-quwah al-ʿamilah: Maslahat al-buhuth al-fanniyyah*, Dossier 11/4/6/8: "Agreements with the aid of the Labour Bureau—Bureau of Suez."

CHAPTER 8

1. There were several such parties in Egypt at the time. Each party cadre considered the differences between them significant, but in this analysis, all such groups are treated as similar. A detailed analysis of some of the differences can be found in Jean-Pierre Thieck, "La journée du 21 Février 1946 dans l'histoire du mouvement nationale égyptien" (unpublished *Mémoire de maitrise*, Paris VII, 1974).

2. Government figures from the 1954–1956 statistical abstracts point in this direction. Textile workers are reported to have worked between 45 and 54 hours weekly for wages of between 193 and 206 piasters a week. On average, all industrial workers worked between 50 and 51 hours per week for pay ranging between 210 and 229 piasters. At least as an order of magnitude we can safely say textile workers were far from below average in the Egyptian context, and the Shubra workers generally received better wages than other textile workers. See Table IV, "Salaire moyen de l'ouvrier et moyenne des heures de travail à la première semaine du mois indiqué, par classes d'activités diverses, selon le code international," in Department of Statistics and Census, Egypt, *Annuaire Statistique* (Cairo: Amiriyah Press, 1957), pp. 230–231.

3. This is actually an overstatement. Some of the utilities were relatively more advanced, being on a par with contemporary British, French, or American norms, but taken as a whole the statement is near enough to the truth to be useful. One French study done in 1938 suggested that at least Cairo and Alexandria had an urban infrastructure comparable to that of "the most modern capitals." See Groupe d'Etude de l'Islam, *L'Egypte indépendante* (Paris: Paul Hartman, 1938), p. 329.

4. Although, as indicated below, not quite as up-to-date in terms of labor relations as the West.

5. There were several Communist organizations with followings among textile workers. I do not discuss them in any detail for two main reasons. First, their followings were to some degree distinct locally and succeeded each other in time rather than competing directly for the same members at the same moment; second, even though they were competitors in other arenas, their differences are not important in the context of this study. As Eric Hobsbawm points out: "At the level of the working-class militant, the doctrinal or programmatic differences which divide ideologists and political leaders so sharply, are often quite unreal, and may have little significance, unless *at this level*—i.e., the worker's specific locality or trade union—different organizations or leaders have long-established patterns of rivalry [italics in original]." See "Bolshevism and

the Anarchists," in *Revolutionaries* (New York: New American Library, 1973), p. 62.

6. See Egypt, *Taqrir lajnat al-tijarah wa al-sinaʿah* (Cairo: Al-Matbaʿah al-amiriyyah, 1925), p. 175.

7. Ibid.

8. In 1948 the Muslim Brothers criticized the Sibahi family for hiring a Jewish accountant during the Palestine War. See *Al-Ikhwan al-Muslimun*, January 9, 1948.

9. See the Egyptian Federation of Industry, *Livre d'Or de la Fédération Egyptienne de l'Industrie* (Cairo: Imprimerie Schindler, 1948), p. 234.

10. See Charles Issawi, *Egypt: An Economic and Social Analysis* (London: Oxford University Press, 1947), p. 86. In absolute terms the growth was from 25 million square meters to 150 million; of these 40 million came from hand looms in 1939. By 1944 hand-loom production was still fairly high: some 50 million square yards. See Husayn Hamdi, *Mushkilat al-batalah* (Cairo: Matbaʿat al-ikhwan al-muslimin, 1944), p. 232.

11. A. I. Gritly, *The Structure of Modern Industry in Egypt* (Cairo: Government Press, 1948), pp. 482–484, for a discussion of site location and the note that "the average level of wages in Mehallah being approximately 70% of that ruling in Cairo and 60% of that ruling in Alexandria, and the fact that labour in rural areas is not highly organized." Mahallah was a historic center of artisan weaving, which may have meant that skilled workers were available cheaply as the factory production increased. There is no doubt they had low wages. One source gives their wages (as well as those in Qaliyub and Kirdasa) as being around three and a half piasters per day. See ʿAbbas Halim, *Al-ʿUmmal al-misriyyun* (Cairo: Matbaʿat al-ʿabbassiyyah al-hadithah, 1934), p. 21.

12. See *ʿAqd al-ʿamal al-mushtarak sharikat al-ghazal al-ahliyyah* (Cairo: 1949), p. 9.

13. Again, see Gritly, *The Structure of Modern Industry*, pp. 481–482. In 1940, Mahallah produced 45 percent of yarn spun; Alexandria and Kafr al-Dawwar 51 percent; and Cairo about 1 percent. Fifty percent of the mechanical looms were in Mahallah; 44 percent in Alexandria and Kafr al-Dawwar; and fewer than 5 percent in Cairo.

14. Ibid., p. 495. This is larger, he argues, than the average American or English plant at that time.

15. Egyptian Federation of Industry, *Livre d'Or*, p. 12.

16. Gritly, *The Structure of Modern Industry*, p. 482.

17. Egyptian Federation of Industry, *Livre d'Or*, p. 40. They were located near Shubra in the villages of Bahtim and Musturud.

18. Richard Marsden, *Cotton Weaving: Its Development, Principles, and Practice* (London: George Bell and Sons, 1895), pp. 174–175.

19. *Al-Yaraʿ*, June 1, 1942. Titled "Justice or Anarchism," the article contrasts the justice of payment by results with the essentially false equality of the lazy, inept worker and the apt, skilled one that allows the former to share the produce of the latter.

20. When Abd al-Qadr Hamada first began working at the silk plant in Helwan, he was offered "a small wage which would increase in proportion to my

work, and I accepted this condition because I had confidence in myself." Unpublished memoir. The Communist newspaper *Al-Jamahir* published an inquiry on factories in the Cairo suburbs of Zaitun and Matariyyah; one worker suggested that piece rates were better because they encouraged equality of opportunity and made owner favoritism less likely in the setting of hourly rates: "We want payment by production so that we're all alike . . . also the factory needs a system that doesn't change all the time." *Al-Jamahir*, September 28, 1947.

21. See *Wizarat al-quwah al-ʿamilah: Maslahat al-buhuth al-fanniyyah*, Dossier 11/4/6/22, where three contracts detailing the arrangements negotiated under the auspices of the Labour Conciliation Board are preserved.

22. See *Al-Jamahir*, April 14, 1947. The article gives ten hours as the time to make fifty meters of cloth and suggests eight piasters as the base rate, with ten piasters paid for working on two machines. As late as 1950, workers in Sharabiyyah (Cairo) were complaining about pay reductions when they were forced to work two machines at the rate previously given for one. *Al-Mustaqbal*, December 4, 1950.

23. See the *Collective Agreement and Higher Committee Decisions Regarding Standardization of Textile Factory Wages and Conditions* (*Sharikat al-ghazal al-ahliyyah al-misriyyah*; ʿAqd al-ʿamal al-mushtarak wa qararat al-lajnah al-ʿulya li-tawhid shurut al-ʿamal wa al-ujur bi-masnaʿ al-ghazal wa al-nasij) (Alexandria: Don Bosco, 1949), pp. 32–33 and 56. There is a slight ambiguity because the contract lists not only "beginner" workers on one loom but also "weavers' helpers," which seems to indicate primarily two sets of names for the same jobs: that is, workers entering the factory who would become fully paid weavers within a relatively brief time, and adolescents who, as assistants, had to spend five years at part pay.

24. See Gamal Eldin Said, "Productivity of Labour in Egyptian Industry," *L'Egypte Contemporaine*, 1948, p. 506.

25. See Mahmoud Amin Anis, *A History of the National Income of Egypt* (Cairo: Société Orientale de Publicité, 1950), p. 776. The sugar and cigarette industries met 100 percent of local demand, according to Anis, and thus did not generally face such problems.

26. Ibid., p. 789.

27. Ibid., p. 790.

28. Marsden, *Cotton Weaving*, p. 354.

29. Ibid., p. 355.

30. William Morris Carson, "The Mehallah Report" (Badr al-Shayn: Ford Foundation, 1953), mimeographed.

31. Gritly, *The Structure of Modern Industry*, p. 532.

32. Taha Saʿd ʿUthman, *Mudhakkirat wa wathaʾiq min tarikh ʿummal misr: al-ʿummal wa al-intikhabat al-barlaminiyyah* (Cairo: Maktabat Madbuli, 1982), p. 82.

33. The report is a memorandum submitted by ʿAbd al-Fattah Muhammad Husayn to the Higher Committee on Labour Problems, a committee on which he was the labor delegate as well as being a member of the subcommittee on textiles. The text of the memorandum is contained in ʿAbd al-Munʿim al-Shafiʿi's *Tarikh al-harakah al-niqabiyyah fi misr* (Cairo: Dar al-thaqafah al-jadidah,

1968), p. 226. The entire memorandum is reprinted on pp. 226–229.

34. Ibid.

35. The following discussion is based largely on comments from the graduates of a technical school set up to train skilled mechanics for Mahallah; the comments were printed in *Al-ʿAmil al-Misri*, April 14, 1930. It should be apparent that I am not describing here relative deprivation but rather an absence of participation and a denial of upward mobility, which was not only systematic but also interpreted as such.

36. *Al-ʿAmil al-Misri*, April 14, 1930.

37. *Al-Iʿtisam*, November 12, 1939. A letter from Mustafa Imam Husayni, graduate of textile technique.

38. See the "Response to the Memorandum of the Owners' Delegate," in ʿAbd al-Munʿim al-Shafiʿi, *Tarikh al-harakah*, pp. 230–242, especially pp. 231–232.

39. Ibid.

40. See Muhammad ʿAbd al-Salam Ahmad, *Bahth mushkilat khirriji al-madaris al-thanawiyyah al-sinaʿiyah* (Cairo: Matbaʿat lajnat al-taʾlif wa al-tarjamah, 1960), pp. 14–16. Almost all the graduates from the years requested (1950–1954) did return the questionnaires—roughly 3,100.

41. It was a given that urban working-class families would take tremendous risks to educate at least one bright young boy for an official post in government. The plot of the novel that catapulted Najib Mahfuz to popular acclaim is set in motion by the contradictory emotions engendered when a working-class father gives up his lump-sum pension so that a favored son may continue in school and gain a clerical position in a ministry. See his *Al-Qahirah al-jadidah*.

42. See *Mudhakkirat Bayram al-Tunisi* in *Turath Bayram al-Tunisi* (Beirut: Manshurat al-maktabah al-ʿarabiyyah, n.d.), pp. 22–23.

43. See ʿAbbas Halim, *Al-ʿUmmal al-misriyyun*, p. 21.

44. Taha Saʿd ʿUthman, *Mahadir wa taqarir al-lajnah al-wizariyyah al-ʿulya al-mukawwanah fi fibrayir sanat 1948* (Dar al-saʿah 12, 1948), especially pp. 17 and 39.

45. *Al-Jihad*, April 19, 1935.

46. *Al-Balagh*, March 29, 1935. "Belgian" here seems to refer to a type of weaving rather than to the nature or ownership of the workshop. Perhaps it refers to the Jacquard loom.

47. Unpublished memoirs.

48. Unpublished memoirs in my possession.

49. *Al-Bashir*, July 15, 1950. The initials of the worker are given as *mim*, *shin* and thus are possibly those of Muhammad Shatta.

50. Personal interview. Almost all the information on Taha Saʿd is drawn from a series of personal interviews given on October 28, November 5, and December 15, 1980, in Cairo.

51. Taha Saʿd ʿUthman, *Al-ʿummal wa al-intikhabat al-barlaminiyyah*. See especially pp. 124–126 for information on Shaykh Zaʿtar.

52. *Al-Iʿtisam*, July 22, 1943. Other branches mentioned include the one at

the railway workshops and the technical school at Musturud, evidence of an interest in the brotherhood in organizing industrial workers. Musturud is within the Shubra region and was the site of several textile factories.

53. *Al-Bashir*, September 2, 1950.

54. Taha Saʿd ʿUthman, *Al-ʿummal wa al-intikhabat al-barlaminiyyah*, p. 132.

55. Interview, Cairo, November 29, 1980.

56. What ʿAmir calls the association is an ʿisaba. Interview, Cairo, November 29, 1980.

57. See *Al-Jihad* for April 30, 1935, for a mention of the Muhammad ʿAli "of the workers of Zaitun and Matariyyah."

58. Probably in each case the factories were within walking distance of the nearby areas in which workers lived or accessible to unscheduled mechanized transport. Regarding buses see Taha Saʿd ʿUthman, *Al-ʿummal wa al-intikhabat al-barlaminiyyah*, pp. 121–122. It seems that there were special bus lines for the factories, as well as private factory-owned vehicles. This suggests relatively compact though perhaps distinct areas within which workers lived and worked. We know that in Alexandria well over half the workers in one large sample walked to work. See Hasan al-Saʿati, *Al-Tasniʿ wa al-ʿumran* (Cairo: Dar al-maʿarif, 1958), pp. 265–266.

59. *Al-Yaraʿ*, November 19, 1942.

60. Al-ʿAskari is quite specific in his memoirs that the inspiration for the hunger strike and its popularity among union members at that time came from Mahatma Gandhi, and he calls the trade unionists active in the struggle to create a union federation at that time "the followers of Gandhi in Egypt" (*khulafaʾ ghandi fi misr*).

61. Taha Saʿd ʿUthman, *Al-ʿummal wa al-intikhabat al-barlaminiyyah*, pp. 83–84.

62. Exactly when and how these men were all recruited into the ranks of Egypt's Leninists is unclear. Some of the articles I have cited as indications of what Leninists thought may have been written before formal induction into a party. Because this study is not concerned with party organizations but with leadership of workers in the organizational setting of unions, and because the ideas of the men involved did not change abruptly at whatever point they formally entered the ranks, it is irrelevant when and how they joined. What is striking, indeed, is precisely the working of the elective affinities between their expressed ideas as early as 1942, when they were certainly not yet Communists, and 1946, when they were. On a larger scale, especially for the period characterized by Zhdanov in the Soviet Union, these men may not have been very good Leninists (i.e., Stalinists), but they were whatever Egyptian Leninism was in its mass incarnation.

63. ʿAli ʿAmir was actually first recruited into a Trotskyist group, which he left when it became apparent that the essentially middle-class members could not take the rigors of prison. They were certainly not *gidʿan* (the plural of *gadaʿ*). He seems to have found the militancy or combativeness of the left appealing initially, whereas al-ʿAskari and Taha Saʿd underwent a lengthier process of recruitment.

64. See *Al-Jamahir*, April 14, 1947, which claims that two-thirds of the factories in the Shubra area were owned by three firms, all of which were associated with such prominent political and economic figures as Sidki, Husayn Haykal, and Husayn Sirri, and at least one figure from Halim's Workers' party. The figure on the concentration of ownership seems too high, but it was not uncommon for one owner to establish several small factories in different areas.

65. Layoffs were rare in the petroleum industry, and although they happened in the tobacco industry, they were not very great because after the 1930s there were simply not that many tobacco workers. In the sugar industry, work was seasonal but relatively stable.

66. Literally, General Union of Mechanized Textile Workers of Cairo and Its Suburbs—*Al-niqabah al-ᶜammah li-ᶜummal al-nasij al-mikaniki fi al-qahirah wa dawahiha*.

67. The revised constitution appeared in the union's newspaper *Shubra* on May 28, 1942. All references to the constitution are to this issue. The original constitution adopted October 13, 1939, does not seem to have been preserved.

68. See Frederick H. Harbison and Ibrahim Abdelkader Ibrahim, *Human Resources for Egyptian Enterprise* (New York: McGraw-Hill, 1958), p. 85.

69. See Taha Saᶜd ᶜUthman, *Nidal ᶜummal al-nasij al-mikaniki fi al-qahirah* (Cairo: Maktabat al-tabaqah al-ᶜamilah, 1946), p. 7. Specifically, Taha Saᶜd cites the danger to skilled workers of layoffs because of "employer preference for agricultural laborers trained in the industry by the laid-off workers."

70. *Shubra*, May 28, 1942.

71. Ibid.

72. It is the specificity of all this—to a degree beyond that required by law, and indeed to a level government officials often despaired of reaching—that I wish to emphasize. Not only were the textile workers in Shubra oriented to the left, they were also organized at an administrative level far in advance of any other union in the country at the time.

73. To avoid the inevitable criticism that my argument here is Eurocentric, let me point out that it represents the distillation, as the succeeding quotes will show, of what the men in the plants in Shubra thought about these questions. They believed in organization as opposed to loose association; they preferred to know where their money went and on what it was spent; they preferred regular elections and an organization that supported itself from dues. Those are their preferences. For the record, though, they also happen to be mine.

74. *Shubra*, May 28, 1942.

75. Ibid., June 4, 1942.

76. Ibid.

77. Ibid., July 9, 1942.

78. Ibid.

79. See Taha Saᶜd ᶜUthman, *Nidal ᶜummal al-nasij al-mikaniki fi al-qahirah*, pp. 9–10.

80. See Groupe d'Etude de l'Islam, *L'Egypte indépendante*, p. 343. A note to the main text says that "those affiliated with the movement of ᶜAbbas Halim have been given the option by their employers in the Misr group enterprises of resigning from Halim's group or being fired."

81. *Al-Jihad*, May 3, 1935.

82. *Al-Jihad*, April 17, 1935.

83. Zaki Badaoui, *Problèmes du travail en Egypte* (Alexandria: Société des publications égyptiennes, 1948), p. 68. The description is from a report given by Dr. Abdel Wahed El-Wakel to a conference on worker housing in 1942.

84. See Andre Eman, *L'Industrie du coton en Egypte* (Cairo: 1943), p. 183.

85. Ibid.

86. Robert Tignor, *State, Private Enterprise, and Economic Change in Egypt, 1918–1952* (Princeton: Princeton University Press, 1984), p. 129.

87. For subsidies, see ibid., p. 130.

88. *Shubra*, July 2, 1942.

89. *Al-Yaraᶜ*, November 26, 1942.

90. Badaoui, *Problèmes*, p. 112; Gritly, *The Structure of Modern Industry*, p. 484, assigns it 27,000 members in the same period.

91. *Al-Yaraᶜ*, November 26, 1942.

92. This is "The Mehallah Report," of course, by William Carson.

93. *Al-Jamahir*, September 6, 1947.

94. See Muhammad Yusuf al-Mudarrik, *Hawla mushkilat ᶜummal al-mahallah* (Cairo: Matbaᶜat al-shabab al-hurr, 1947), p. 18. For threats of firings see *Al-Jamahir*, September 6, 1947.

95. See *Al-Jamahir*, April 28, 1947.

96. See *ᶜAmil al-Mahallah*, December 13, 1947.

97. *Al-Jamahir*, September 6, 1947.

98. Mudarrik, *Hawla mushkilat ᶜummal al-mahallah*, p. 9.

99. William Morris Carson, "The Mehallah Report" (Badr al-Shayn: Ford Foundation, 1953), mimeographed, p. 3.

100. Ibid., pp. 2–3.

101. This is not quite the concept of surplus value as enunciated by Marx, but it is close, and one can see in it a transitional understanding from the view that only colonialism exploits the workers to one that there is an inherent systematic set of relations in the plant that governs the allocations of the product for wages. Whether the concept of surplus value is itself accurate is far less important than the view both that it corresponds to a set of relations perceived by the workers in the industrial plant and that it is an essentially systematic analysis toward which the workers appeared to be moving rather than a completely personalistic view.

102. See al-Mudarrik's memoirs in *Al-Thaqafah al-ᶜUmmaliyyah*, May 15, 1968. As the WFTU had not yet split and the British TUC as well as the American CIO were still involved, the WFTU was still "left," although its orientation toward the world Communist movement was already marked.

103. See al-ᶜAskari's memoirs in *Al-ᶜAmal*, November 8, 1976.

104. *Al-Ikhwan al-Muslimun*, April 28, 1947.

105. Ibid., April 29, 1947.

106. Ibid., April 30, 1947.

107. See Muhammad Hasan Ahmad, *Al-Ikhwan al-Muslimun fi al-mizan* (Cairo, 1946), pp. 98–99.

108. *Al-Ikhwan al-Muslimun*, February 2, 1948, reports that a Commu-

nist demonstration occurred outside the Ahliyyah plant when twelve "youths" shouted "long live the unity of the peoples," which seems to have interested the workers. The members of the brotherhood in the plant "explained" the meaning of the slogan to the workers and approved the arrival of the police; four demonstrators were arrested with bombs and explosives after having "changed into" workers' clothes.

109. See, for example, *Al-Jamahir*, May 5, 1947, for a story on two Sibahi plants in Shubra al-Khaima being closed and the attempts by the local union to keep the plants in operation.

110. *Al-Ikhwan al-Muslimun*, February 25, 1948. See the mention of the telegram sent to al-Banna by the new leaders.

111. *Al-Ikhwan al-Muslimun*, March 6 and 7, 1948. As at Mahallah, the phrase "outside agitators" referred to Communists.

112. *Al-Ikhwan al-Muslimun*, March 2, 3, 14, 19, 1948.

113. *Al-Ikhwan al-Muslimun*, January 15, 1948.

114. Despite several strikes at the Egyptian Jute Company works in Shubra, the brotherhood never mentioned the nature of its ownership, which was partly Egyptian, but on whose board of directors also sat Alexander Keown-Boyd, the British police chief mentioned in chapter 4.

115. See *Al-Jamahir*, September 28, 1947. This was a different group of Communists, closely associated with the newspaper *al-Jamahir*, rather than the earlier group in Shubra, which had been associated with *Al-Fajr al-Jadid*.

116. See the ʿAqd al-ʿamal al-mushtarak sharikat al-ghazal al-ahliyyah, p. 49.

117. Ibid., see p. 19 for a definition of work norms—the number of looms to be tended for each pay category—and p. 49 for a discussion of incentive-based pay scales.

CHAPTER 9

1. During this period, a relatively liberal parliamentary regime was in place, largely defined as a Wafd parliamentary government.

2. See, for example, Jean and Simonne LaCouture, *Egypt in Transition* (New York: Criterian Press, 1958), p. 384, for an example of the use of Suez Canal workers against the canal administration in 1951 and of similar situations later.

3. See Mahmoud Abdel-Fadil, *The Political Economy of Nasserism* (Cambridge: Cambridge University Press, 1980), p. 34.

4. Ibid., p. 47. See al-Banna's introduction to a pamphlet by Ibrahim Nusayr, *Min asbab al-batalah wa al-aristuqratiyyah al-niqabiyyah* (Cairo: Matbaʿat Yusuf, 1963), where he argues that it was the military regime that realized earlier proposals by nationalist officials (such as Nusayr) for guaranteed positions for workers. In 1951, Nusayr had published a book entitled *Sayhat al-ʿummal*, which he described as demanding "immunity of the unions from the tyranny of the employers. . . . It should not be permissible to fire employees unless it is established that the worker damaged the mutual interest [of the worker and the owner—*al-maslahah al-mushtarakah*] and with the proviso that the family of the man fired not be denied the right to live." Nasir evidently went further and actually suggested that there be absolutely no right to fire because

firing amounts to "destruction and murder of men, wives, and children." See pp. 9–10, where al-Banna cites the earlier pamphlet. He then notes that by 1963 the Nasser government had "forbidden firing or made it very difficult." Ibid., p. 10. Al-Banna, it will be recalled, was the object of left criticism, as I showed in chapter 8, as a propagandist of ʿatf.

5. Archives of the Suez Canal Company, No. PO/320/38/CF, in Folder 412. The letter is dated March 11, 1953, and was sent from Ismailia.

6. Al-ʿAmal, August 29, 1977. Cherine is the French spelling for the name I transliterate as Shirin.

7. See Nusayr's book, mentioned above, for details.

8. Nusayr, Min asbab. See especially pp. 15–20, and the allegation on p. 19 that union leaders had already ceased holding general meetings to ensure themselves of control over relatively lucrative positions in various union presidencies.

9. Not all peasants own the land they work on, but they do believe they have a moral title to continue using it, just as artisans may possess a skill or a set of tools, and thus presume to own a workshop or a bench in a workshop even without legal title.

Select Bibliography

GENERAL SOURCES

Abdel-Fadil, Mahmoud. *The Political Economy of Nasserism.* Cambridge: Cambridge University Press, 1980.

Abrahamian, Ervand. *Iran between Two Revolutions.* Princeton: Princeton University Press, 1982.

Abu-Lughod, Janet. *Cairo, 1001 Years of the City Victorious.* Princeton: Princeton University Press, 1971.

Abu-Lughod, Janet. "Varieties of Urban Experience: Contrast, Coexistence, and Coalescence in Cairo," in *Middle Eastern Cities*, ed. Ira Lapidus. Berkeley: University of California Press, 1969.

Anis, Mahmoud Amin. *A Study of the National Income of Egypt.* Cairo: Société Orientale de Publicité, 1950.

Apter, David. *The Politics of Modernization.* Chicago: University of Chicago Press, 1965.

Ayrout, Henry Habib. *The Egyptian Peasant.* Boston: Beacon Press, 1963.

Baer, Gabriel. *Egyptian Guilds in Modern Times.* Jerusalem: Israeli Oriental Society, 1964.

Baer, Gabriel. *Studies in the Social History of Modern Egypt.* Chicago: University of Chicago Press, 1969.

Barbour, R. M. *The Growth, Location, and Structure of Industry in Egypt.* Washington, D.C.: Praeger Publishers, 1972.

Barois, J. *Irrigation in Egypt.* Washington, D.C.: Government Printing Office, 1889.

Bassaty, Fatma Rakha el-. "Le Changement sociale dans une ville égyptienne, Damiette, dans le 20ème siècle." Ph.D. diss., Université de Paris, 1978.

Beinin, Joel. "Class Conflict and National Struggle: Labor and Politics in Egypt, 1936–1954." Ph.D. diss. University of Michigan, 1982.

Beling, Willard. *Modernization and African Labor.* New York: Praeger Publishers, 1965.

Beling, Willard. *Pan-Arabism and Labor.* Cambridge, Mass.: Harvard University Press, 1961.

Bendix, Reinhard. *Work and Authority in Industry.* New York: Wiley, 1956.

Berger, Elena. *Labour, Race, and Colonial Rule.* Oxford: Clarendon Press, 1974.

Berger, Morroe. *Bureaucracy and Society in Modern Egypt.* Princeton: Princeton University Press, 1957.

Berque, Jacques. "Classes Sociales," in *De l'Euphrate à l'Atlas.* Paris: Editions Sindbad, 1978.

Berque, Jacques. *Egypt: Imperialism and Revolution.* Washington, D.C.: Praeger Publishers, 1972.

Blackman, Winifred S. *The Fellahin of Upper Egypt.* London: Frank Cass, 1968 (first ed. 1927).

Briggs, Martin. *Through Egypt in War Time.* London: Fisher Unwin, 1918.

Brinton, Crane. *The Anatomy of Revolution.* New York: Vintage, 1952.

Brown, Kenneth. *People of Salé.* Cambridge, Mass.: Harvard University Press, 1976.

Burawoy, Michael. *Manufacturing Consent.* Chicago: University of Chicago Press, 1979.

Burns, Elinor. *British Imperialism in Egypt.* London: Labour Research Department, 1928.

Butler, Harold B. *Report on Labour Conditions in Egypt with Suggestions for Future Social Legislation.* Cairo: Government Press, 1932.

Butzer, Karl W. *Early Hydraulic Civilization in Egypt.* Chicago: University of Chicago Press, 1976.

Calhoun, Craig. *The Question of Class Struggle.* Chicago: University of Chicago Press, 1982.

Cammett, John M. *Antonio Gramsci and the Origins of Italian Communism.* Stanford: Stanford University Press, 1967.

Carson, William Morris. "The Mehallah Report." Badr al-Shayn: Ford Foundation, 1953. Mimeographed.

Chesneaux, Jean. *The Chinese Labor Movement 1919–1927.* Stanford: Stanford University Press, 1968.

Chorley, Katharine. *Armies and the Art of Revolution.* Boston: Beacon Press, 1969.

Cohen, Robin, and Richard Sandbrook (eds.). *The Development of an African Working Class.* London: Longman, 1975.

Colombe, Marcel. *L'Evolution de l'Egypte, 1924–1950.* Paris: G. P. Maisonneuve, 1951.

Couland, Jacques. *Le Mouvement Syndical au Liban, 1919–1946.* Paris: Editions Sociales avec le concours de CNRS, 1970.

Couland, Jacques. "Regards su l'histoire syndicale et ouvrière égyptienne (1899–1952)," in *Mouvement ouvrier, communisme, et nationalismes dans le monde Arabe,* ed. René Gallisot. Paris: Editions Ouvrières, 1978.

Damachi, Ukandi Godwin. *The Role of Trade Unions in the Development Process.* New York: Praeger Publishers, 1974.

Deeb, Marius. *Party Politics in Egypt: The Wafd and Its Rivals, 1919–1939.* London: Ithaca Press, 1979.

Doeringer, Peter B., and Michael J. Piore. *Internal Labor Markets and Manpower Analysis.* Lexington, Mass.: D. C. Heath, 1971.

Durkheim, Emile. *The Division of Labor.* New York: Free Press, 1966.

Edelman, Bernard. *Le Légalisation de la classe ouvrière.* Paris: Christian Bourgeois Editeur, 1978.

Edwards, Richard. *Contested Terrain.* New York: Basic Books, 1979.

Egyptian Federation of Industry. *Livre d'Or de la Fédération Egyptienne de l'Industrie.* Cairo: Imprimerie Schindler, 1948.

Engels, Friedrich. Introduction to *Class Struggles in France.* New York: International Publishers, 1964.

Fedden, Robin. *The Land of Egypt.* New York: Charles Scribner's Sons, 1939.

Galatoli, Anthony. *Egypt in Midpassage.* Cairo: Urwand and Sons, 1950.

Geertz, Clifford, Hildred Geertz, and Lawrence Rosen. *Meaning and Order in Moroccan Society.* Cambridge: Cambridge University Press, 1979.

Goitein, S. D. *A Mediterranean Society,* Vol. 1, *Economic Foundations.* Berkeley: University of California Press, 1967.

Goldberg, Ellis. "Bases of Traditional Reaction: A Look at the Muslim Brothers." *Peuples Méditerranéens/Mediterranean Peoples,* January–March 1981.

Gran, Peter. *The Islamic Roots of Capitalism.* Austin: University of Texas Press, 1978.

Gritly, A. I. *The Structure of Modern Industry in Egypt.* Cairo: Government Press, 1948.

Groupe d'Etude de l'Islam. *L'Egypte indépendante.* Paris: Paul Hartman, 1938.

Handley, William. "The Labor Movement in Egypt." *The Middle East Journal,* vol. 3, no. 3, pp. 277–292, July 1949.

Hansen, Bent. "Wage Theory for LDC's," in *Working Papers.* Berkeley: Economics Department, University of California, Berkeley, October 1982.

Haraszti, Miklos. *Worker in a Worker's State.* New York: Universe Books, 1978.

Harbison, Frederick H., and Ibrahim Abdelkader Ibrahim. *Human Resources for Egyptian Enterprise.* New York: McGraw-Hill, 1958.

Harbison, Frederick H., and Ibrahim Abdelkader Ibrahim. "Some Labor Problems of Industrialization in Egypt." *The Annals of the American Academy of Political and Social Science* 305 (1956): 114–124.

Hassan, Chihata Saafran. "Essai sociologique." Ph.D. diss., University of Paris, 1948.

Huntington, Samuel. *Political Order in Changing Societies.* New Haven: Yale University Press, 1969.

Hussein, Mahmoud. *Class Conflict in Egypt, 1945–1970.* New York: Monthly Review Press, 1973.

International Labor Organization. *L'OIT et les pays Nord-africains et du Proche Orient.* Geneva: International Labor Organization, 1935.

Issawi, Charles. *The Economic History of the Middle East, 1800–1914.* Chicago: University of Chicago Press, 1966.

Issawi, Charles. *Egypt: An Economic and Social Analysis.* London: Oxford University Press, 1947.

Jenkins, J. Craig. "Why Do Peasants Rebel? Structural and Historical Theories of Modern Peasant Rebellions." *American Journal of Sociology* 88 (1982): 487–514.

Jenks, Leland. *The Migration of British Capital to 1875.* New York: Alfred E. Knopf, 1927.

Johnson, Chalmers. *Peasant Nationalism and Communist Power.* Stanford: Stanford University Press, 1962.

Johnson, Chalmers. *Revolutionary Change.* Boston: Little, Brown, 1966.

Jowitt, Kenneth. *Revolutionary Breakthroughs and National Development: The Case of Romania, 1944–1965.* Berkeley: University of California Press, 1971.

Kaplan, Temma. *Anarchists of Andalusia, 1868–1903.* Princeton: Princeton University Press, 1977.

Karaali, Abd al-Azim. "L'Egypte à l'age industriel." Ph.D. diss., Faculté des Lettres de Bordeaux, 1952.

Kay, Geoffrey. *Development and Underdevelopment: A Marxist Analysis.* London: Macmillan, 1975.

Kirchheimer, Otto. "Confining Conditions and Revolutionary Breakthroughs." *American Political Science Review* 59 (December 1965): 964–974.

Laqueur, Walter Z. *Communism and Nationalism in the Middle East.* London: Routledge, Kegan Paul, 1961.

LeFranc, Georges. *Les Expériences Syndicales Internationales.* Paris: Aubier, 1952.

Lenczowski, George. *Soviet Advances in the Middle East.* Washington, D.C.: American Enterprise Institute, 1971.

Lenin, V. I. *Selected Works.* 3 vols. Moscow: Progress Publishers, 1967.

Lewis, Bernard. "Communism and Islam," in *The Middle East in Transition,* ed. Walter Z. Laqueur. New York: Frederick A. Praeger, 1958.

Lewis, Bernard. "The Islamic Guilds." *The Economic History Review,* vol. 8, pp. 20–37, November 1937.

Liebesny, Herbert. *The Law of the Near and Middle East.* Albany: State University of New York Press, 1975.

Longrigg, Stephen H. *Oil in the Middle East.* London: Oxford University Press, 1961.

Lowit, Thomas. *Le syndicalisme de type soviétique.* Paris: Armand Colin, 1971.

Ma'oz, Moshe. *Ottoman Reform in Syria and Palestine.* Oxford: Clarendon Press, 1968.

Malek, Anouar Abdel. *Egypt: Military Society.* New York: Random House, 1968.

Maraghi, Aziz al-. *La législation du travail en Egypte.* Paris: Librairie Technique et Economique, 1937.

Marsden, Richard. *Cotton Weaving: Its Development, Principles, and Practice.* London: George Bell and Sons, 1895.

Marsot, Afaf Al-Sayyid. *Egypt's Liberal Experiment, 1922–36.* Berkeley: University of California Press, 1977.

Marx, Karl. *Capital.* New York: Modern Library.

Marx, Karl. *Grundrisse.* London: Penguin Books, 1973.

Marx, Karl. *Selected Letters.* New York: International Publishers, 1939.

Maxwell, Francis. *Economic Aspects of Cane Sugar Production*. London: Norman Rodger, 1927.

Mazuel, Jean. *Le Sucre en Egypte*. Cairo: E. & R. Schindler, 1937.

Meisner, Maurice. *Li Ta Chao and the Origins of Chinese Marxism*. Cambridge, Mass.: Harvard University Press, 1967.

Michelat, Guy, and Michel Simon. *Classes, religion, and comportement politique*. Paris: Presses de la FNRS et Editions Sociales avec le concours de CNRS, 1977.

Migdal, Joel. *Peasants, Politics, and Revolution*. Princeton: Princeton University Press, 1974.

Millen, Bruce. *The Political Role of Labor in Developing Countries*. Washington, D.C.: The Brookings Institution, 1963.

Monica, Madeleine Della. *La Classe Ouvrière sous les Pharaons*. Paris: Librairie d'Amérique et d'Orient, 1975.

Olson, Mancur. *The Logic of Collective Action*. Harvard Economic Series, 124. Cambridge, Mass.: Harvard University Press, 1965.

Piorie, Michael J. "On the Technological Foundations of Economic Dualism," in *Working Papers*. Cambridge, Mass.: Department of Economics, Massachusetts Institute of Technology, May 1973.

Polanyi, Karl. *The Great Transformation*. Boston: Beacon Press, 1957.

Prinsen Geerligs, H. C., and R. J. Prinsen Geerligs. *Cane Sugar Production 1912–1937*. London: Norman Rodger, 1938.

Rabinowitch, Alexander. *The Bolsheviks Come to Power*. New York: W. W. Norton, 1976.

Radwan, Samir. *Capital Formation in Egyptian Industry and Agriculture, 1882–1967*. London: Ithaca Press, 1974.

Radwan, Samir, and Robert Mabro. *The Industrialization of Egypt*. Oxford: Clarendon Press, 1976.

Raymond, André. *Artisans et commerçants au Caire pendant le XVIIIe siècle*. Damascus: Institut Français de Damas, 1973.

Redfield, Robert. *The Little Community*. Chicago: University of Chicago Press, 1958.

Richards, Alan. *Egypt's Agricultural Development, 1800–1980*. Boulder, Colo.: Westview Press, 1982.

Robertson, C. J. *World Sugar Production and Consumption*. London: John Bale, Sons & Danielson, 1934.

Rodinson, Maxime. "Les problèmes des partis communistes en Syrie et en Egypte," in *Marxisme et monde musulman*. Paris: Editions de Seuil, 1972.

Sabel, Charles. *Work and Politics*. Cambridge: Cambridge University Press, 1982.

Safran, Nadav. *Egypt in Search of Political Community*. Cambridge, Mass.: Harvard University Press, 1961.

Said, Gamal Eldin. "Productivity of Labour in Egyptian Industry," *L'Egypte Contemporaine*, 1948, pp. 493–506.

Sandbrook, Richard. *Proletarians and African Capitalism*. Cambridge: Cambridge University Press, 1975.

Shwadran, Benjamin. *The Middle East, Oil, and the Great Powers, 1959.* New York: Council for Middle Eastern Affairs, 1959.

Skocpol, Theda. *States and Social Revolution.* Cambridge: Cambridge University Press, 1979.

Springborg, Robert. "Patterns of Association in the Egyptian Political Elite," in *Political Elites in the Middle East,* ed. George Lenczowski. Washington, D.C.: American Enterprise Institute, 1975.

Suny, Ronald G. *The Baku Commune, 1917–1918.* Princeton: Princeton University Press, 1972.

Thompson, E. P. *The Poverty of Theory and Other Essays.* New York and London: Monthly Review Press, 1978.

Thompson, E. P. "Time, Work Discipline, and Industrial Capitalism." *Past and Present,* December 1968.

Tignor, Robert. *Modernization and British Colonial Rule in Egypt, 1882–1914.* Princeton: Princeton University Press, 1966.

Tignor, Robert, and Gouda Abdel-Khalek. *The Political Economy of Income Distribution in Egypt.* New York: Holmes and Meier, 1982.

Tilly, Charles. *From Mobilization to Revolution.* Reading, Mass.: Addison-Wesley, 1978.

Tomiche, F. J. *Syndicalisme et certains aspects du travail en la République Arabe Unie 1900–1967.* Paris: G. P. Maisonneuve et Larose, 1974.

Touraine, Alain. *La Conscience Ouvrière.* Paris: Editions du Seuil, 1966.

Vallet, Jean. *Contribution à l'étude de la condition des ouvriers de la grande industrie au Caire.* Valence: Imprimerie Valencienne, 1911.

Waterbury, John. *Hydropolitics of the Nile Valley.* Syracuse: Syracuse University Press, 1979.

Weber, Max. *From Max Weber.* New York: Oxford University Press, 1972.

Weber, Max. *General Economic History.* New York: Greenberg, 1927.

Zeitlin, Maurice. *Revolutionary Politics and the Cuban Working Class.* Princeton: Princeton University Press, 1967.

ARABIC SOURCES

Aḥmad Ṣādiq Saʿd. *Safḥāt min al-yasār al-miṣrī.* Cairo: Maktabat Madbūlī, 1976.

Amīn ʿIzz-al-Dīn. *Tārīkh al-ṭabaqah al-ʿāmilah al-miṣriyyah fī al-thalāthīnāt (1929–1939).* Cairo: Dār al-shaʿb, 1971.

Amīn ʿIzz-al-Dīn. *Tārīkh al-ṭabaqah al-ʿāmilah al-miṣriyyah min sanat 1919 ila sanat 1929.* Cairo: Dār al-shaʿb, 1970.

Amīn ʿIzz al-Dīn. *Tārīkh al-ṭabaqah al-ʿāmilah al-miṣriyyah mundhu nashaʾ-atihā hattah sanat 1919.* Cairo: Dār al-ʿarabi li al-kitāb, n.d.

Egypt. *Majmūʿat qawānīn al-ʿamal fī misr.* Cairo: Al-Maṭbaʿah al-amīriyyah, 1954.

Egypt. *Taqrīr lajnat al-tijārah wa al-sināʿah.* Cairo: Al-Maṭbaʿah al-amīriyyah, 1925.

Egypt. *Taqwīm al-mamlakah al-miṣriyyah.* Cairo: Al-Maṭbaʿah al-amīriyyah, 1926.

Fāḍil Zakī Muḥammad. *Al-fikr al-siyāsī al-ʿarabī al-islamī*. Baghdad: Wizārat al-iʿlām, al-jumhūriyyah al-ʿirāqiyyah, 1976.

Hasan al-Bannā. *Mudhakkirāt fī al-daʿwah wa al-dāʿiyyah*. Cairo: Dār al-shabāb, 1977.

Hizb al-ʿAmal. *Dustūr ḥizb al-ʿāmal*. n.d.

Hizb al-ʿAmal al-Ishtirākī. *Barnāmaj li ḥizb al-ʿamal al-ishtirākī wādī nil*. 1949.

Husayn Hamdī. *Mushkilat al-baṭālah*. Cairo: Maṭbaʿat al-ikhwān al-muslimīn, 1944.

Ibrahim Nāsir. *Min asbāb al-baṭalah wa al-aristuqrātiyyah al-niqābiyyah*. Cairo: Matbaʿat Yusuf, 1960.

Jamal al-Banna. "*ʿArd li kitab ma hiya al-niqabah*," in *Dirāsāt ʿummāliyyah*. 1972.

Labib Shuqayr Muḥammad. *Ittifāqiyyāt wa ʿuqud al-batrul fi al-bilād al-ʿarabiyyah* (*Part One*). Cairo: Maʿhad al-dirāsāt al-ʿarabiyyah al-ʿāliyyah, 1959.

Mālikah ʿIryān. *Kitāb markaz miṣr al-iqtiṣādī*. Cairo: Matbaʿat Raʿmsis, 1923.

Masʿad Muḥammad al-Bashkār. *Dalīl Dūmyāṭ*. Damietta: Dār al-Nīl, 1948.

Muʾtammar niqābāt ʿummāl miṣr. *Mashrūʿ lāʾihat al-niẓām al-asāsī li muʾtammar niqābāt ʿummāl miṣr*. Cairo: Maṭbaʿat al-risālah, 1946.

Muḥammad Anīs. *Dirāsāt fī wathāʾiq thawrat sanat 1919* (*Part One*). Cairo: Al-Maktabah al-anglū al-miṣriyyah, 1963.

Muḥammad Fahmi Lahitah. *Al-ʿadālah al-ijtimāʿiyyah*. Cairo: Maktabat al-nahḍah al-miṣriyyah, 1946.

Muḥammad Husayn Haikal. *Al-siyasah al-miṣriyyah wa al-inqilāb al-dustūrī*. Cairo: Maṭbaʿat al-siyāsah, 1931.

Muḥammad Ḥusayn Ḥaykal. *Mudhakkirāt fī al-siyāsah al-miṣriyyah*. Cairo: Maktabat al-nahḍah al-miṣriyyah, 1951.

Muḥammad Ḥusnī al-ʿUrābī. *Ma hiya al-niqabah?* Cairo, 1931.

Muḥammad Rushdī. *Al-Tatawwur al-iqtiṣādī fī misr*. Cairo: Dār al-maʿarif bi miṣr, 1972.

Muḥammad ʿAbd Allah Abu ʿAli. *Al-Tanẓim al-ijtimāʿī li al-sināʿah*. Alexandria: Al-Hayʾah al-ʿāmmah al-miṣriyyah lial-kitāb, 1972.

Najīb Mahfūz. *Al-Summān wa al-kharīf*. Beirut: Dar al-qalam, 1972.

Nawal ʿAbd al-ʿAziz Rāḍi. *Aḍwāʾ jadīdah ʿalā al-ḥarakah al-niqābiyyah*. Cairo: Dār al-nahḍah al-ʿarabiyyah, 1977.

Niqābat ʿUmmāl maṣnaʿ takrīr al-sukkar bi al-hawamdiyyah. *Al-Lāʾihah al-asasiyyah al-muʿaddalah*. Cairo, 1950 (A.H., 1369).

Raʾuf ʿAbbās. *Al-ḥarakah al-ʿummāliyyah al-miṣriyyah fī dauʾ al-wathāʾiq al-briṭāniyyah min sanat 1924 ilā sanat 1927*. Cairo: ʿAlam al-kutub, 1975.

Raʾuf ʿAbbās. *Al-ḥarakah al-ʿummāliyyah fī miṣr min sanat 1899 ila sanat 1952*. Cairo: Dār al-kātib al-ʿarabī, 1968.

Rifʿat Al-Saʿīd. *Tārīkh al-ḥarakah al-ishtirākiyyah fī miṣr min sanat 1900 ila sanat 1925*. Cairo: Dār al-thaqāfah al-jadīdah, 1975.

Rifʿat Al-Saʿīd. *Tārīkh al-munaẓẓamat al-yasāriyyah al-miṣriyyah min sanat 1930 ila 1950*. Cairo: Dar al-thaqāfah al-jadīdah, 1977.

Sayyid Qandil. *Al-ʿAmil wa al-niqābah*. Cairo: Dār al-tibāʿah al-miṣriyyah al-ḥādithah, 1949.

Saʿd Zaghlūl. *Āthār al-zaʿīm Saʿd Zaghlūl: ʿAhd wizārat al-shaʿb.* Cairo: Maṭbaʿat dār al-kutub, 1927.

Saʿd ʿAbd al-salām Ḥabīb. *Mashākil al-ʿamal wa al-ʿummāl.* Cairo: Maktabat al-nahḍah al-miṣriyyah, 1951.

Sulayman al-Nukhayli. *Al-ḥarakah al-ʿummāliyyah fī miṣr wa mawqif al-sihafah wa al-sultah al-misriyyah minha min sanat 1882 ila sanat 1952.* Cairo: Ruz al-Yusuf Press, 1968.

Ṭāha Saʿd ʿUthman. "Mudhakkirāt wa wathāʾiq min tārīkh al-ṭabaqah al-ʿāmilah." *Al-Kātib,* July, August, September, and November 1971 and January, February, March, April, May, and July 1972.

Ṭāha Saʿd ʿUthman. *Niḍāl ʿummāl al-nasīj al-mikānīkī fī al-qāhirah.* Cairo: Maktabat al-ṭabaqah al-ʿāmilah, 1946.

Ṭāriq al-Bishrī. *Al-Ḥarakah al-siyāsiyyah fī miṣr min sanat 1945 ila sanat 1952.* Cairo: Al-Hayʾah al-miṣriyyah al-ʿāmmah li al-kitāb, 1972.

ʿAbd-al-munʿim Al-Ghazzali. *Tārīkh al-ḥarakah al-niqābiyyah al-miṣriyyah min sanat 1899 ila sanat 1952.* Cairo: Dār al-thaqāfah al-jadīdah, 1968.

ʿAbd-al-munʿim Nasr Al-Shāfiʿī. *Baʿḍ mashākil al-ʿamal fī miṣr.* Cairo: Dār al-nahḍah al-ʿarabiyyah, 1939.

ʿAbd-al-raḥmān Al-Rāfiʿ. *Fī aʿqāb al-thawrah al-miṣriyyah (Part One).* Cairo: Dar al-shaʿb, 1969.

ʿAbd-al-ʿaẓīm Ramadān. *Al-Sirāʿ bayna al-wafd wa al-ʿarsh, 1936–1939.* Beirut: Al-muʾassasah al-ʿarabiyyah li al-dirasāt wa al-nashr, 1979.

ʿAbd-al-ʿaẓīm Ramaḍān. *Taṭawwur al-ḥarakah al-waṭaniyyah fī miṣr min sanat 1937 ila sanat 1948.* Beirut: Dār al-waṭan al-ʿarabī, 1978.

ʿAbd-al-ʿaẓīm Ramaḍān. *Taṭawwur al-ḥarakah al-waṭaniyyah fī miṣr min sanat 1918 ila sanat 1936.* Cairo: Dār al-kātib al-ʿarabī, 1968.

ʿAbd-al-ʿaẓīm Ramaḍān. *ʿAbd al-nāṣir wa azmat māris sanat 1954.* Cairo: Maṭābiʿ rūz al-yūsuf, 1976.

ʿĀṣim Aḥmad al-Disūqī. *Miṣr fī al-ḥarb al-ʿālamiyyah al-thāniyah.* Cairo: Al-munaẓẓamah al-ʿarabiyyah li al-tarbiyah wa al-thaqāfah wa al-ʿulūm, 1976.

Index

Compositor: G & S Typesetters, Inc.
Printer: Braun-Brumfield, Inc.
Binder: Braun-Brumfield, Inc.
Text: 10/13 Sabon
Display: Sabon